Political Communication

Political Communication
A New Introduction for Crisis Times

Aeron Davis

Polity

First published in 2019 by Polity Press

Polity Press
65 Bridge Street
Cambridge CB2 1UR, UK

Polity Press
101 Station Landing
Suite 300
Medford, MA 02155, USA

ISBN-13: 978-1-5095-2899-8 (hardback)
ISBN-13: 978-1-5095-2900-1 (paperback)

A catalogue record for this book is available from the British Library.

Typeset in 10.5 on 12 pt Plantin by Fakenham Prepress Solutions, Fakenham, Norfolk NR21 8NL
Printed and bound in Great Britain by T.J. International Limited

The publisher has used its best endeavours to ensure that the URLs for external websites referred to in this book are correct and active at the time of going to press. However, the publisher has no responsibility for the websites and can make no guarantee that a site will remain live or that the content is or will remain appropriate.

Every effort has been made to trace all copyright holders, but if any have been overlooked the publisher will be pleased to include any necessary credits in any subsequent reprint or edition.

For further information on Polity, visit our website:
politybooks.com

Contents

Acknowledgements

I have many people to mention here. First, I want to thank the many amazing students who have taken the MA Political Communication at Goldsmiths. I have learnt a lot from our exchanges over the years. Many thanks are also owed to the colleagues and visiting lecturers who have taught with me on the course: James Curran, Natalie Fenton, Des Freedman, Paolo Gerbaudo, Vana Goblot, Mike Kaye, Gholam Khiabany, Jack Mosse, Emily Seymour, Jón Gunnar Ólafsson and Catherine Walsh.

Over the years, I have gained much-needed subject advice, inspiration and personal support from: Peter van Aelst, Olivier Baisnée, Mike Berry, Rod Benson, Lisa Blackman, Clea Bourne, Roger Burrows, Aditya Chakrabortty, Andy Chadwick, Jean Chalaby, Stephen Cushion, Lincoln Dahlberg, Will Davies, Will Dinan, Danny Dorling, Joe Earle, Bob Franklin, Lee Edwards, Becky Gardiner, Peter Golding, Dan Jackson, Jonathan Hardy, Dave Hesmondhalgh, Dan Hind, Sukhdev Johal, Anu Kantola, Bong-hyun Lee, Colin Leys, Jo Littler, Andrew McGettigan, David Miller, Tom Mills, Liz Moor, Mick Moran, Angela Phillips, Chris Roberts, Heather Savigny, Nick Sireau, Bev Skeggs, Peter Thompson, Daya Thussu, Polly Toynbee, Howard Tumber, Janine Wedel, Karel Williams, Dwayne Winseck, Simon Wren-Lewis and Kate Wright.

I'm also very grateful to John Thompson, Mary Savigar, Ellen MacDonald-Kramer and everyone at Polity who advised on this project.

Last of all, I must, of course, mention the love and support of my close family: Anne, Hannah, Miriam, Kezia, Kelly, Helen and Neville.

Aeron Davis
October 2018

Part I

Introductory Frameworks

1

Introduction

The End of Old Certainties and Paradigms in Political Communication

They say that everyone remembered what they were doing the day John F. Kennedy was shot (22 November 1963). I wasn't born yet but I do remember other such days: the day the Falklands/Malvinas conflict began (1982), images of the Berlin Wall being knocked down (1989), the multiple playbacks of two passenger airplanes crashing into New York's Twin Towers (2001), the collapse of Lehman Brothers (2008), and the growing tide of protestors in Egypt's Tahrir Square (2011). Each of these endlessly reported events left observers with a sense of shock and disbelief, and a feeling that things would never be the same again.

For me, as with many others, two such days stand out in 2016. The first was after the British went to the polls to vote on continuing membership of the European Union on 23 June. I woke up early in Amsterdam to get the result no one thought possible just a couple of months earlier. Geert Wilders was on the radio promising that the Dutch would soon follow the British out of the EU. No one in either the UK or continental Europe could predict what would follow. The second was the day US citizens voted for a new president on 8 November. I was chairing an event with Wolfgang Streeck on his new book (*How Will Capitalism End?*). He confidently predicted a Clinton victory to the three hundred or so in the audience, as had all but one of my one hundred students in the lecture hall the day before. Again, no one quite believed that the alternative of a Trump Presidency could ever happen. The same feelings of fear and the unknown quickly spread.

Both events did not simply produce freak outcomes. In multiple ways, they made the conventional wisdom about media and politics appear suddenly outdated. The large majority of academics, journalists, experts and pollsters all got it wrong. The winning campaigns tore up the tried and tested playbooks. The established parties were as much at war with each other as with their opponents. Electorates swung wildly and did not behave as they should. Mainstream media, now struggling for economic viability, was frequently distrusted or ignored by citizens. US and UK politics seemed to have suddenly fallen down a deep, dark rabbit hole.

The historical upheaval was not just an Anglo-American problem, to be linked to those nations' neoliberal policy frameworks and first-past-the-post electoral systems. Countries across Europe, with different political and economic systems, were also throwing up erratic results. Parties that had dominated for decades were virtually wiped out. In 2015 the radical left party Syriza won power in Greece. In 2017, Macron's fledgling En Marche! beat Marine Le Pen's Front National, edging out France's traditional main parties to win the Presidency in France. The 2018 Italian election resulted in a new governing coalition of the populist Northern League and Five Star Movement parties led by Giuseppe Conte, a lawyer without parliamentary experience. The Dutch and Germans experienced elections where mainstream parties lost substantial ground and took many months to form fragile, uneasy coalition governments. Far-right, populist and extremist parties have been on the rise across Europe, from the newer democracies of the East, to those seemingly more stable nations of Northern Europe and Scandinavia.

Change and uncertainty could be seen everywhere else too. In 2017, moves began for the impeachment of presidents in South Korea, Brazil and South Africa. In 2018, Lopez Obrador won the Presidency in Mexico with another fledgling party. Jair Bolsonaro, an extreme far-right politician, was victorious in the Brazilian presidential elections. Populist leaders consolidated their holds on power in Japan, Turkey, China, India and Russia. A new world order was emerging as US power waned. Other nations, notably China and Russia, who offered their own brand of authoritarian capitalism, began challenging the liberal cosmopolitan vision of globalization. Democracy watchers recorded clear democratic declines across the globe for the first time in decades.

It is these various signs of historical upheaval that have given me the impetus to write this book. In early 2016, having taught political communication for the best part of two decades, I felt confident in engaging with a clear set of theories and debates. Suddenly, as I began teaching the new cohort that Autumn, the discussions and arguments I had set out and participated in now appeared increasingly redundant. The subject text books, even recently published ones, looked to be describing a past era (my own included). Debates around professionalized parties set against ideologically driven ones now seemed less relevant after Donald Trump's victory. Discussions of the steady mediatization of politics appeared confused when mass, legacy news outlets were going bust everywhere. Traditional media effects research looked redundant when so much of the population got their news in scraps from social media and elsewhere.

The lectures were packed with new students wanting to work out what was happening and where it was all leading. Each week, they and I began charting new territories, still unsure as to what the final destination looked like.

What was becoming clear was that several long-prophesized tipping points had finally been reached. Traditional left–right political spectrums were no longer the clearest means of identifying or cohering a party. The legacy media of the public sphere was dying. Social media was rapidly reconfiguring the basis on which politics and journalism operated. Electorates were more volatile than they were aligned. Economics and economic policy-makers no longer seemed to be describing real economies. Parties began looking more like new social movements. Meanwhile, pollsters and forecasters appeared to be as reliable as astrologers. No one could tell the difference between an 'expert' and a propagandist. And all the while, national publics were increasingly fragmenting into ever more polarized echo chambers.

The Fourth Age of Political Communication and Democratic Crisis

In the 1990s, Jay Blumler published two prominent interventions in the field of political communication: one focusing on *crisis* and the other emphasizing fundamental *change*. In 1995, with Michael Gurevitch, he published *The Crisis of Public Communication*. This pulled together their decades of research on UK and US politics and media to identify a series of worrying trends. An ever more powerful media were reshaping politics to the detriment of democracy. Blumler followed this up in 1999 with an article co-authored with Dennis Kavanagh in the journal *Political Communication*, entitled: 'The Third

Age of Political Communication: Influences and Features'. This focused on change more than crisis. The first age, in the two decades after the Second World War, was the 'golden age' of parties and presses. Party memberships were large, citizens loyal and print media deferential. The second age, from the 1960s to 1990s, was driven by the introduction of limited-channel national television, taking politically interested audiences away from their partisan presses. While engaging more citizens, TV politics also created 'an emptier and less nourishing communication diet'.

They then documented the features of what they saw as an emerging 'third age' at the turn of the century. This had developed, on the one hand, out of wider social shifts, such as individualization, secularization, economization, aestheticization and rationalization. On the other, it was also linked to the growing 'media abundance, ubiquity, reach' of the new 24-hour, multiple channel environment. The trends they tried to highlight were: the increased professionalization of parties which now prioritized media strategy in political policy-making; intensifying competition everywhere, both for parties and media; an anti-elitist and short-term populism replacing traditional political ideologies; a growing diversification of media outlets, topics and agendas, that now encompassed 'identity politics'; and a less homogenous and more fragmented audience that could pick and choose its news sources. Two decades later, all those trends remain observable now. Some, like anti-elitist populism and audience fragmentation, have progressed considerably.

However, we have also been witnessing other distinct trends across politics, media and communication. The most obvious of these has been in the area of communication technologies. In the 1990s, multi-channel TV and a partisan press dominated in many wealthy countries. The internet was an interesting distraction. Smart phones, social media and many of the titans of today's online age did not exist. Now, these digital tools are beginning to dominate political communication in much the way TV or the press did in earlier ages.

In a 2013 keynote address Blumler suggested that digital communication could be driving democracies towards a fourth age of political communication. The trends of the third age, such as communication abundance, audience selectivity and 'centrifugal diversification', had been spurred on by developments in the online world. He speculated that this could mean the end of the top-down, 'pyramidical model' of elite to mass communication. Instead, a new 'two level political communication ecology' of elites and masses was emerging. If so, such conclusions led him to believe that 'the model of political communication process that dominated our scholarship in the past, my own included, is kaput'.

Since then, others too have pointed towards the emergence of a possible new fourth age. Some, such as Magin et al. (2016) have limited their discussions to the impact of the digital on conventional politics. For them, the fourth age is about new communication rather than crisis. Others, such as Bennett and Pfetsch (2018), have looked to wider shifts in politics, institutions, democracy and the public sphere. They, like Blumler, insist changes to the political communication environment have been equally driven by larger social trends and are concerned about the larger threats to the public sphere. In addition to the social shifts observed by Blumler and Kavanagh in 1999, have emerged a powerful set of trends, each of which poses threats to contemporary democracies. These include: advanced neoliberalism, financialization, aspects of globalization, population growth and migration, inequality extremes, global warming and environmental devastation, and the instability of established national institutions.

All these trends, combined with the events of the last half decade, have led me towards three contentious conclusions. One, several core foundational elements of the scholarly field of political communication are in desperate need of a rethink (see also Davis, 2010a; Bennett and Iyengar, 2010; Bennett and Pfetsch, 2018). Two, modern democracy itself is in the midst of an existential crisis as weighty and disturbing as any since 1945. The trends of 'post-democracy', outlined by Crouch (2004) and others, are coming to fruition as the key institutions, norms and practices of politics and communication have become significantly eroded.

Three, whether seen as causing democratic crisis or not, the fourth age of political communication has well and truly arrived for mature democracies. The full impact of the changes and transitions has become clearer within the last half decade. Leaving aside the very valid objections to the idea of set 'ages', what are the defining features of today's democratic crisis and fourth age of political communication? Those recorded and explored in the following chapters include:

• *A significant weakening of state institutions'* ability to enact policy or operate accountably: as globalization and financialization spread, it becomes increasingly difficult for politicians and bureaucrats to manage economic, environmental and other policy areas, to collect corporate taxes, maintain regulations, etc.

- *The development of large, complex policy areas and risks* beyond the understanding of most leaders: key policy areas, such as those covering finance, new technologies, health and the environment, have become so complex that few, including those in charge, understand them and the risks involved.
- A pronounced *break-down of faith in political institutions, experts and elites*: not only have people become increasingly untrusting of politicians and political organizations, they are more critical of elites and experts of all kinds.
- *Ideologically fragmented parties*: Once large and stable political parties have either been wiped out or fractured into multiple factions, immobilizing them in the process.
- *Cultural identity and nationalist challenges* to traditional left–right politics: increasingly, issues of race, nation, gender, sexuality, immigration and the environment cut across established class divides and economic policy differences.
- Rapidly growing *unstable new parties, interest groups and social movements*: new parties and social movements can now grow rapidly to sizeable entities that challenge their opponents, but they can fade or become paralysed just as quickly.
- *Hollowed-out legacy news media operations*: the business model of many established news organizations, especially in the print press, has been broken, either bankrupting them or turning them into shadows of what they were.
- Unaccountable and untraceable news and information flows across *social media networks*: in many countries, and among specific audience demographics such as younger voters, a majority get their news and share political information and opinion using social media, not legacy news producers.
- Problems of *information overload and 'truth'*: political information and opinion continue to grow exponentially, leaving individuals struggling to find valid sources and verifiable, objectives facts and information. This is exacerbated by the activities of internet bots and the deliberate dissemination of fake news and information on social media.
- *Unaligned and very volatile electorates*: numbers of strongly aligned voters are now outnumbered by undecideds, with election-period swings getting much larger and pollsters finding it hard to make accurate predictions.
- *Audiences fragmented and polarized* across multiple divides: as numbers and types of media have multiplied so audiences have increasingly been subject to both separation and intensification

of exchanges. There are multiple areas of division, from age to education, wealth to political interest, race and gender to region.

- *A growing divide* between the world of public, visible, symbolic politics, on the one hand, and that of private politics, encompassing opaque policy-making, lobbyists and experts, on the other.

Each of these elements is transforming political communication systems substantially. They severely undermine the core foundational norms, values and institutions of established political systems everywhere, and democracies in particular. They present substantial challenges to political actors of all kinds and to scholars trying to observe and analyse what is happening.

Defining Political Communication and Defining My Approach

This book has several objectives, one of which is to challenge and broaden the boundaries of the discipline. But, to do that, one has to begin by clarifying what the discipline covers. Demarcating the boundaries of political communication is tricky because agreeing what constitutes 'politics' and communication around politics is tricky. McNair's 6th edition (2017: 4) introduction to the subject offers the following definition:

> '*purposeful communication about politics*'. This incorporates: '1 All forms of communication undertaken by politicians and other political actors … 2 Communication addressed *to* these actors by non-politicians such as voters and activists. 3 Communication *about* these actors and their activities, as contained in news reports, editorials and other forms of media …'

McNair's (2017) definition is as good a place to start as any and offers a degree of flexibility. But, he also acknowledges that what counts as a political actor or a politically relevant form of communication is open to debate. Like most writers on the topic, he makes selective choices about the actors, processes, communication forms and events he focuses on. A glance at Kenski and Hall Jamieson's (2017) handbook suggests that the major actors and concerns of the discipline are elected politicians and parties, election campaigns and media effects on voters. This very much relates to formal politics and institutions in democracies. In contrast, Doris Graber's 10th edition (with Dunaway, 2017) of *Mass Media and American Politics*, orients itself towards mass news media as it relates to a variety of formal political actors, processes and reporting conditions.

These well-regarded authors have made their own selective decisions about what counts. Their books offer relatively little on other types of political actor or process beyond governments, legislatures and legacy media. But, of course, politics involves many other types of participant, activity and type of communication. Political communication goes beyond election campaigns, and includes day-to-day party conflicts and compromises over policy, budgets and the ups and downs of politicians. Wars, disasters, demonstrations and technical debates around the environment or the economy all involve communication and media coverage that is political.

There are many additional kinds of political actor too. Governments and parliaments are supported by extensive bureaucracies and often unseen but influential civil servants. Corporations, interest groups, trade unions, religious institutions, think tanks and others all contribute to political parties with their ideas, funds and organizational support. They also lobby government ministers and civil servants. Politics is now full of professional communication intermediaries, in public relations, marketing, advocacy and so on. Citizens are not just voting fodder but frequently become political actors, when making financial contributions, demonstrating, organizing around local issues, or sharing alternative news stories through Facebook.

Communication in or about politics also takes many forms. Mass news media (print, broadcast, online) and the practices of journalism are the most obvious form. There are also the ever-growing plethora of specialist publications, political websites and social media networks. So too, we might consider interpersonal communication, of the kind that takes place between journalists and political sources, lobbyists and government bureaucrats or across social networks. We might also think more about political culture as politicians appear in entertainment programmes, celebrities become politicians, or social media spreads satirical memes across online networks.

The discipline has other forms of exclusion. Many scholars only count surveys and quantitative studies, while others prefer qualitative approaches or engage with complex social theory. Most cannot avoid national and cultural biases, often interpreting the wider world in relation to their own national norms, actors and institutions. Some attempt to separate the political from wider social, economic and technical changes and influences, while others insist on linking all these things, at times losing focus in the process.

These divides were very apparent in the early days of the discipline's development and can still be seen. But there is also a wider appreciation of the various approaches, actors, theory and interdisciplinary nature of the subject. So too, there is now a greater understanding of difference and variation across nations and systems. This book attempts to reflect the plurality of the work now being produced but, of course, it makes its own selective choices, and can't avoid its own Anglo-centric biases.

Bearing all this in mind, the book's approach is guided by the following objectives. The first is to document the challenges to some of the established paradigms that have defined the field in recent decades. As the various chapters argue, evolving trends have now become tipping points, in some cases fatally undermining the institutions, organizations and democratic models which have sustained polities. In other words, a paradigm shift is required. If it becomes harder to establish and sustain political parties, news media operations, state institutions and public spheres, then the norms and ideals associated with them have to be rethought too. Intellectually, scholars must re-evaluate their models, assumptions and norms. Practically, nations must step in to either resuscitate these institutions and principles or replace them with something else.

Second, the book is presented as an advanced introduction to the subject of political communication. Each chapter offers a bridge between the old and the new. The old covers the debates, institutions and actors that have defined the field for some years. Key organizations, such as parties, news media, interest groups, voters and government institutions are introduced, as are long-running debates around, for example, professionalization, new technologies and mediatization. So too are ways of evaluating systems, such as public sphere theory or comparative systems research, as well as discussions of the larger disruptive forces undermining all this. Having set out the traditions, each chapter then explores how recent trends and tipping points are challenging our understanding of systems, actors and communication.

The final objective is to bring together diverse approaches and findings from a mix of disciplines. These are primarily from politics, media and journalism, drawing on a combination of theory, quantitative and qualitative studies. But, there are also attempts to stretch the subject boundaries, pushing into adjacent disciplines where appropriate. These include sociology, economics, international relations, cultural theory and political economy. At the same time, the book is, of necessity, more focused on Western democracies generally and the US and UK in particular. That does not mean to assume some form of crude universalism or that English-speaking democracies are 'more advanced'.

Outline of the Book

Part I introduces the core concerns and parameters of the book. Chapter 2 sets out different ways through which we might think about what 'good' democratic political and media systems might look like. It skirts through philosophers and democratic theorists from the French Revolution, Dewey and Lippman to Jürgen Habermas, as well as setting out more recent comparative systems work. It asks: are the tensions inherent in democracies, between liberty and equality, representative and direct democracy, becoming too difficult to reconcile?

Chapter 3 looks at the question of crisis in politics and media in twenty-first century democracies. As with previous periods of such talk the discussion becomes one of whether we are experiencing a worrying break-down in democracy or merely a period of unnerving change. Should we frame what's happening now in terms of Blumler's 1995 'crisis' book or his 1999 new 'age' article? How are the great disrupters of globalization, neoliberalism and new ICTs, reconfiguring democratic governance and, perhaps, making it untenable?

Part II focuses on the formal institutions and actors of political systems: parties, news media and government institutions. Chapter 4 traces the evolution of political parties and election campaigning, as ideologically driven parties first became mass, catch-all organizations and then electoral-professional entities. In this shift, ideological direction and clearly aligned constituents were balanced off against professional campaigning and technocratic governance. Are such debates still important when traditional ideologies are riven with fault lines and professionalized parties neither trusted nor stable?

Chapter 5 turns to traditional news media operations. Even though the internet has powerfully disrupted the legacy news environment, it still plays a major role in institutional politics. Thus, long-running debates between political economists and liberal sociologists, about whether or not legacy news media have retained their autonomy, fourth estate and 'truth'-seeking values, remain important. However, as the business model of national news production collapses, do both positions still hold any relevancy?

Chapter 6 explores the evolving literature on media–source relations. Such dynamics are fundamental to political communication, whether politicians and journalists are cooperative or in conflict, and whether media is overly managed by states or, vice versa, politics is becoming overly mediatized. However, what happens to such relations when both parties and media have become increasingly precarious, fragmented and populist in nature?

Part III turns away from formal politics and institutions to cover media effects, public engagement, interest groups and new social movements. Chapter 7 looks at citizens, unpacking two related discussions on political participation and media influence. The first re-evaluates the literature on why publics are participating less in formal politics. The second, skips through varied phases of effects research alternating between 'strong' and 'limited' paradigms. Both discussions find their way to a similar conclusion. That is that in the UK and US, publics are gravitating towards three general groups: two polarized and ghettoized but engaged factions, and a third increasingly disaffected and disengaged group that has turned its back on mainstream media and formal politics altogether.

Chapter 8 moves on to civil society, interest groups and the policy process. It asks what kind of groups and organizations are able to influence government legislation and media content most often and why. Long-term debates have focused on conflicting accounts of insiders and outsiders, resource-rich and poor, and varying opportunity structures. These perspectives have now become overlain by two key developments: the rise of fast-emerging and moving new social movements, and the growth of powerful elite intermediary professions (lobbyists, accountants and lawyers). Together, they are expanding the gap between public, visible politics and private, shadowy policy and regulation.

Part IV explores the big disrupters of democratic political communication. Chapter 9 begins with the economy, often regarded as the most important voting issue and point of ideological division between left and right parties. Since the 1980s neoclassical economics and neoliberalism have increasingly come to dominate systems of national economic management and global governance. However, a series of problems for developed economies have been exacerbated by the financial crash of 2007–8. Hard economic realities now suggest such forms of capitalism are threatening democracy itself, yet few alternatives are emerging.

Chapter 10 concentrates on the latest waves of digitally facilitated political communication. Classic fault lines, between techno-optimists and pessimists, technological determinist and social-shaping approaches have been played out in investigations of parties, news organizations, interest groups and individual participation. While optimists have been confronted with a harsh reality check, pessimists have been forced to admit the depth of the changes confronting the political communication environment. The anarchic, wild west of a public sphere emerging suggests that democratic media theory needs an urgent rethink.

Chapter 11 introduces and melds diverse literatures on globalization and international political communication. In recent decades, advocates have argued that globalization has stabilized and improved the economic fortunes of nation states, more than making up for the losses of state sovereignty. Likewise, enthusiasts have linked the new international communication infrastructure to an ideal vision of cosmopolitanism and an emerging global civil society. However, while transnational communication continues to expand in multiple ways, social, economic and political trends have not followed the expectations of the global elite. As a consequence, there is a public backlash against globalization, a lack of faith in Western-style free-market capitalism and democracy, a new cold war and a breakdown of international cooperation.

Chapter 12 pulls together the findings of the previous chapters. It concludes that we have both entered into a new age of political communication, and that democratic systems are indeed in a state of crisis rather than simply change. Too many key institutions of democracy – in theory and practice – are struggling to survive and fulfil their basic functions. In which case philosophers, scholars and political actors need to go back to first principles, rethinking the norms, institutions and practices of modern, representative democracies.

2
Evaluating Democratic Politics and Communication

This chapter is all about attempts to evaluate politics and communication in democracies. On the one hand, that involves identifying the ideals, norms and values that we might associate with healthy polities. On the other, it involves scrutiny of the institutions, systems and practices that make up the communication ecology of politics.

Clarifying these elements, and the debates that are linked to them, is important for a few reasons. For one, they offer a framework for evaluating what we have, both as a whole and in terms of the individual parts. Second, they aid us in making judgements about whether and to what degree democracy is in crisis. Third, they help identify the range of alternatives on offer, enabling discussion of what might change or be adopted in future.

The chapter links three related literatures. The first of these returns to first principles by outlining the basic philosophy and ideals of democracy as they relate specifically to media and communication. These emerged in political and philosophical treatises, and in response to major political events such as the French Revolution and US Declaration of Independence. In particular, the focus is on general liberal notions of Liberty, Equality and Sovereignty (or Sorority). The second literature is that tied to Jürgen Habermas's historical account of the public sphere, its associated ideals and varied modern equivalents. The third area is comparative systems work, a line of research which has expanded considerably in the last two decades.

Although these literatures are distinct they share a set of norms, values and tensions, each of which sit at the heart of both old and new debates about democracy and communication. These move through abstract notions of what makes for 'good' democracy to discussions of systems and institutions, to more concrete evaluations of what Nancy Fraser (1997) calls 'actually existing democracies'.

Public Communication Ideals and Representative Democracy

Democracy developed historically in opposition to more autocratic forms of rule. The concept of democracy came from the ancient Greeks and literally means 'the rule of the citizen body'. Athenian democracy was practised in some city-states as an alternative to tyrannical rule. That said, participation still excluded the majority, and forms of democracy were limited and usually short-lived.

Similar oppositions to tyranny developed later in Europe's early modern period. Rule by the 'divine right of kings', aided by the nobility and church, became increasingly challenged by parliaments, civil wars and the emerging bourgeoisie. A common set of liberal ideals, involving the participation, rights and responsibilities of individuals and the citizen body, was developed in philosophical treatises. Direct confrontations with English monarchs such as against James II in 1689, the US overthrow of British rule in 1776, and the French Revolution of 1789, all produced new declarations and bills of rights. Each of these contributed to transforming ideals into codified constitutions, law and democratic institutions. In turn, such elements were frequently adopted in the constitutions of emerging democracies through the twentieth century as well as in the 1948 Universal Declaration of Human Rights. They are still central, even as their interpretation has become more contested and their application ever more complicated (see Ball and Dagger, 2013; Held, 2006, for an overview).

The larger role of public communication in relation to such democratic ideals was not usually considered. Little was set down much beyond the insistence on freedom of speech and of the press, as contained in the US First Amendment. But, for some key thinkers in earlier centuries (e.g., Thomas Paine, Thomas Jefferson, John Stewart Mill, Jeremy Bentham), it was a crucial element they paid attention to in their writing. They themselves benefited from the rise of mass printing and the dissemination of new ideas through political pamphlets and newspapers. Accordingly, they looked to print media as an important component of a new, more democratic politics (see Keane's overview, 1991).

Their twentieth-century counterparts (e.g., Walter Lippmann, John Dewey, Jürgen Habermas) pondered the importance of public communication too and added broadcast media into the mix. Current-day thinkers wrestle with the additional mediums of the internet and mobile communication. Clearly, whatever the predominant modes of public communication, it is essential for a number of core operating features of democracy. The ways that a state establishes legitimate public authority, how citizens become informed about issues and electoral candidates, how those in charge are held accountable, and how individuals get a wider hearing for their concerns, all require widely shared, reliable and accessible forms of communication. Accordingly, a set of normative 'ideal' media and public communication functions in democracies have emerged (see Keane, 1991; Norris, 2000; Curran, 2002, for discussions).

What are these core ideals and how do they apply to public communication in democracies? Three core concepts come up in virtually every treatise or declaration of rights: Liberty, Equality and some sense of binding Sovereign Nationhood (or Sister/Brotherhood). They are most simply summed up in the most memorable motto of the 1789 French Revolution, enshrined in the constitutions of later French Republics, as 'Liberté, Égalité, Fraternité'. To put it a (bit too) simply, Liberty, Equality and Fraternity/Sorority are the equivalent of democracy's primary colours.

All three concepts have varied interpretations and applications in democratic theory. Liberty initially referred to physical freedom of the individual (hotly contested in past eras of empire and slavery), and also to the need to be free from the coercion of monarchs and tyrannical states. But, it also came to be interpreted as freedom to participate politically, and freedom of all actions and opinions which did not curtail the freedoms of others. Its interpretations shift across law, politics and society. The Equality principle put all individuals on the same standing, declaring all were born equal, and therefore should have equal rights to free speech, religious affiliation, property and so on. But, what else should be included here is debatable. Equality of health, education and economic means are considered by some to be essential to guarantee 'equality of opportunity' but such factors are ignored or denied by others. And, of course, all societies produce inequality to varying degrees; something which then automatically produces varying life chances from birth onwards.

Sororities/Fraternities (not the kind in US colleges) of necessity demarcate who is to be included, be it on the national, regional or other level. Those 'citizens' who are, make up the general will, contribute to the public good, and have obligations as well as rights. Pretty much every form of democratic citizen body to emerge in earlier centuries, including for much of the twentieth century, has had its exclusions denoted by a combination of gender, race, property, wealth, official citizenship, legal freedom, age and so on.

In relation to public communication, these core ideals are typically interpreted in the following ways. Under liberty, the media has a role to play to support individual liberties and freedom of speech by keeping governments and their leaders in check. This entails holding them up to public scrutiny and exposing corruption and abuses of power. Thus, mainstream news media take on a 'watch-dog role' and have been regarded as the 'fourth estate' (government, parliament and judiciary making up the first three). In terms of political communication, equality translates to equal access to information and to expression of opinion. As democracies advance, so it is argued that the maximum amount of people possible must be able to intervene in public debates on issues that affect them. It is equally important that the maximum amount of people must be informed about relevant political and social changes. A healthy democracy contains a plurality of opinions from different peoples, parties, organizations and institutions.

In relation to national sovereignty or sorority, there is the general sense of public media and communication pulling all citizens together. Political and media systems provide the shared communicative architecture that holds democratic, consensual nation states together. They offer shared platforms for information circulation, deliberation and debate, allowing the citizen body to come to reasoned, rational and fair decisions about the rule of law and the distribution of resources.

These basic ideals are fairly easy to agree on. Historically and in the present, democracies are concerned with balancing the elements of liberty, equality and sovereignty. It is rare to find a politician or newspaper editor in democracies arguing against any of them. Even authoritarian leaders, radical revolutionaries, billionaire media moguls and alt-right news website owners selectively proclaim their merits from time to time.

But, they also co-exist only in an ongoing state of tension. Individual rights sit uncomfortably alongside ideals of equality and community. Practically speaking, it's not possible to give everyone complete freedom or make everyone equal or to give everyone an equal voice. States must act with strong authority and efficiency in the name of the wider public body but also retain respect for individuals. A series of checks and balances on state power needs to be in operation but these should not overly hinder new legislation, the delivery of agreed laws or the defence of the nation.

How nations have sought to tackle the big policy questions of the day often reflects these differences of ideal emphasis too: military intervention, the financial crash, tackling global warming, refugee crises and a series of counter-terrorism measures. Countries like the US, UK and Australia obstruct measures to curtail global warming or financial risk-taking as they impinge on the freedoms of individuals, companies and markets. Nordic nations have taken an opposite view. Responses to the economic and refugee crises have alternated between nationalist, fraternity-related and free market, individual liberty sentiments. Decisions to impose austerity budgets or extend welfare nets and more Keynesian-type economic stimuli, balance liberty and equality considerations.

All of these tensions are further exacerbated by practical considerations of representation and participation in the large, complex democracies we have now (as opposed to smaller, direct forms of democracy). The question is: how much should or can ordinary citizens participate in large, representative democracies? Should representative polities encourage more 'minimal' and 'representative' or more 'maximal' and 'direct' forms of participation (Crouch, 2004). On the one hand, more representation and participation suggest a stronger, deeper democracy will result. As Almond et al. (2010: 23) state 'the more citizens are involved and the more influential their choices, the more democratic the system'. On the other, greater participation offers its own complications and can hinder effective government.

Here, there has been a long-running split between supporters of 'liberal' limited, rational choice models of representative democracy, and advocates of greater 'republican', participatory democracy. In 1920s America, Walter Lippmann and John Dewey publicly disagreed on this issue. Lippmann was sceptical of journalism and public opinion, seeing politics being guided by expert and political elite opinion, with ordinary citizens being too disinterested and/ or unqualified to engage or challenge them. Alternatively, Dewey argued forcefully for greater individual-level participation in everyday politics of all kinds and believed journalism should be configured towards facilitating greater citizen engagement.

Political theorists have continued to gravitate towards one pole or other in this debate. For many (e.g., Schumpeter, 1942; Dahl, 1989; Kateb, 1992), representative forms of democracy, in spite of their many flaws, are the only practical options for large, complex societies. The more technically advanced and specialist modern societies become, the more they come to rely on experts and knowledge that ordinary citizens or indeed rulers themselves, cannot possess. Elite competition through the ballot box both maintains representation and prevents authoritarianism returning. For others, ideal democracy requires more inclusive participation on every social and political level and, accordingly, good democratic processes should encourage that (MacPherson, 1965; Dryzak, 2002). Otherwise, elites end up ruling on their own behalf more than for their people (see Lukes, 2005).

In effect, representative democracy continually generates conflicts and uncomfortable compromises, first between those competing ideals, and second, between abstract ideals and practical considerations around representation and participation. So, it follows that modern democracies, in theory and practice, always operate as a series of compromises. All nations and systems balance them in different ways, offer alternative interpretations of how they are best achieved, and often lean towards one ideal or another.

Unsurprisingly, such differences also have a direct bearing on discussions about the most ideal media and public communication systems required to support democracy. Those more on the political left emphasize equality and greater participation in media. Those on the right gravitate towards liberty and more limited participation.

Jürgen Habermas and the Public Sphere

One of the most well-known attempts to develop a theory of public communication in democracy is that of Jürgen Habermas's *The Structural Transformation of the Public Sphere* (1962). Since its publication in English (1989) the work has been widely used, particularly in UK and European studies of journalism, politics and political communication. It offers historical, philosophical-ideal and sociological-empirical elements. It unravels a historical account of the development and importance of public communicative spaces in emerging democracies in early modern Europe. At the same time, it provides a terminology and set of idealized norms by which democracies of all kinds can be empirically observed and evaluated.

The book has two parts. The first traces the historical evolution of bourgeois public spheres of communication in Britain, France, Germany and elsewhere. These, which emerged primarily in the eighteenth century, created the public communicative spaces essential for more democratic systems of government to emerge. They developed through physical forums, such as clubs and coffee houses, but also via printed works, such as newspapers, books and political pamphlets. Thus, were created communicative spaces which floated between states and private individuals and linked to a wider and more pluralist form of public opinion; the same spaces and publications where liberal principles of equality, liberty, participation and so on became more defined and accepted. As such, these bourgeoise public spheres were central to challenging the older, top-down ruling orders of monarchy, nobility, church and autocratic state.

These public spheres developed some important, progressive practices. For one, involvement, to a degree, was decoupled from social status which meant more inclusiveness and more extensive participation. That in turn resulted in subject agendas being opened up. There was a sense for those concerned of the 'public good' and a need to establish what would work for the wider citizenry. Such notions facilitated more altruistic practices of 'rational deliberation' and 'critical publicity'. Although such spaces remained limited and exclusionary, they provided the models and parameters for the more inclusive, citizen-based forms of modern democracy that would later materialize. In effect, Habermas's account, while upholding individual liberty, put greater emphasis on the ideals of equality and sorority.

The second part of Habermas's book, influenced by his Frankfurt School roots, describes the 'refeudalization' of these same public spheres during the nineteenth and twentieth centuries. In many ways, the very driving forces that brought public spheres into being, such as the growth of capitalism, the bureaucratic state and mass democracy, also set in motion their corruption. It became harder to identify them as autonomous spaces, operating independently of state and individuals and on behalf of the wider public good. Mass media, as the main component of modern public spheres in large, representative democracies, figured centrally. Increasingly commercialized and mediated public spheres inevitably became polluted with promotional and self-serving material. Rational debate was replaced by self-interested rhetoric and passive consumerism.

Habermas's work, when first published in English in 1989, was quickly subjected to a number of criticisms (see collection in Calhoun, 1992; Fraser, 1997; Goode, 2005). Many took issue with the historical accuracy of the account. It was based on limited source material, rather idealized and did not fully acknowledge the general exclusion of much of the population. Its constituent groups remained predominantly wealthy, male and educated. Like the ancient Athenian polis, eighteenth-century public spheres had a limited membership and so could support more direct, participatory democratic practices. An important point is that the practices and norms of its past would be very difficult to reproduce in much larger, national public spheres.

For others, Habermas's rather critical account of twentieth-century mass media and democracy was rather too negative. It unfavourably compared a complex, flawed present with an idealized, partial history. His insistence on inclusive, rational and participatory public dialogue in an era of large-scale, representative democracy was both naïve and impractical. For these scholars (Thompson, 1995; Dahlgren, 1995; Kellner, 2000) mass media and culture continue to have a central part to play, both positive and problematic, in the modern public sphere.

In spite of these historical criticisms, many scholars argued that the greater strength of Habermas's work lay in the concepts and framework it offered for judging and evaluating modern democratic communication systems. The original ideals, such as inclusiveness, open subject agendas, altruistic rational deliberation and the wider public good, each reflected wider normative thinking on democracy. Thus, even as political systems and media evolve and multiply, public sphere norms and practices may still be documented, compared and judged.

Ironically, Habermas himself had already moved on to explore other public communication issues (notably, 1977, 1987) by the time his book was published in English. He acknowledged many of the historical and practical problems of his original work (1992) while still advocating the core democratic values at its heart. In 1996, he then published *Between Facts and Norms*. This offered a new evaluative framework in line with large, complex, modern democracies, with their elaborate civil societies and formalized parliamentary institutions. He observed a 'two-track' system that channelled the multiple spheres of civil society through to legislative bodies which then deliberated and produced law. Consequently, he put far less emphasis on the generalized, mass-mediated public sphere itself, which he continued to regard with suspicion. Instead, far more was put on citizens participating in multiple, overlapping spheres, in which shared interests and values are identified informally, to be channelled to the heart of the formal, contemporary public sphere: that of parliament itself (see account in Davis, 2010a). Rehg and

Bohman (2002), among others, adapted Habermas's schema to develop specific criteria for assessing the application of his ideals to parliaments.

While Habermas bypassed the mass media, political communication scholars continued to focus on multiple media formats and mediatized public spheres. Some used his ideals and framework to assess or proscribe changes to current-day mass media systems (Dahlgren and Sparks, 1992; Hallin, 1994; Curran, 2002). Others looked at how they might apply to online public spheres and counter-public spheres (Coleman and Blumler, 2009; Fuchs, 2014; Fenton, 2016b). Dahlberg (2001) and Polat (2005) offered early schema for assessing public sphere principles at the digital level. Others still, look beyond the nation state, perceiving the existence of European-level, global or transnational public spheres (McNair, 2006; Fraser, 2007; Castells, 2008; Volkmer, 2014).

Despite the continuing appeal of Habermas's public sphere concept and critical-normative framework, difficult questions remain. On a practical level, are governments and societies now so large and complex that they make the basic concept invalid?

States are now wide-ranging, conflicted mixtures of networks and institutions. Civil societies, with their plethora of organizations, associations and communication forums, even more so. The few mass media outlets that once dominated their national public spheres have become surpassed by numerous smaller and specialist alternatives, from the digital to the international; often resembling polarized 'sphericules' rather than collective public spheres. Expertise and complexity, non-human as well as human technical agency, mean that most publics neither have the understanding or desire to participate in many facets of politics that affect them. Rational deliberation, if it was ever really practised, seems to be rather implausible in today's world of spin, advertising and media management. The boundaries of nation states are now entirely porous as peoples, cultures, businesses, finance and governing institutions criss-cross the globe (see discussion of several of these issues in Livingstone and Lunt, 2013; Kellner, 2014; Bennett and Pfetsch, 2018). All of which means that it may no longer be useful to apply public sphere frameworks to an evaluation of 'actual existing democracies' (Fraser, 1997), and actual existing media systems.

Alternatively, perhaps it is the ideals themselves that are redundant. Is it still feasible to attempt to apply a set of political and communication ideals from the eighteenth and nineteenth centuries to twenty-first-century political spaces, problems and populations?

Comparing Politics and Communication in Actually Existing Democracies

This takes us onto looking at the actual institutions and systems through which politics and communication operate in large, complex, representative democracies. Studies here are still concerned with the core ideals of liberty, equality and sovereignty, as well as with issues of representation and participation. The protection of individual freedoms and rights, political checks and balances, equality of life chances and expression, and a sense of a shared society and national identity, are all considerations that inform the now weighty comparative literature on media and political systems. Such work is very useful, both for interrogating and evaluating one's own system, and for setting out the range of alternatives on offer.

Before introducing some of this work it is important also to note a few of its flaws. For a start, comparative researchers, however cosmopolitan in intent, still interpret and frame research through their own nation-state eyes. Country-influenced parameters and values are hard to avoid, and typologies may be crudely imposed regardless of fit. Researchers have a tendency to favour particular systems and ideological preferences in their data collection and analysis (Norris, 2000; Zhao and Hackett, 2005; Hardy, 2008). Second, using the nation state as the de facto unit of measurement and comparison is flawed, quite simply because there are so many dimensions and variables to take into account which cannot be isolated. Lastly, nation-state boundaries are becoming harder to define and there seems an increasing degree of international political and media system convergence (Swanson and Mancini, 1996; Hallin and Mancini, 2011).

Starting with political systems and institutions, the world's many democracies contain a number of similar features. These include such components as regular free and fair elections, competitive party systems, autonomous judiciaries and independent news media. But, there is considerable variation in terms of how such systems and institutions have emerged historically. Every state has placed varying emphases on the competing ideals of liberty, equality, representation and participation.

Comparative politics scholarship has a long and more wide-ranging history with debates encompassing many variables and correlations (see Lijphart, 1999; Almond et al., 2010; Hague and Harrop, 2013). One key source of comparison, directly linked to representation, focuses on electoral systems. The most common system now is some form of proportional representation (PR), employed in much of Europe and South America. Voting procedures ensure that the seat distribution in a parliament reflects the wider popular vote and, most often, encourages several parliamentary parties and coalition governments. The main alternative is a first-past-the-post electoral system, used in the UK, US, Canada, India and several African nations. Such systems directly link individual politicians to their constituencies and, in most cases, are dominated by two major parties, with one party taking control of government. There are also some notable variations on these two systems, such as Germany and Mexico's MMP (Mixed Member Proportional), or Japan and South Korea's MMM (Mixed Member Majoritarian) systems.

The question of representation also relates to the demographic make-up of members of Parliament. Most surveys of elected members reveal an over-preponderance of older males from more privileged backgrounds. Women, ethnic and religious minorities, and the young, are generally under-represented. No system is, or can be, truly representative but some are more socially reflective of their societies than others. In terms of gender balances, for example, 42% of MPs in South Africa's main parliament are women but only 9% of Japan's Parliament are (IPU, 2017).

Another key issue regards the checks and balances of power in a political system, between the executive (government), parliament and judiciary. In Sweden, parliamentary committees are able to substantially alter government proposals but cannot do so in the UK. In some states, like Germany, Canada and the US, constitutional courts allow judicial reviews of new legislation. This has not traditionally been the case in Sweden and the UK. Balances of power can also be observed in the relationship between central government and regional or federal politics, or between government and non-government regulatory institutions.

The strength of civil society and the levels of civic participation are further indications of democracy. Some countries encourage more voting and more elected officials. So, the US has frequent national elections (including mid-term ones) and a large number of locally elected officials. Switzerland conducts regularly referenda on policies and legislation several times per year. Participation also includes membership of interest groups and other forms of activity, varying from joining union strikes and public demonstrations to contacting political representatives and signing petitions (see Putnam, 2000; Pattie et al., 2004; Couldry et al., 2010). For example, according to the 6th Wave of the World Values Survey (2010–14), 48% of Swedes were union members next to only 2% of Turks.

Each of these factors influences normative evaluations in comparative work. Lijphart (1984, 1999) developed a typology that identified more 'majoritarian' or more 'consensus' systems of government across thirty-six nations. Consensus systems, typified by Switzerland and Belgium, tend to produce multi-party legislatures, coalition governments, use PR electoral systems, have stronger parliaments, and encourage the devolution of state power to other institutions and regions. Majoritarian systems, typified by the UK and India, have traditionally been led by single parties, have weaker checks and balances and less devolution beyond the centre. In terms of democratic ideals, majoritarian systems put more emphasis on liberty, and consensus ones on sorority/fraternity and equality.

Lijphart then suggested that 'Consensus' systems of government are democratically stronger than 'Majoritarian' ones such as the UK 'Westminster Model'. However, the differences between systems, and the health of their democracies, are not so clear cut in crisis times. Just over the last two decades several states have devolved power to regions, established constitutional courts, central banks and other independent regulatory institutions. Major parties everywhere, whether operating in multi-party or two-party systems, are increasingly split. Far-right parties, with anti-democratic leanings, have grown substantially larger in many consensus systems in the last decade.

In parallel to this academic work there have been multiple attempts by think tanks and international bodies to classify and quantify elements of democracy. The US-based Freedom House, the UK's Economist Intelligence Unit (EIU) and Sweden's Institute for Democracy and Electoral Assistance (IDEA), have each developed comprehensive criteria for evaluating the relative strength of democracy in all states. Such things as a nation's electoral process, the strength of its civil liberties and political rights, its political participation levels, and its checks on government, are scored and aggregated to produce a final score. In 2016, the EIU determined that there were nineteen full and 57 flawed democracies. Freedom House concluded there were 87 free and 59 partly free democracies.

Table 2.1 contains a sample of sixteen nations from around the world of varying sizes, democratic strengths and political systems: **A**rgentina, **A**ustralia, **B**razil, **Ch**ile, **G**ermany, **H**ong Kong, **H**ungary, **I**ndia, **I**taly, **J**apan, **P**oland, **S**outh Africa, **S**weden, **T**urkey, the **UK** and the **USA**. The table notes some of these comparative factors:

Table 2.1: Comparing Political Systems

	Ar	Au	Br	Ch	Ge	HK	Hu	In	It	Ja	Po	SA	Sw	Tu	UK	US
1. Popul Size [1]	44	23	207	18	81	7	10	1290	62	127	39	55	10	81	65	327
2. Democy Rank [2]	49	10	51	34	13	68	56	32	21	20	52	40	3	97	16	21
3. Voting System [3]	PR	PR	PR	PR	Mx	Mx	Mx	Mj	PR	Mx	PR	PR	PR	PR	Mj	Mj
4. Last Elec Turn Year, % [4]	2015 81	'16 91	'14 81	'13 49	'17 76	– –	'14 62	'14 66	'13 75	'14 53	'15 51	'14 73	'14 86	'15 85	'17 69	'16 65
5. Particp Score [5]	6.1	7.8	5.6	4.4	7.8	5.6	4.4	7.2	7.2	6.7	6.7	8.3	8.3	5.0	7.2	7.2
6. Civil Lib Sc [6]	2	1	2	1	1	–	2	3	1	1	2	2	1	5	1	1
7. Union Mem % [7]	10	21	14	13	12	19	4	17	14	10	11	36	48	2	19	16

1. CIA, July 2017 Estimates (millions)
2. Economist Intelligence Unit, democracy ranking (1 being top), 2016
3. Voting System: **P**roportional **R**epresentation, **M**ajority/First Past the Post, **M**ixed
4. IDEA (2017) Last election turnout, year and percentage voting
5. Economist Intelligence Unit, political participation score 1–10 (10 being best), 2016
6. Freedom House, civil liberties score on scale of 1–10 (1 being best), 2017
7. World Values Survey, trade union membership % in 6th wave (2010–14), Italy, UK and Hungary in 5th wave (2005–9)

(1) population size of a country, (2) Freedom House's rating of a nation's democracy, (3) whether it has a majoritarian, PR or other electoral system, (4) the last election turnout, (5) Economist Intelligence Unit's political participation score, (6) Freedom House's civil liberties rating, (7) percentage who are trade union members.

Moving onto comparative work on media and political communication, one approach has been to collect detailed, individual nation studies, and then isolate and attempt to correlate specific phenomena (e.g., Swanson and Mancini, 1996; Gunther and Mughan, 2001; Esser and Pfetsch, 2004). Others develop typologies within which nations may be placed. Siebert et al.'s *Four Theories of the Press* (1956), Curran and Park's *De-Westernizing Media Studies* (2000), and Hallin and Mancini's (2004) *Comparing Media Systems*, are three examples. Curran and Park placed their mix of nations along two axes: democratic to authoritarian political systems and state-regulated to free market media. Hallin and Mancini, produced a tripartite typology ('polarized pluralist', 'democratic corporatist', 'liberal') to describe the systems of sixteen Western democracies.

A commonly debated issue in comparative media systems work is whether states should have a greater or lesser role when it comes to the funding, ownership and general regulation of media (Keane, 1991; Hardy, 2008). As market advocates argue, individual liberties are best protected through media that are free from state control. State-owned media are less likely to hold the state itself to account. Governments, both authoritarian and democratic, have a long history of abusing their positions of power in relation to news reporting. However, as those on the left maintain, large, powerful media companies are equally capable of pursuing the interests of their owners or organizations, regardless of democratic ideals or public good principles (McChesney, 1999; Curran, 2002; Freedman, 2008). Market-led news media result in commercially oriented content, producing 'softer', less informed and investigative reporting and less informed citizens (Benson and Hallin, 2007; Aalberg and Curran, 2012; de Vreese et al., 2016). Thus, a stable state, active state regulation and/or financial support can be necessary conditions for an autonomous, public service-minded media to flourish. Looking at Table 2.2 below, it seems that in democracies at least, journalists are far more concerned with owner than political interference.

Historically, the US has taken a market-led approach, emphasizing free speech and individual liberties (McChesney, 1999). It has never had a sizeable public service broadcasting (PSB) presence and just a few conglomerates have come to dominate across all media and communication sectors (Bagdikian, 2014). It is one of the few democracies to neither give free broadcast time to political parties nor to impose limits on political advertising. In contrast, European countries have had a strong PSB sector historically. Although declining in recent decades they have maintained a clear market share in many nations (Hardy, 2008). They have also retained stronger limits on media ownership and clear restrictions on political campaign advertising.

Two further features of media systems, noted in Hallin and Mancini (2004, 2011), are national variations in journalist culture and modes of news consumption. In their 2004 study, they identified a 'North Atlantic' professional model of reporting, with an emphasis on autonomy, objectivity and balance (see also Chalaby, 1996). In contrast, in several 'Polarized Pluralist' Southern European nations, such as Spain and Italy, journalism was less developed as a distinct profession, and political and media elites worked more closely together. In their 2011 comparisons 'beyond the Western World', they and their contributors argued that the polarized pluralist model was most common among new, emerging democracies. They also suggested that international trends were converging towards the professional model of reporting.

News consumption habits also vary considerably in relation to literacy rates, wealth and history (Hallin and Mancini, 2004). Southern European nations, such as Spain or Greece, traditionally have had relatively low levels of newspaper circulation compared to Northern Europe and Japan. In many poorer democracies, such as Brazil, Mexico or South Africa, a large proportion of news consumption has been via radio (Norris, 2004). Internet penetration rates, and thus access to online news, varies considerably between wealthier and poorer nations. Currently, a sizeable group of people in several states in South America, Eastern and Southern Europe use social media or messaging apps as a key source of news. Those in the UK and Scandinavia are more likely to go direct to online news sites (Reuters, 2017).

Several measures of media, related to the autonomy, funding, culture and consumption of news are recorded in Table 2.2 below. The measures are: (1) Freedom House's freedom of the press ranking, (2) national internet penetration rates, (3) the percentage of the public who have paid for online news, (4) public trust in news media, (5) the percentage of journalists with a degree in journalism, (6) the degree to which journalists see their remit as including

Table 2.2: Comparing Media Systems

	Ar	Au	Br	Ch	Ge	HK	Hu	In	It	Ja	Po	SA	Sw	Tu	UK	US
1. Freedom of the Press Score, 2017 [1]	46	22	47	29	20	42	44	43	31	27	34	38	11	76	25	23
2. Net Penetr % [2]	69	85	66	78	88	74	80	35	66	91	72	52	93	58	93	89
3. Pay for News Online [3]	10	13	22	9	7	21	10	-	12	11	16	-	20	0	6	16
4. Trust in News [3]	39	42	60	47	50	42	31	-	39	43	53	-	42	40	43	38
5. Jnlm Degree [4]	71	70	91	87	37	69	68	72	50	13	-	70	68	32	41	79
6. Hold Pol to A/C [5]	4.0	3.6	3.6	3.9	2.8	4.1	3.1	3.8	3.3	4.5	-	3.6	4.4	4.1	3.3	4.3
7. More Influence by Politicians/ or Owners [6]	O	P	O	O	O	O	O	O	O	-	-	O	O	P	O	O

1. Freedom House, Freedom of the Press Score, 2017 (lowest is most free)
2. Internet Penetration Rates 2016, at Internet Live Stats
3. Reuters Institute Digital News Report 2017
4. Ppercentage of public who ....
5. Worlds of Journalism 2012–16. % of journalists with specific degree in journalism.
6. Worlds of Journalism 2012–16. Journalists see role as monitoring/scrutinizing political leaders. Average score on 1–5 Scale, 5 being highest
7. Worlds of Journalism 2012–16. Comparison of average journalists experience of influences by politicians and owners. More influence by Politicians or Owners.

scrutinizing and monitoring political leaders, (7) whether journalists feel more influenced by politicians or media owners.

As with comparative political systems work, national distinctions are now not so clear cut. Recent international trends in news production and consumption have been towards more free-market producers and multiple, dispersed media. News outputs in the UK and US, supposedly guided by more professional objective practices, appear to be becoming more partisan and polarized (the opposite of what Hallin and Mancini, 2011, argued). The 2017 Reuters digital news report identified the US as being the most polarized of the thirty-six in its report (see also Newman and Fletcher, 2017). With digitalization of news, more people in more nations can access more news at low cost than ever, and alternative news producers are springing up everywhere. But, the quality of those general outputs seems of rather softer and poorer quality than before (de Vreese et al., 2016; Aalberg, 2017). These suggest a decline in shared, public sphere-types of media. Thus, across mediated democracies of all kinds, ideals of equality and sorority are on the decline and that of individual liberty is in the ascendancy.

We now have a number of means of classifying and evaluating political and media systems according to certain normative values. However, several authors identify other indicators used to judge the health or 'quality' of democracies. For example, certain measures of democratic wellbeing relate to wealth and the state of the economy, being recorded in levels of growth, inflation and unemployment. In 2016, the US had a per capita income of $57,436, while India's was $1,723. An important measure of national equality is the Gini Coefficient. Another such measure is the UNDP's (United Nations Development Programme) Human Development Index (HDI), combining life expectancy, education levels and living standards. Increasingly, per capita levels of CO_2 emissions, energy use and environmental waste, are seen as significant measures. Yet another measure is the aggregate feelings of 'trust' in political institutions or 'happiness' of a national population. Several such indicative measures are included in Table 2.3.

Conclusion

Where does this chapter lead us in terms of identifying the ideals and values, institutions and practices, which are most appropriate for sustaining healthy democracies? What is the best balance of liberty

Table 2.3: Wider Evaluations of Democracy

	Ar	Au	Br	Ch	Ge	HK	Hu	In	It	Ja	Po	SA	Sw	Tu	UK	US
1. Per Capita GDP [1]	56	10	69	54	17	14	55	141	25	20	57	91	11	60	19	7
2. UN HDI Rank [2]	45	2	79	38	4	12	43	131	26	17	36	119	14	71	16	10
3. Gini Coefficient [3]	43	30	50	51	27	54	28	35	32	31	31	63	25	40	32	45
4. Women Parlm [4]	39	29	11	16	37	-	10	12	31	9	28	42	44	15	30	19
5. CO_2 Emissions [5]	4.7	15.4	2.6	4.7	8.9	6.4	4.3	1.7	5.3	9.5	7.5	9	4.5	4.5	6.5	16.5
6. Trust in Govt [6]	32	30	41	31	44	59	16	46	26	24	16	46	60	59	32	33
7. Very Happy? [6]	34	35	35	24	23	23	17	37	18	32	22	39	41	38	51	36

1. IMF 2016 (Index of 187 countries), per capita GDP world ranking
2. United Nations Development Programme, Indices 2016, Human Development Index (Index of 188 countries)
3. CIA, 2016, Gini Coefficient data calculations from 2006–15. Higher mark is more unequal.
4. IPU, 2017, percentage of women that make up the lower or single parliament.
5. CIA, 2014 CO_2 emissions, metric tons per capita.
6. World Values Survey, % in 6th wave (2010–14), Italy, UK and Hungary in 5th wave (2005–9)

and equality, participation and representation, and which systems and institutions are most likely to achieve this?

At one end of various spectrums comes the United States, a large, prosperous nation with extensive old and new media infrastructures. The US unequivocally comes down on the side of liberty over equality. Its governance continues to emphasize individual liberties, such as a free press and the right to bear arms, despite a political system strongly influenced by the wealthy and very high rates of incarceration and gun-related deaths. It is a majoritarian, first-past-the-post system, but also one that has a high level of checks and balances. Electoral turnout and trust in institutions, parties and media has been low for decades. It is a strong promoter of free markets and deregulated industry and media, and lower taxes. Compared to many European nations it spends less per capita on public health and welfare. It is also one of the most unequal societies, in terms of income and life expectancy, of any advanced economy. It scores poorly in terms of its low percentage of women in its legislature and high levels of CO_2 emissions. It is classed as 'democratic neoliberal' (Curran and Park, 2000) or 'liberal' (Hallin and Mancini, 2004).

At another end comes the far smaller Nordic countries such as Sweden and Finland. They too are comparatively wealthy and have extensive old and new media infrastructures. They favour equality and sorority over liberty. They practise more consensual politics, using PR electoral systems, with state power balanced across institutions. Electoral turnout and trust in institutions is rather higher. Both in terms of economic policy and media, there is a greater emphasis on state support and regulation, and higher taxes and redistribution. They score well in terms of women's representation in Parliament and wider forms of political participation. They are classed as 'democratic regulated' (Curran and Park, 2000) or 'democratic corporatist' (Hallin and Mancini, 2004).

The UK hovers between these two ends but for some years has been edging closer to the US in various ways. It's a medium sized nation with a per capita income a bit below the other three but ahead of many other developed economies. Like the US, it is a majoritarian system but has fewer checks and balances holding back governments. Economically, it has chosen the more markets, less regulation and lower taxes route. But, at the same time, it is used to spending European levels of public money on health and welfare. Its broadcasting system is dominated by the publicly funded BBC, but its press operates in a highly competitive market and is polarized politically. Thus, the BBC and NHS suggest elements of equality and sorority, but its economic system and press sector, something driven more by individual liberty.

In many ways, the polarization in parties and populaces caused by the votes for Brexit and Donald Trump reflect the heightened tensions between liberty, equality and sovereignty/sorority. British policy-makers want access to the single market but not free movement of people. EU members insist the two go together. Americans value cheap goods and services bought by globalization but not the loss of home-grown industries that have accompanied this. Free market arguments emphasize global competition and free movement of capital, businesses and individuals. But, this is conflicting with a sense of collective national identity or national sorority. And, it's an odd combination of nationalism, collectivism, individualism and market freedoms that have left the supporters and politicians of many major parties in the UK, US and continental Europe very split.

3

Political Communication and Crisis in Established Democracies

This chapter looks at the question of crisis in politics and media in established democracies. Discussions of democratic crisis emerge periodically in political communication. Political legitimacy crises were widely debated amid the economic challenges of the 1970s. They featured frequently in writing on politics and media in the late 1990s and early 2000s, as long-term declines were recorded in political trust, voting levels and news consumption. In the late 2010s they have returned once again.

For some, notions of crisis are always overblown. They are better conceived of as cycles of change where modern media and politics are reconfigured by wider social forces. Things are not better or worse, just different. Trends over a century instead suggest that citizens and democracies are in far better shape now. By this thinking we are simply experiencing another (fourth) age of politics and communication.

However, during this decade, talk of crisis has begun to look like more than just another temporary dip in the long advance of democracy. A prolonged economic crisis has left extreme debts, instability and inequality. Long-established political parties have fractured or been shoved to the margins. The business model that underpinned news journalism has been broken. The global order now looks increasingly unstable and beset with threats. Environmental concerns, from global warming to resource scarcities, are becoming critical.

The chapter is in three parts. The first covers two sides of the earlier crisis debate. The second argues that just in the last decade, a series of more fundamental tipping points for democracies have been reached. The third looks at some of the wider causes of this, focusing on three broad disrupters of democracy: globalization, neoliberalism and new information and communication technologies (ICTs).

Crisis Talk: Substantial or Superficial?

The 1990s and 2000s saw a plethora of accounts of democratic crisis. These revolved around the disengagement of governments, political parties and media from their publics. Each suggested that a long-term state legitimation crisis could be developing (Crozier et al., 1975; Habermas, 1977).

Part of this was a sense that governments had become increasingly disengaged from and less accountable to their citizens. For some, this was best explained by the general process of 'depoliticization' observed across mature democracies in the UK, Continental Europe, North America and elsewhere (Flinders and Buller, 2006; Hay, 2007; Mair, 2013). Since the 1970s, a combination of corporate public management practices, free market economics and directives from global institutions such as the IMF and World Bank, have all encouraged the same things: smaller, less-interventionist government, technocratic rather than political management, the handing over of power to 'non-political' regulatory institutions and experts, and the outsourcing of public services and functions to the private sector. Such trends have been particularly pronounced in more neoliberal countries like the UK (Burnham, 2001; Moran, 2003; Bowman et al., 2015). Consequently, many of the levers of state management have been steadily handed to non-democratically accountable institutions and experts.

A similar thesis of disengagement has developed in relation to political parties, their members and the wider citizenry (Dalton and Wattenberg, 2002; Crouch, 2004; Hay, 2007; Tormey, 2015; Chapter 4, this volume). Originally, parties emerged to represent particular groups in society. But, over time, increasing professionalism transformed them, organizationally, ideologically and managerially. Organizationally, an influx of experts from marketing and media relations, elevated for their skills rather than their political ideals, became more central to party activities. Ideologically, policy construction and elections became more oriented towards centre ground politics and swing voters. Managerially, parties have come to be dominated by professional, career politicians who spend more time with wealthy donors and media moguls than members. In effect, today's 'electoral-professional' parties have become distanced, physically and communicatively, from publics. They are no longer representatives of 'the people'.

Politicians and bureaucrats have thus colluded in their own depoliticization and the ceding of political power to non-accountable or representative professionals and organizations. Democratic politics, linking governance to public 'opinion- and will-formation', has suffered. Almost imperceptibly, democracy has been 'hollowed out'.

There has also developed an established crisis literature in media and political communication (Blumler and Gurveitch, 1995). For some, news media is quite simply failing in its duty to properly report and inform citizens. As competition in the industry has grown and news consumption declined, so news has become more simplistic and entertainment-oriented (Hall Jamieson, 1996; Franklin, 1997; Delli Carpini and Williams, 2001; Davies, 2008). Coverage has replaced investigative reporting and informed policy discussions with soundbites, personalities, negative stories and horse-race coverage. All of which leaves publics struggling to engage positively with the political process.

For political economists it is more than general failure. Rather it is bias as news producers are far more oriented to elite interests than public ones (Herman and Chomsky, 2002; Curran and Seaton, 2003; Bagdikian, 2004). Governments and large corporations own most media, are its main reported sources, its biggest advertisers and main suppliers of public relations material. All of which suggests that journalists have an uphill battle when it comes to fulfilling their 'fourth estate' remit and 'speaking truth to power'.

Such concerns have been exacerbated by the steady erosion of income for traditional legacy news organizations in most mature democracies. For decades, aggregate newspaper readerships and advertising spends have slowly declined. Slowly but surely the traditional business model on which legacy news media has operated for centuries is becoming unsustainable (McChesney and Nichols, 2010; McChesney and Pickard, 2011; Chapter 5, this volume). Continuing survival means more cuts in editorial resources, more reliance on the subsidies and sponsorship of the powerful, and more non-news and extremist content. Consequently, public trust and consumption of news media continues to edge down.

Those pursuing the crisis line found their most worrying findings in surveys of publics. These revealed a strong decline of faith in institutional politics and media. Robert Putnam's studies (1993, 2000) observed a general drop in forms of 'social capital' and civic participation, as fewer joined local associations, social or political groups. In turn, they had less trust in national political and state institutions. Such themes were explored in the US, Europe and elsewhere (Putnam, 2002; Dalton, 2004; Hay, 2007; Mair, 2013). The clearest evidence of this was in the long-term decline in voter turnout in many democracies. From the 1950s to the 1990s turnout dropped 10% across the nineteen OECD democracies for which time-series data existed. New turnout lows were reached in Japan in 1995 (44.9%), in the US in 1996 (49%), and in Canada in 2000 (54.6%). Putnam (2002: 406) noted that membership of political parties had dropped from 14%, in the 1970s, to less than 6% in the 1990s.

Disengagement manifested itself in other ways too. The World Values Survey, repeated periodically since 1981, provided extensive data on declining levels of public trust in institutions. Dalton and Wattenberg (2002: 264) found that, of the nineteen nations surveyed in the 1990s, only 38% of their publics had confidence in their national governments. 38% had confidence in their parliament, 32% in their press and just 22% in their political parties. Hay (2007), drawing on 2004 polls, found that aggregate trust (those with trust minus those without) in political parties was minus 69 in the USA and minus 63 in the EU. In the mid-1970s, Gallup polls of the US public's trust in the mass media were at 72%. By the end of the 1990s they were at the low fifties, and by the end of the 2000s the low forties. Since 1983 Ipsos-MORI have asked the UK public about their trust in the national media. Response levels have fluctuated but not been above 22% in any year of this century. Figures for both nations drop far lower if applied just to tabloid journalism.

For several scholars in the 2000s, the wider trends all pointed towards a growing democratic crisis. For Colin Crouch (2004) we were moving towards a state of 'post-democracy'. For Colin Hay (2007) citizens in democracies had come to 'hate politics'. For John Keane (2009) we were potentially looking at the 'death of democracy'.

However, for others, crisis talk is just talk. For Pippa Norris and Ronald Inglehart, there was not a substantive 'crisis' to speak of. Such notions were superficial and an over-pessimistic reaction to changing times. We were not going through a crisis so much as another anxiety-inducing period of disruption. Over the longue duree, democracy has spread and most people in the world are far better off than they were a century ago.

Looking back, crisis talk appears to be a regular phenomenon. It often repeats old concerns while ignoring the longer-term pathway of progress. Wars, economic collapses and periods of social unrest disrupt but are temporary. The Second World War was followed by decades of welfare reform, growth and prosperity. The 1970s economic and political crises led to new forms of political and economic management and further extended periods of growth and prosperity. In the longer-term, publics have thrived as democracy has developed. They are substantially better off than they were a century ago. They have experienced steady increases in living standards, education levels and healthcare provision, all leading to rising lifespans. In 1900, average global life expectancy was forty. By 2014 it had reached 71.5. Although the figures do not show the huge variations across regions and classes, clear rises have taken place virtually everywhere.

It is the same with news media. Complaints about the fakery and failings of 'yellow journalism' have been regularly made since the 1880s (Williams, 1997; Campbell, 2003). The death of news generally, and the newspaper in particular, has been predicted with each new technological advance and new medium over the same period (Curran, 2009). Yet, currently, there are more news producers and more news content available than ever before.

What we really experience are temporary cycles of democratic disruption and renewal (Norris, 2000, 2002, 2004). Modern parties may have become more professional-electoral in outlook, but they are also better communicators and more responsive to the wider citizenry when developing policies (Lees-Marshment, 2001). Those parties that are not, become marginalized and ejected, leaving space for new, more responsive ones to emerge. Alongside a changing party system has come the expansive growth of civil society, with its range of flourishing interest groups and alternative media (Castells, 1997, 2001; Della Porta and Diani, 1999; Downing, 2001). Membership of political parties may have declined but that of NGOs, such as Amnesty, Greenpeace or the Danish Refugee Council, have all risen considerably. In fact, their member numbers often dwarf those of formal parties. Just, as readership and trust in mass media is declining, so we have a new wave of online publications, blogs, tweets and social networking spaces (Coleman and Blumler, 2009; Chadwick, 2013; Dalhgren, 2013; Castells, 2015). New technologies are being used in the service of large, new protest movements – from established Western democracies to authoritarian regimes in the Middle East and Asia. In effect, politics, media and participation are simply being reconfigured with multiple, vibrant alternatives springing up everywhere. Citizens have not lost interest in politics but have simply redirected it elsewhere.

Despite the growing apathy and cynicism of voters, democracy seems essentially sound in other ways. The number of democracies tripled in the last decades of the twentieth century. In 1975, forty-six nations conducted competitive elections. By 2015, that number was 132 (IDEA, 2017). In the early 2000s in all those countries surveyed where trust and voting had been declining, between 88% and 98% of the public polled still believed in democracy as a system of government (see Hay, 2007). They may be critical of their leaders and parties but they remain strongly supportive of their own democratic political system.

Putting this information together, Inglehart, Norris and others concluded that the problem of 'democratic deficit' was one of perception rather than substance. Inglehart's thesis (1977, 1990, 1997) was that established capitalist democracies have produced a 'postmaterialist' generation. When democracies mature, and economic and physical security is achieved, wealthier and more literate citizens adopt postmaterialist values. Their education makes them more critical and demanding but not necessarily more active and participatory. Investigations of political participation in the UK and US (Hibbings and Theiss-Morse, 2002; Dalton, 2004; Webb, 2007; Hansard, 2009) find that many want a say but rather fewer are prepared to be substantially involved. Fewer still have an understanding of the processes and complexities of today's modern 'multi-dimensional policy space'. Thus, expectations and criticisms of governments rise while an appreciation of those in power decline.

In effect, for Inglehart, Norris and others, it is all about public perceptions. Their real argument is that we never had it so good. We are all too busy with our Facebook accounts, Jimmy Choo shoes and sports teams to notice or care. For those with a keener interest in politics, our critical faculties are more advanced than our understanding.

These same authors continued to present aspects of this thesis through this decade. In 2011, Norris revisited her 'democratic deficit' arguments. Although more open to questioning the roles of the mass media, government and public institutions, she still returned to her basic position: low levels of trust and political legitimacy were more a matter of perception; they waxed and waned according to current events; and support for democracy was as strong as ever. In 2016, Inglehart and Norris argued that the rise of Donald Trump represented a 'cultural backlash' more than a reaction to substantial failings in US and EU economic and political systems.

An IDEA report on the global state of democracy in 2017, similarly emphasized the importance of reflecting more on long-term gains than short-term instabilities. Applying their own set of metrics, the authors determined that most global democratic trends in most regions of the world had been positive over the past four decades. On a range of measures, from civil liberties and welfare provision to representative government with appropriate checks and balances, trends continued to move in progressive directions. Despite some recent 'backsliding' in some newer democracies, the majority of systems had proved themselves 'resilient' to adversity. As they concluded, in response to more crisis talk (2017: 8): 'Over the past forty years most aspects of democracy have advanced, and democracy today is healthier than many contend.'

Tipping Points for Democracy Reached

With hindsight, the 1990s and 2000s now appear to be periods of relative tranquillity and prosperity. Several key events and new data suggest that capitalist democracies everywhere are facing huge challenges. In the last half decade in particular, the crisis debate has taken on a renewed sense of purpose. Although some would continue to argue that this is just another transitional point for modern democracy, I would argue that the challenges are far more profound than that.

Some key twenty-first century events and trends have unsettled nations and called into question some of the core functions and institutions of US-style capitalist democracy. The 2001 attack on New York's twin towers, set in motion a series of wars in the Middle East as well as terrorist attacks around the world. The 2007–8 global financial crash led to a global recession with a range of consequences for all economies. At the same time, the geopolitical balance of economic and political power began altering. Russia adopted a more aggressive and expansionist foreign policy while China's rapidly growing economy became more integrated into the global system. The new digital economy began reconfiguring industries, media and social relations. The effects of climate change, extreme inequality and large-scale migration, became more visible. Much publicized revolts against economic and political injustice took place across Europe, the US and the Middle East in 2011 (see Chapter 8). Thus, once again, critics began asking if the twentieth-century model of capitalist democracy was now reaching a dangerous tipping point (Crouch, 2011; Streeck, 2014).

For those taking the change-not-crisis position, there remains quite a bit of evidence to suggest that their larger analysis still holds good. The number of countries holding direct parliamentary elections continued to rise into the 2000s (IDEA, 2016). The voting and survey data from 2010 to 2015, although hardly positive, does not suggest a substantial break-down is close at hand. Voter turnout is still edging down but no dramatic collapse has taken place (IDEA, 2016: 23–5). The 1990s average of 70% had dropped to 66% in 2011–15. The fifth (2005–9) and sixth (2010–14) waves of the WVS (World Values Survey), although still negative about governments and parties, were not markedly different from earlier waves. In several cases, the aggregate figures for confidence and trust in institutions had improved marginally. General support for 'democracy' still scored highly everywhere. The average aggregate score, for the sixty countries asked to rate the 'importance of democracy' in the 6th WVS wave, was 8.24 out of 10. All of which lends support to Norris's thesis of trust 'waxing and waning' but democracy fundamentally remaining strong.

However, there are also some clear signs that democracy is not just going through a temporary dip. The Economist Intelligence Unit (EIU, 2016) recorded that half the 167 countries it evaluated annually had experienced a decline in their aggregate democracy scores over the previous decade. The biggest drops were in North America, Western and Eastern Europe. They now classified states such as the US, Italy and Japan as 'flawed democracies' (see also EIU, 2018). Freedom House (2017) recorded that sixty-seven countries had experienced declines in political rights and civil liberties since the previous year, while only thirty-six had registered gains. The number of countries with a decline had outnumbered those with a gain in every year of the last decade, with numbers of net declines for the last three years, 2014–17, being 29, 29 and 31. They noted that 2016 had been the first year since they began monitoring democracies in which the number of 'free countries' dropped and the number of 'not free' increased.

Something also important to note is that the global aggregate numbers cover over the large variations across nations and regions. For example, although global average voter turnout has dropped 12% since the 1950s, it has declined 20% in Europe since the 1980s (IDEA, 2016). While support for 'democracy' per se remains high, it has been dropping more significantly in certain regions like Eastern

Europe, as well as among certain demographics such as younger voters (IDEA, 2017). A growing proportion, over a quarter in some nations and among some demographics, now wonders if democracy is still the best political system (see also EIU, 2016; Stefan and Mounk, 2016). Some countries, like the US, Australia, Brazil, Japan, South Korea, Mexico, Poland and Spain, have a series of strong negative WVS trust survey scores, often in conjunction with low electoral turnouts. This combination is very concerning for such nations, making their citizens more accepting of less democratic parties, leaders and systems.

Tipping points have also been reached in news media. The problems of a declining news business model and lack of public trust in media have become much more acute everywhere. The slow downward trends in consumers and advertising revenues, detectable in the last decades of the twentieth century, became rather sharper after 2000. The global economic recession, combined with new ICTS, meant revenues started dropping substantially after 2007. One study found that the newspaper market declined by between three and 30% in every OECD country between 2007 and 2009 (OECD, 2010, see Table 3.1). The top publications of almost every OECD country either stagnated or declined markedly between 2001 and 2008. Papers like *Hankook Ilbo* (Korea), the National Post (Canada) and Le Progres (France) experienced circulation drops of 50% or more. The US and UK have been particularly hard hit here. In 2012 Pew calculated that the US newspaper industry had shrunk 43% and lost 28% of journalist jobs since 2000. In that time, on average, fifteen papers had gone bankrupt each year. Sales of most national UK newspapers are now between a quarter and a half of what they were at the turn of the century.

At the same time, news media has developed a growing trust problem in multiple nations. A broken business model, that left a growing editorial resource gap, made news output more reliant on outside subsidies and resources, and less able to challenge corporate funders and governments. More citizens began getting their news from social media and other online sources, many of which operated with less professionalism and integrity. Fake news has grown and can be quickly disseminated across online platforms. Populist politicians, such as Donald Trump, Boris Johnson and Benjamin Netanyahu, have exploited uncertainty and distrust to create their own fake truths and news. By 2016, trust in news, news organizations and journalists in general, had reached fairly low points everywhere, declining clearly over the previous five years (Reuters, 2017).

Table 3.1 looks at some of these shifts in relation to the sixteen sample nations compared in Chapter 2: **A**rgentina, **A**ustralia, **Br**azil, **Chi**le, **G**ermany, **H**ong Kong, **H**ungary, **I**ndia, Italy, **J**apan, **P**oland, **S**outh Africa, **Sw**eden, **Tu**rkey, the **UK** and the **USA**. According to the Economist Intelligence Unit's *Democracy Index*, twelve of the sixteen suffered a decline in their rating from 2006 to 2016. Although the 'importance' of, and 'support for', democracy remains high, there has been a clear drop from earlier surveys. Nine of the twelve nations that were included in both the fifth and sixth waves of the WVS, saw a decline, while three saw a rise. Confidence levels in government, political parties and the press have had ups and downs but, in most countries, remain fairly negative. Only four of the thirteen nations that were in the 2010–14, 6th WVS wave, had a positive aggregate rating for confidence in government. Only three had so for the press and none for political parties.

By the middle of this decade, it suddenly felt like actual political tipping points had been reached in several democracies around the world. The tipping points were revealed in a series of election results. Against all expectations, in 2016, Britain voted to leave the European Union, Donald Trump was elected President of the United States, Italy rejected Matteo Renzi, and Brazil impeached Dilma Rousseff. The political systems of each of these nations was thrown into turmoil. Established parties looked broken and governments decidedly unstable. In 2017 the French Presidency was contested for the first time by candidates from none of the major established parties, and the Korean President Park Geun-hye was impeached. Following their 2017 election, the Dutch took almost nine months to pull together an uneasy ruling coalition government of four parties. Likewise, Angela Merkel's Christian Democrats lost significant ground in their election and struggled to put together a precarious majority administration over six months. In Mexico in 2018, for the first time in nearly a century, a candidate from neither main party was elected President. Italy became ruled by a coalition of two extreme, populist parties, one of which was led by a professional comedian. Brazil took a lurch to the far right with the election of Jair Bolsonaro.

To add to this, far-right parties (UKIP, Front National, Golden Dawn, Jobbik, DPP, AfD, PVV) began making serious challenges across Europe and upending long-established parties and coalitions. Mostly right-wing populist parties became part of coalition governments in eleven democracies (Inglehart and Norris, 2016) and, even where relatively small, ate into the voter base of larger, centrist

Table 3.1: Wider Evaluations of Democracy

	Ar	Au	Br	Ch	Ge	HK	Hu	In	It	Ja	Po	SA	Sw	Tu	UK	US
EIU Change 06–16 [1]	+ .33	– .08	– .48	– .11	– .19	+ .39	– .81	+ .13	+ .25	– .16	– .47	– .5	– .49	– .66	+ .28	– .24
Import Demcy [2]	– .58	– .2	– .17	+ .41	– .16	NA	NA	+ .69	NA	– .24	+ .01	– 1.15	– .27	– .52	NA	– .16
Drop in News 07–09 [3]	NA	– 2	NA	NA	– 10	NA	– 9	NA	– 18	– 15	– 11	NA	– 7	– 16	– 21	– 30
Confidence in Govt [4]	– 34.7	– 38.3	– 17	– 31.3	– 9.6	+ 19.3	NA	+ 1.7	NA	– 40	– 61.7	– 4.2	+ 21.3	+ 20.3	NA	– 34.7
Confidence in Parties [5]	– 66.4	– 72.0	– 67.2	– 64.8	– 49.7	– 43.5	NA	– 23.1	NA	– 56.8	– 79	– 22.8	– 12.9	– 26.7	NA	– 72.8
Confidence in Press [6]	– 13.8	– 65.4	– 17	– 2.3	– 10.3	– 18.6	NA	+ 40.1	NA	+ 45.5	– 40.4	+ 10.4	– 26.4	– 17.8	NA	– 52.5

1. Economist Intelligence Unit Democracy Index Score change from 2006 to 2016 (on scale of 1–10)
2. World Values Survey, 'Importance of Democracy' question, % change from 5th wave, 2005–9, to 6th wave, 2010–14
3. % Drop in Newspaper Market 2007–9, OECD report (2010)
4. World Values Survey, 'Confidence in Government' aggregate % score, 6th wave, 2010–14
5. World Values Survey, 'Confidence in Parties' aggregate % score, 6th wave, 2010–14
6. World Values Survey, 'Confidence in Press' aggregate % score, 6th wave, 2010–14

parties. In turn, this either threatened their ability to hold together stable, ruling coalitions, or pushed them to adopt more extreme policies. Elsewhere, powerful populist politicians also got into power, or consolidated their positions, in China, the Philippines, Turkey, Russia, India, Hungry and Poland.

Looking beyond media and politics, it is also clear that democracies have not found answers to a number of other major crises fast approaching. As yet, nation states, whether acting unilaterally or together, are moving too slowly to avert human-made crises caused by: global warming, energy dependence on fast-depleting fossil fuels, ongoing conflicts in the Middle East, drastic forthcoming global water and food shortages, rising inequality, increased levels of migration and refugees, and an aging and increasingly unhealthy population.

Combining the trends with many recent election results suggests to me that capitalist democracy is going through more than a temporary downward blip. International and national instability can be detected in multiple places. Challenges, such as the threat of nuclear war, the impacts of global warming and mass migration, or further financial crashes, seem to be everywhere. Currently there appear frightening parallels to the 1930s: global financial crisis, struggling and unstable economies, unhappy and distrustful populations, populist aggressive leaders offering radical solutions, rising levels of nationalism and racism, international stand-offs and threats of economic and military conflict.

The Great Disrupters

Whether democracies are experiencing an extended period of change or approaching an existential crisis, it is important to identify some of the great disrupters of current-day nation-state democracy. The three broad ones highlighted here are globalization, neoliberalism, and new information and communication technologies. Each is discussed in more depth in Chapters 9, 10 and 11.

Globalization is one clear force that, whether positive or negative for national democracies, is certainly transforming them. Globalization, by most definitions, involves greater interconnectedness and inter-action across national borders (see Held and McGrew, 2003; Steger, 2009). Advances in transport and communication have facilitated more international, mobile networks of industrial production, finance, culture, communication and people. Similarly, it seems clear that an increasing amount of state politics and communication is bound up with inter-governmental and transgovernmental institutions.

For its many advocates, globalization has been largely positive for nation states and their publics. The losses to national sovereignty have been more than made up for by the gains. International bodies have integrated diverse social, legal and economic systems. They have brought stability and efficiency, warding off large-scale trade wars and global conflicts (Slaughter, 2000; Held, 2002). Globalization has also enabled the cross-border exchange of culture and communication and contributed to the development of a 'global public sphere' (Volkmer, 2014; McNair, 2016). This in turn has been vital for the evolution of a form of 'global civil society' with a shared sense of 'cosmopolitan identity' (Beck, 2006; Albrow and Glasius, 2008). In such perspectives globalization, while transforming nation states, is also supporting and securing them too.

For others, globalization has become far more damaging to national democracy than stabilizing. As several argue, the power of nations to exert influence over larger political, economic and environmental issues appears to be waning. In many accounts (Strange, 1996; Cerny et al., 2005; Krugman, 2008; Stiglitz, 2017) the international organizations and markets of 'turbo capitalism' have come to control or influence capital flows that are far in excess of those managed by states and political leaders. The largest transnational corporations and financial institutions now control more funds than most of our largest economies. Climate change, international migration, food, energy and other resource shortages develop beyond the control of most individual nations.

Such developments are severely eroding national sovereignty and notions of citizenship. It thus becomes clear, to publics as well as politicians, that casting votes for national parties may have little impact when it comes to influencing global warming, international financial markets or mass migration. There is also a growing concern about the maintenance of national culture and identity. A limited number of global media companies and brands increasingly dominate national media, homogenizing culture as they go (Herman and McChesney, 1997; Thussu, 2007). Various aspects of globalization, such as multi-culturalism, immigration or the relocation of industries abroad, appear to directly threaten local communities and cultures.

For several commentators, the success of Donald Trump, the vote for Brexit and the rise of far-right populism elsewhere, have each been driven by a rejection of globalization. In a 2016 working paper, Inglehart and Norris (2016), interpreted such shifts in Europe and the US as being explained by a 'cultural backlash'. This pitted increasingly unhappy 'populists', often inhabiting rural areas, against urban, 'cosmopolitan liberals'. David Goodhart (2017) presented a similar thesis in relation to the UK. He argued that a new form of 'socio-cultural politics' was challenging the traditional 'socio-economic politics' of left and right. For Goodhart, the new divide was between static, socially conservative 'somewheres', who felt threatened by globalization and immigration, and a smaller, mobile, liberal group of 'anywheres', who had been thriving.

Neoliberalism has proved to be another great disrupter of national democracies. The term has become a catch-all phrase, covering a set of political regimes, economic policies and broader ideas linked to individualism, free choice and free markets (see Larner, 2000; Harvey, 2007; Davies, 2014). Its advocates became increasingly influential in governments from the 1970s onwards. Adopting neoclassical economics, neoliberals are in favour of markets and market-based solutions to economic problems, and for the roll-back of the state wherever possible. In policy terms this has meant the privatization and deregulation of nationalized industries and markets, the reduction of welfare state support systems and trade union power, lower taxes and open trading borders.

Neoliberalism was taken up first by Chile's Pinochet regime in the 1970s, and then the Thatcher and Reagan administrations in the 1980s (Mirowski and Plehwe, 2009). Slowly but surely, its ideas and practices became more widely disseminated, coming to influence most types of capitalist democracy, be they mature, developing, more liberal or more socialist. International institutions, like the World Bank, IMF (International Monetary Fund) and OECD (Organization for Economic Co-operation and Development) helped build a more global consensus for it.

Like globalization, neoliberalism has both supported and challenged states and their economies. For its many advocates, neoliberal principles of economic and political management were instrumental in stabilizing economies everywhere following the 1970s economic crisis. Neoliberalism has offered a direct alternative to corrupt and inefficient state regimes, over-powerful unions and corporate vested interests. It has integrated disparate regimes into an international economic system, contributing to world-wide economic growth and prosperity. Billions of people, particularly in developing economies, have been lifted out of poverty (IDEA, 2017).

However, for its critics (Harvey, 2007; Mirowski, 2009; Crouch, 2011), neoliberalism has been extremely damaging to nations. As a basic philosophy, it is antithetical to democratic states, even as it relies on them to operate. It seeks to shrink government power and activity, not just in the operation of the economy but in many aspects of politics, welfare, education and so on. In so doing, it replaces democratically elected and accountable politicians with unelected, unaccountable business leaders. Eventually, democracy and free-market capitalism become locked in a death embrace in which all-powerful markets bring down democratic governments, ruining market economies in the process (Dean, 2009; Varoufakis, 2016; Streeck, 2017).

Three clear by-products of neoliberalism have contributed to the destabilization of capitalist democracies. One, growing levels of inequality have accompanied its rise from the start, becoming more extreme over time. The gap between the top 1% (or 0.001%) and the rest has increased many-fold, with many middle and low-income workers seeing their real incomes stagnate or drop (Piketty, 2014; Oxfam, 2017). Second, deregulated free markets have brought a great deal of economic instability. Industries have shifted from developed to developing economies, leaving large areas suffering economic and community decline. International trade imbalances have grown.

Third has come financialization, a process which has seen the financial sector expanding many times faster than the real economy (see Epstein, 2005; Krippner, 2011; Palley, 2013). The rise of big finance has brought large-scale financial instability and taken investment away from local, material economies. The global financial crisis in 2007–8 set off a world-wide economic crisis, bankrupting many nations like Greece, Ireland and Iceland. Others, such as Spain, Italy, the UK, Japan, the US and China, have gone into huge debt. For many, neoclassical economics neither predicted nor explained the crash. It seems to offer few ideas for fixing fundamental problems, like rising inequality, mounting debt, wage stagnation and future crashes (Keen, 2017).

For these critics, Brexit, Trump and the instabilities encountered in many other nations, are best explained by neoliberalism and its by-products. The anti-elite, anti-cosmopolitan, anti-globalization backlashes were because capitalism had stopped functioning for a majority of people. Their voting patterns and lack of trust in democratic institutions, politics and business elites, are a direct result of the failed neoliberal economic policies of centrist parties of both left and right (Muller, 2016; Frank, 2016; Barnett, 2017).

The third major disruptive force for democracies has been new ICTs (information and communication technologies). The internet, digitalization, wireless technology, mobile phones, and advanced computing power, have combined to reconfigure politics, media and communication.

Their emergence has been accompanied by a positive narrative that echoed previous waves of technological advance. For several early observers, there was a clear line about democracy's failings, for which new media offered potential solutions (Norris, 2002; Castells, 2001; Coleman and Gotze, 2001; Trippi, 2004). Modern democracy, with its distant politicians and limited news media, were inhibiting citizen participation and engagement. The internet, as a cheap, many-to-many medium, offered a range of potential means to re-engage citizens. This included multiple new, low-cost platforms to deliberate on, and a challenge to establishment gate-keepers, whether in politics or news media.

Indeed, the earlier years of the internet were positive, and promised to fulfil the visions of its various cheerleaders (Tapscott and Williams, 2007; Beckett, 2008; Jenkins, 2009). Governments facilitated digital petitions, votes and consultations, and published far more information about their activities online. Interest groups, from Oxfam to Occupy, were able to compete with their better funded government and corporate opponents. New social movements flourished. Politicians, once on the periphery, from Howard Dean to Bernie Sanders and Jeremy Corbyn, were able to bypass their Washington and Westminster media-political establishments to raise funds, organize their supporters and communicate to large numbers of citizens. New online news media outfits, alternative publishers, political blogs and discussion forums all mushroomed.

However, early optimism about digital democracy has given way to more realist and pessimistic assessments as new ICTs have affected every area of society. Parties and interest groups deliberate little more with their members than before, preferring to use digital media to broadcast and fundraise rather than engage. Multiple new industries, parties, news websites and interest groups have failed to sustain themselves in the online environment. Digital divides have continued, leaving many countries and peoples behind and excluded. Old media monopolies have merely been replaced by news media ones such as Facebook, Amazon, Alphabet (Google) and Apple. Lastly, it is also clear that states and corporations are increasingly using the power of new media tracking and big data capabilities to monitor and influence behaviour in ways George Orwell never dreamed of (see variously Morozov, 2012; McChesney, 2013; Fuchs, 2014; Tufekci, 2014a; Curran et al., 2016; Srnicek, 2016). All of which suggest that, on balance, new ICTs have failed to re-energize democracies.

More than that, the most recent developments, put together, amount to a destruction of the communicative architecture of the public sphere. First, the internet is largely responsible for the collapse of the business model of mainstream news journalism. This is important for all news media as legacy news operations fund professional reporting and, even if not followed directly, provide much of the news content for aggregator sites and social media. Second, the news audience is fragmenting and ghettoizing at an alarming rate (Turow, 2012; Reuters, 2017; Sunstein, 2018). A combination of consumer choices, algorithmic-led social media and advertising, is separating and polarizing the news audience. The divides between hard-core Republicans and Democrats, UK Remainers and Leavers, rich and poor, young and old, appear to be growing. Third is the emerging evidence of well-funded and organized misinformation and fake news campaigns. Much of this takes place out of sight through social media but also easily spreads to conventional media.

Conclusion

As I have argued here, the current state of crisis for democracies is now substantial. For whatever reasons, democracies old and new no longer seem to be operating in the best interests of their larger populations. Long-term deficiencies in the logics of centre-ground politics, free market economics, technological advance and globalization, have produced larger problems that policy-makers have few answers to. The negative trends, such as declining electoral turnouts and lower trust in political institutions, can no longer be simply dismissed as the responses of a 'postmaterialist generation'. The declining measures of democracy over the last decade, reversing the trends of more than half a century, are evidence of this. So are the many turns to more radical, often less democratic alternatives, in conjunction with the growing power of more authoritarian nations.

In many ways, the threat to democracy is as great as at any time since the Second World War; perhaps more so. But, unlike the 1930s, global warfare is too devastating an outcome to fathom. In contrast to the 1930s or 1970s there is as yet no alternative economic paradigm on offer. Unlike all past periods of crisis, there is no simple way back once global warming reaches certain levels. The same is true as global population rises get too great to be sustained by declining natural resources.

There are many possible explanations for the current democratic crisis. Three explored here are globalization, neoliberalism and new ICTs. Each has been heralded as a positive step forward for capitalist democracies. In each case, the positive rhetoric has been partly fulfilled. But, in each case, they have also undermined nation states, eroding sovereignty, political accountability, and contemporary public spheres. They have moved forward, driven by logics and objectives that have little to do with democracy's core ideals. They have done so at a pace that has been too quick for public institutions and media operations to adapt to. If democracies are to survive, national polities must rethink their responses to these trends. Simply embracing them on their own terms and accepting them as inevitable developments is not an option.

Part II
Institutional Politics and Mass Media

4

Political Parties and Elections

This chapter looks at political parties and election campaigns. Parties and elections sit at the heart of any democracy. Parties are the main organizations through which citizen interests are aggregated and turned into concrete policies and blueprints for governance. Elections are the mechanism by which parties compete for votes; the prize being temporary control over the institutions of government and policy process (see Dalton and Wattenberg, 2002; Webb, 2007). Thus, how parties evolve and communicate with publics is of fundamental interest.

Over the last century, the ways parties emerge, are managed and communicate, has changed enormously. Traditionally, parties developed organically to represent specific interests. They had clear supporter bases and adopted consistent ideological positions. As democracy evolved, and parties became more institutionalized, they moved first to becoming mass, 'catch-all parties', and second into 'electoral-professional parties'. This evolutionary path has had its admirers and detractors. For supporters, the shift meant parties were better communicators, more attuned to publics, ruled rationally and professionally rather than ideologically. But, for critics, the transition has meant that parties became too oriented towards elite interests and winning elections rather than representing their members and the wider public.

Developments over the last decade leave us wondering about the future of traditional parties of all kinds. Whether taking strong ideological positions or operating on a more professional, centre-ground basis, voters are losing faith all round. The professionals – the pollsters, the electoral strategists and 'expert' policy-makers – no longer seem to be getting it right as voter behaviour becomes more cynical and volatile. In the growing spaces opening up, more extreme party alternatives, with neither clear ideologies and supporter bases nor professional party machines, are gaining ground and even winning elections. This leaves us asking questions about the future of party-oriented democratic politics. Are we witnessing the demise of traditional party politics or, perhaps, a challenge to the kinds of centrist, professional-electoral parties that have dominated in recent decades? Are party-based electoral systems still the best way for democracies to link publics and governments or are we in need of a more fundamental overhaul?

The chapter is in four parts. These essentially trace the rise and fall of the modern electoral-professional party. The first traces the origins and evolutions of parties, from specific interest-based, amateur entities to their electoral-professional manifestations now. The second reviews the arguments and evidence put by the supporters and critics of such developments. It interrogates whether the professionalization of parties has been a cause of or solution to public disaffection and democratic decline. Part three reviews some key events and election outcomes of the last half decade. These suggest that the combination of increasingly volatile voting patterns, ideological fragmentation and a more dispersed media environment, mean that traditional parties in general are struggling to survive. Part four then offers a different thesis. That is that it is the electoral-professional party model itself that has failed. It concludes by briefly reviewing the kinds of fast-evolving, populist parties succeeding currently. Neither of the party alternatives now on offer – being managed by detached technocrats nor irrational ideologues – offers much positive for democracies.

From Traditional Political to Electoral-Professional Parties

Going back to the first half of the twentieth century and earlier, political parties tended to emerge organically. That is, they developed to represent clear constituent groups and interests in society: industrial workers, religions, racial and ethnic groupings, geographical regions, land owners and so on. Funding, organization and policies each emanated from such groups.

Under these circumstances, traditional parties were local, voluntary and amateur. Parties relied on members for finance and to manage local operations. Campaigning was oriented around local issues, networks and communication. In turn, supporters had a strong 'partisan alignment' to those parties. They remained loyal over decades regardless of changing leaders, social conditions and policies.

Party ideologies were also simpler and clearer. There have been various attempts to classify traditional party ideologies (see Ball and Dagger, 2013; Dalton, 2017; Heywood, 2017). The most common has been the left–right spectrum, moving from communism to socialism at one end, to conservativism and fascism at the other. Things were complicated by competing pulls such as nationalism, ethnicity and religion. But, at the same time, parties of left and right managed to develop fairly enduring positions on economic management, the role of the state and other related policy areas.

Left parties are linked to notions of equality. This originally translated into affiliations with lower economic classes, labour unions and workers' rights. It has spread to also cover equality issues in relation to gender, race, religion and sexuality. The left has also been more associated with state intervention in the economy, pushing for higher tax and redistribution, greater welfare spending and management of national industries. Right-leaning parties have leaned towards individual liberties, promoting competition and justifying inequality. They have been more associated with business and land owners, and higher economic classes. They have promoted free-market economics, smaller welfare states, privatization and lower taxation and redistribution. When they have advocated stronger state intervention it has been in policing and defence, and in upholding socially conservative values.

Such differences traditionally helped distinguish Labour from Conservatives in the UK, Democrats from Republicans in the US, Social Democrats and Christian Democrats in Germany, Socialists and Republicans in France, the BJP from the Indian National Congress in India, and so on.

However, as the twentieth century progressed, much of this changed. Parties evolved, becoming more national and professional, less ideological and more oriented towards the larger citizen body. Citizens became less attached to specific parties, with paid membership dropping and partisan alignment weakening (see accounts in Dalton, 2004; Hay, 2007; van Biezen et al., 2012; Hershey, 2017). Depending on the account, this evolution has been driven more by either wider society shifts ('demand-side') or by the internal dynamics of parties themselves ('supply side').

From the demand-side perspective, a set of grander societal trends has forced parties to adapt to or die. One of these is demographics (see Inglehart, 1990; Norris, 1999; Dalton, 2004; Lees-Marshment,

2008). Economies, occupations, religious affiliations and living circumstances have all changed substantially. The working classes, once employed in heavy industry and farming, have declined in number. Union membership has plummeted. In the UK case, for example, in 1951, 64.9% were classified as 'working class' but by 1997, the figure was 34.1%. In 1979, 52.7% of employees were unionized but by 1997 the number had dropped to 27.3% (Heath et al., 2001). Many more people now migrate to large urban areas for employment and work in smaller, more fragmented units, in the service and gig economies. In fact, as recent research on class suggests (Savage, 2015), the older distinctions between upper, middle and lower class, are now far less applicable. Instead societies have several, fragmented class divisions. Such changes have eroded the traditional class and regional ties that existed between parties and voters.

Ideological foundations and certainties have broken down in other ways too. Between 1989 and 1991, communist regimes toppled across Russia and Eastern Europe, leaving Francis Fukuyama (1992) to declare 'the end of history'. Globalization, international migration and multi-culturalism challenged traditional cultures, communities and associations. So too, religion, feminism, nationalism, ethnicity and environmentalism, have each interacted with traditional left–right politics. Single issue politics and movements have flourished as individuals have preferred to devote their energies to interest groups like Greenpeace, Amnesty, the Pro-Life movement or National Rifle Association.

Another significant cause of change, with an impact on party-citizen interaction, has been the advent of mass, broadcast media. Coinciding with the evolution of 'mass' parties, television changed the organization of party campaigning itself (Maarek, 1995; Blumler and Kavanagh, 1999; Wring, 2005; Hershey, 2017). National television appearances proved to be far more cost-efficient, in terms of time, money and organization, than local campaign operations. Consequently, parties reoriented themselves towards national media and away from local members and communication. Despite the internet's rise, television remains the most influential medium when it comes to making judgements about parties and political leaders (Reuters, 2017).

Whether driven by external or internal factors, parties have adapted and reinvented themselves multiple times. The first general shift was towards becoming larger, 'mass' or 'catch all parties' (Kircheimer, 1966). To gain political power required appealing to other groups of voters. This meant more flexible ideologies, making policy compromises and developing additional policy positions. It also required the development of more professional party organizations, employing a range of policy experts and communication professionals.

That led to a second shift as they became more 'electoral-professional' parties. As various studies have documented (Blumler and Gurevitch, 1995; Swanson and Mancini, 1996) large parties across the globe became more 'professionalized' (or 'Americanized'). They evolved centralized structures, rigid campaign hierarchies and brought in a range of outside professional experts and commercial practices. For Blumler and Kavanagh (1999) this rise in professionalization within parties was one of the key features of the 'third age' of political communication. Multiple studies since, in politics and political communication (Heffernan, 2003; Lilleker and Lees-Marshment, 2005; Hay, 2007; Mair, 2013; Scammell, 2014; Hershey, 2017), have documented the ongoing aspects of this.

Professionalization began with the replacement of amateur party organizers with outside expert practitioners, mostly from the commercial world. Professions employed included advertisers, public relations practitioners, pollsters, marketing specialists, journalists, television producers, professional writers, film makers, media trainers and image consultants. This started in the US in the early 1970s, and in the UK in the late 1970s (Scammell, 1995; Hall Jamieson, 1996; Denton and Woodward, 1998; Davis, 2002; Franklin, 2004). In the UK, leading advertising and public relations firms, such as Saatchi and Saatchi, Lowe-Bell and Shandwick, developed long-term accounts with the Conservative Party during the 1980s (Scammell, 1995). Labour followed some years later, with key former professionals such as Phillip Gould, Peter Mandelson and Alistair Campbell being central to Labour's reinvention as New Labour (Wring, 2005).

Similar developments have been documented in many nations subsequently (Lilleker and Lees-Marshment, 2005; Maarek, 2011; Scammell, 2014; Hershey, 2017). Today, party leaders and managers are surrounded by a mix of temporary consultants and permanent advisers. Political consultants, such David Axelrod, Jim Messina and Lynton Crosby, as well as international agencies, like WPP, Omnicom and Publicis, offer their advice and services to parties and governments across the world.

Professionals evaluate policy ideas and develop communication strategies in conjunction with extensive polling and market research activities. Voters are surveyed, interviewed and focus-grouped.

Methods of identification and classification have become more complex and varied with each decade. Measures began with class, dictated by income and profession, and soon came to include indicators like age, race, gender and education. Qualitative data, such as the use of 'psychographics', used theories of social psychology to identify and segment consumers through motivations. 'Lifestyle research' built up general accounts of attitudes, opinions and beliefs, as well as detailed media consumption habits. More recently, this is being increasingly combined with big data collected from social media, purchasing habits and other mobile and online applications that record and track individuals (see Tufekci, 2014a; O'Neill, 2017).

From this mixture very detailed pictures of voters, their motivations, finances, political dispositions and media uses are developed. Data is aggregated at a number of levels, from the national, to the state, voting constituency, and even housing block. At the most basic level, strategists work out who will likely vote for their party regardless, who will never vote for their party and, most importantly, who might vote. It is these latter 'floating voters' and 'marginal seats' or 'swing states' that get most attention, especially in first-past-the-post electoral systems like the UK, US and India. Such groupings are then targeted above others in an election period.

The market research extends to the party itself, its brand, its policy proposals and its leaders. What is the party's general 'brand', its associations, stronger and weaker policy areas in the eyes of voters? Right leaning parties usually poll stronger on defence, the economy and law and order. Left leaning ones do better on education, health and welfare, racial and gender equality. Accordingly, right-wing parties get more votes from older white males, the upper and middle classes; left-wing parties from younger, poorer, non-white and female voters. Particular policies, in areas from housing and transport, to immigration and taxation, are tested on different demographics.

Political leaders have become 'brand representatives' for their parties (Hall Jamieson, 1996; Corner and Pels, 2003). How they are presented, understood and seen to relate to 'ordinary voters', is crucial information for party strategists. Accordingly, potential leaders are market-tested. Actual leaders and senior party figures are media-trained and employ full-time media advisers. They also have extensive make-overs. Mrs Thatcher had her teeth done, her clothes changed, her hair restyled and elocution lessons, transforming her from hesitant junior minister to commanding 'iron lady'. Male presidents, from Bill Clinton and Silvio Berlusconi to Donald Trump, have spent small fortunes on hair management.

Accumulated market-research and analysis is then used to develop communication strategy. Policy proposals and manifestos are tested and adapted. Advertising budgets are carefully targeted at particular media and regions. Party conferences and national media appearances are intricately managed and negotiated. Campaigns take on a distinctly military feel as parties prepare their electoral campaign 'war books' many months in advance. Future news agendas, advertising hits, political appearances and 'lines of the day' are all planned out in detail. 'Media monitoring' and 'rapid rebuttal' units are set up. Speeches are written by teams. Debating politicians are prepped and tested ad infinitum, while 'spin doctors' try and influence the interpretations of reporters watching those debates.

In the modern era of campaigning, electoral-professional parties became extremely effective and ruthless operations. Like big news organizations, financial investment ventures or modern military units, they functioned 24/7. Such professionals are considered essential components of any party seriously competing for office.

However, the successful adaption towards professionalization could only be achieved with certain trade-offs. Professionals gained an increasing amount of power within parties, often becoming closer to leaders than lower-ranking politicians and even some senior figures. The costs of employing professionals and their services, rather than relying on voluntary amateurs, meant that organizational costs rose significantly and steadily. In turn, that resulted in a growing dependency on locating big funders. Inevitably, various organizational tensions developed: between the local and national, core foundational members and newer floating members, the ideologically 'pure' and the more pragmatic, committed amateurs and trained, paid professionals. Ultimately, as parties broadened their appeal and became more electorally focused, so ordinary members felt more removed and traditionally supportive voters became less clearly aligned.

Evaluating the Implications for Citizen–Party Relations

While most observers agree that the professionalization of party organization and communication have reconfigured party–voter relations, there is quite a contrast in the evaluations presented. Such differing assessments are directly related to whether one holds parties themselves responsible for the current high levels of pubic distrust and low levels of electoral turnout. For supporters, professionalization has been a positive development for publics and democracies as well as parties. For critics, however, party professionalization is itself a major cause of political dissatisfaction and thus a weakening of democracy generally.

Advocates of professionalization, review these developments as being healthy and productive responses to wider social trends (Scammell, 1995, 2003; Newman, 1999; Norris, 2000, 2004). The adoption of modern political marketing techniques has made parties more representative because marketing, if done correctly, is a consultative, two-way process. Jennifer Lees-Marshment (2008, 2011, 2015; Lilleker and Lees-Marshment, 2005) has done most to develop a positive interpretive framework here. According to the 'Lees-Marshment model' (2008) parties went through a historical metamorphosis through the twentieth century, akin to marketing's evolution itself. Those that survived and prospered, did so by following this shift. Those that did not were shunted to the electoral margins eventually suffering extinction.

In her history, traditional parties were product-oriented (POPs). They had basic ideologies that they attempted to sell directly to electorates. Then came more sophisticated sales-oriented parties (SOPs). These still took ideological positions and sold themselves, but they used modern commercial marketing and promotional practices to do so. The final step in the evolution was market-oriented parties (MOPs). MOPs did not just use marketing to sell but to also develop policies in two-way dialogues with citizens and stakeholders. If done properly, parties both freed themselves from the constraints of ideological dogma and, also, become more consultative in relation to citizens. Thus, Lees-Marshment regarded Margaret Thatcher as a 'marketing pioneer' of MOP for the Conservatives in 1979. She regarded Tony Blair's New Labour in the same light. However, Michael Foot's Labour in 1983, and John Major's Conservatives in 1997 lost because of a reversion to POP-style politics. The electoral highs and lows of these and other parties across the world are best explained through such an analysis (Lilleker and Lees-Marshment, 2005; Maarek, 2011; Lees-Marshment, 2015).

Similar, industry-inspired arguments are put forward for the use of modern advertising and public relations techniques in political communication (Grunig and Hunt, 1984; Grunig, 1992; Scammell, 1995; Nessman, 1995). Government and party communication, instead of being a crude top-down affair, has come to be more 'two-way symmetrical' in nature. Professional public relations operations do more to engage party employees and members. They are more cost-effective and turn complex, technical discussions into user-friendly formats, intelligible to ordinary citizens. For Norris (2000), McNair (2011) and others, professional communication is a positive, pragmatic response to the messiness and complexity of modern politics. It means that people may be more cynical and critical but they are also better informed and more engaged than they once were.

Ultimately, what has emerged is a sort of technical-managerial political class who govern the country in a more neutral, logical, responsive and expert way. Ideologies and dogmas, which once infected decision-making, are replaced by evidence-based policy production and responsive government. Thus, as these same authors infer, professionalization strengthens rather than undermines core features of democracy. A win-win situation.

However, for critics the professionalization of parties has generated more negative than positive consequences. They offer a number of objections. First of these is that parties have moved further away from ordinary members and far closer to wealthy donors and special interests (Crouch, 2004; Hay, 2007; Magleby, 2011; Hershey, 2017). As campaign expenditures have continued to rise, so parties have to spend more time fund-raising and enticing rich supporters. In the UK, between 2001 and 2017, the Conservatives spent £63 million and Labour £49 million in parliamentary elections (UK Electoral Commission, 2017). A considerable sum but tiny compared to the US, where regulation is looser and money dominates campaigns. In 1974 total campaign expenditure for all candidates to the Senate and House of Representatives was $72.4 million. In 1976, presidential candidates spent a total of $66.9 million. (Ferguson, 2012: 296–7). By 2016, $2.4 billion was spent on the presidential race and $6.5 billion in total (OpenSecrets, 2017). Just 158 families and their companies contributed half of all money raised for the 2016 presidential race (Hershey, 2017: 296). In each of the four elections prior to 2016 (2000–12), the candidate with the most funds won. At vital points, extreme differences in available funds, left one side advantaged (see Dover, 2010; Farrar-Myers, 2011; Magleby, 2011).

Second, the increasing influence of commercial promotional practices and personnel has resulted in the downgrading of policy and citizenship. Scammell's (2014) exploration of political marketing cites a global survey of campaign professionals. Asked about what factors were 'very important' for ensuring success, 86% of US communicators said 'budget/money' while only 47% said 'issues'. In Europe and Latin America 'the candidate' scored highest – around

79–84% – while 'issues' were only 36–41%. As several have pointed out (see critiques in Wring, 2005; Washbourne, 2005; Savigny, 2006), consumers and products are not equivalent to voters and policies. Citizenship relates to wider collective notions of society while consumption is all about individual fulfilment. Policies are not simple products with discrete uses, but are complex, interrelate with other policies and interests, and have various consequences over time. Selecting parties involves selecting not one but multiple policies and individuals.

Third, professionalized parties have tended to converge in a number of ways, making it harder for voters to discern the differences between them (Hall Jamieson, 2005; Dover, 2010; Magleby, 2011). Major parties adopt almost identical textbook campaign approaches. Challengers sell a vision of progressive 'change', blocked by incumbents, while incumbents stress their safe 'experience' over untried challengers. All sides emphasize leader personalities rather than policies and political visions. Likewise, since the 1970s, there has been considerable convergence in the stated ideologies and policy stances of major political parties. This convergence has been particularly pronounced in left-wing parties such as the UK Labour Party, German Social Democrats and US Democrats (Heath et al., 2001; Curtice, 2005; Entman, 2005; Frank, 2016; Luce, 2017). For decades, left and right in several countries have come to share broad agreement on a number of policy issues: privatization, low taxes, globalization, free trade, deregulation, weakened unions, foreign policy in the Middle East, reduced welfare spending, and so on.

Fourth, communication professionals are not particularly interested in 'two-way communication', 'citizen-dialogues' or 'enhanced public spheres'. They are more oriented towards dominating the public communication space and winning elections (Hall Jamieson, 1996; Franklin, 2004; Sussman, 2011; Frank, 2016). That often means 'spin', 'pseudo-events' and negative attacks, rather than attempts at positive communication. Campaigns, particularly in majoritarian electoral systems, have become increasingly focused on relatively small sets of voters who are deemed necessary to winning an election. Electioneering, aided by digital tracking and big data analysis, focuses on 'swing voters' and marginal constituencies or states. Indeed, the number of 'battleground' areas in the US has steadily declined as candidates devote almost all of their time and advertising budgets to roughly a fifth of all states. In 2004, eleven states got 92% of all candidate visits and 96% of the advertising. In 2008, 98% of all campaign events and advertising took place in fifteen states (Fairvote, 2008). No candidate visited thirty-five of the states at all. In 2012 99.6% of all campaign advertising was in just ten swing states (Fairvote, 2013). Unsurprisingly, many voters feel generally alienated by such campaigns, leading to a long-term drop in voter turnout; something that is more pronounced in those uncontested states ignored by candidates.

Put together, professional-electoral parties have also become 'modern cadre' parties (Crouch, 2004). The predominant 'cadre' at the top of a party is more closely tied to campaign professionals, external advisers and corporate funders, rather than traditional party workers, ordinary members or citizens. For van Biezen et al. (2012: 42) the transformations have been such that 'political parties ... have all but abandoned any pretensions of being mass organizations'.

The Dramatic New Threat to Established Party Politics

For better or worse the electoral-professional (or 'cadre'), centrist party came to be the dominant model at the end of the twentieth century and start of this one. There were clear problems (see Chapter 3) as the long-term links between parties, members and citizens appeared to be weakening. Steady drops in voter turnout, party membership, and political trust, were all signs of a flawed system. However, until this decade, none of that seemed to matter very much. As Norris and Inglehart had been arguing, support for democracy remained constantly high everywhere and parties in mature democracies appeared fairly stable. Electoral volatility was far more associated with the newer ('third and fourth wave') democracies in Latin America, Asia, Africa and Eastern Europe (Mainwaring et al., 2017).

All that changed in the decade following the global financial crisis (2007–8). The slow negative political trends began dipping more harshly in some countries. Electoral volatility spiked up and older, established parties began struggling for coherence and power. This shift affected parties in quite diverse electoral and economic systems in democracies.

The UK, US and Australia initially seemed more immune to developments. Their first-past-the-post electoral system has resulted in a long-enduring political landscape dominated by two parties with little room for alternatives to emerge. People may have been increasingly disenchanted with politics in both countries but the main parties of left (Democrats, Labour) and right (Republicans, Conservatives) still dominated. Then strong fault lines appeared in these parties and governance began breaking down. In the UK, the 2010 election produced no overall winner and resulted in an uneasy coalition government for the first time since the mid-1970s. The 2017 election showed this was no one-off as, once again, a minority government resulted, and marginal seats jumped in number (Renwick, 2017). In between came the 2016 vote on continuing European Union membership. Against all expectations, the vote was to leave. Since 2015 both main parties have been bitterly divided and increasingly factional, making Brexit negotiations virtually impossible.

In the US, the Democrats saw splits between its Washington establishment and its more radical, younger left. The Republican Party juggled its Tea Party faction, as well as tensions between its libertarian market and socially conservative elements. Such divisions aided the advance of Donald Trump in 2016. Although he stood as the Republican nominee, he was clearly 'an outsider' with no political experience and was shunned by many in his own party. In Australia in 2018, yet another political split and coup within the ruling party left the country governed by its sixth prime minister in eleven years.

The political earthquakes taking place were not confined to English-speaking majoritarian political systems. Long-established parties across Europe, used to dominating their multi-party parliaments for decades, were reduced to small, powerless rumps. In 2016, Italian Prime Minister Matteo Renzi was forced to resign after a failed attempt at political reform. By 2018, Italy had ended up with a political novice as prime minister (Giuseppe Conte) leading a coalition of the Northern League and the 5 Star Movement, two populist, anti-elite parties. In 2017 both Brazil and South Korea impeached their presidents, while South Africa forced out their president in early 2018. In the French presidential elections, both main parties were rejected. Emmanuel Macron won at the head of a party barely a year old, with Marine Le Pen's Front National coming second. In Mexico, in 2018, Andrés López Obrador, became the first President from a party other than the PRI or PAN, the two parties that had dominated Mexican politics since 1929. In Brazil, Jair Bolsonaro, for many years a marginalized politician, won the Presidency.

Elsewhere, populist far-right parties grew in support across much of Europe, taking votes and seats from more established centrist parties. Even the more stable democracies of Scandinavia saw nationalist parties, like the Swedish Democrats, Danish People's Party and True Finns, gain considerable support. By 2016 such parties formed parts of ruling coalitions in eleven Western democracies, including

Austria, Switzerland and Italy (Inglehart and Norris, 2016). In 2017, the Netherlands foiled the rise of the right-wing populist Geert Wilders but then struggled to form a ruling coalition, taking over seven months to agree a government. Angela Merkel's CDU lost substantial ground to parties like the AfD in Germany's election and, like the Dutch, took over half a year to agree a new uneasy coalition with the SPD. Where they were not in power, such parties still pushed the centrists further to the right. Elsewhere, nations that had been consolidating their democracies, like Turkey, Hungary and Poland, began adopting more authoritarian practices as their ruling parties clamped down on judiciaries, media and political oppositions.

Despite these dramatic political shifts being in very different democracies, there do appear to be some common causes and features. One of these was the more substantial level of dealignment and electoral volatility, not usually associated with older democracies. Volatility measures the degree to which voters switch their support to either existing or new emerging parties. This rise was first noted in Southern European nations like Italy, Spain, Portugal and Greece (Conti et al., 2018); the same ones that were badly affected by the economic slump and subsequent EU policy responses. Volatility spiked in each of these countries but then also began to grow in more Northern, less economically affected states like France, the Netherlands, Germany and Norway. Chiaramonte and Emanuele (2017) noted that average volatility in Western Europe was 8.32% in the 1946–68 period and had crept up to 12.76% in the 1992–2015 period. Just in the period after 2010, the average jumped to 18.01%.

Such volatility has been equally apparent in the UK and US. In the 2016 US presidential election, Trump's support swung as much as 19% and Clinton's 9%. In the 2016 EU Referendum there were several points when the Remain campaign, which lost the actual vote, held an 18% poll lead. In the 2017 UK election, the Conservatives began with a 20-point poll lead over Labour but ended the campaign, a few weeks later, with a 2.4% lead. Such swings had rarely been recorded for decades.

A second key feature of recent party-based politics is fragmentation of the traditional left–right axis that had previously distinguished parties and aligned them with voter groups. On the one hand, the economic policies of both centre left and centre right parties moved closer together. On the other hand, stronger ideological fault lines have developed that cut across parties and voter groups. The most important of these recently have been recorded around nationalism and cultural identity (Inglehart and Norris, 2016; EIU,

2017; Goodhart, 2017). Inglehart and Norris (2016: 3) extended their earlier work on changing cultural values to explain the shift with their 'cultural backlash' thesis. They reviewed survey data on opinions and attitudes in Europe, observing 'a new cultural cleavage dividing populists from cosmopolitan liberalism'. Populists are anti-establishment (business and political), have a preference for strong leaders, are more nationalistic and mono-cultural, and prefer traditional social and family (Christian) values. They are set against cosmopolitan liberals, oriented towards globalization, multi-culturalism, liberal pluralist democracy, and progressive social values. The 2016 vote for Trump was a triumph for populists.

Goodhart (2017) offered a very similar analysis in relation to the UK and the vote to leave the EU. In his account the divide is between 'somewheres' and 'anywheres'. Anywheres, consisting of 20 to 25% of the public, are more educated, wealthier, urban, socially liberal, global in outlook and mobile. Somewheres, who make up 50% of the population, are socially conservative, less educated, situated in small towns and rural areas, and have a strong sense of community, place and traditional values. They rail against a 'double liberalism' that is both social (e.g., gay marriage, multi-culturalism) and economic (globalization, foreign investment, immigration). The Economist Intelligence Unit (2016: 23–4) sums up the new schisms thus:

> The old left–right political distinctions do not mean that much nowadays; instead the battle lines are being drawn over issues such as globalization versus national sovereignty, cosmopolitanism versus national identity, and open borders versus immigration controls.

All these studies, while emphasizing different schisms, also agree there is now a complex mix of ideological pulls – economic, nationalist, gender, race, class, age and other – which are separating constituent groups in society beyond traditional left–right lines. The same electoral and survey data shows even starker differences in the demographic profiles of voters on different sides of each of these elections. The multiplicity of media sites has exacerbated these differences too. Those, separated by left or right politics, age, gender or race, tend to gravitate towards very different sets of media too (Reuters, 2017; Chapter 5, this volume). All of which makes party media management, policy development and political branding increasingly difficult for all parties (Blumler, 2013).

Put together, the evidence suggests that mainstream parties and political leaders are now experiencing impossible new challenges.

Traditional forms of party organization and governance are becoming untenable. One pessimistic conclusion would be that political parties in general are doomed.

The End of Parties or Just the End of the Electoral Professional Party?

An alternative conclusion might be that it is the centrist electoral professional party that is doomed rather than parties per se. The evidence suggests that there is a direct challenge to everything associated with the professional electoral party itself. For a start, recent elections have dramatically defied the predictions of professional campaign insiders, as well as outside commentators, journalists and pollsters (see accounts in Jackson et al., 2016; Lilleker et al., 2016; Thorsen et al., 2017). The polls predicted that the 2015 UK election would result in a hung parliament with a Labour-led coalition taking power; the Conservatives won a working majority. Most experts gave the 2016 Leave and Trump campaigns minimal chances of winning; they did. The 2017 UK election was going to be a landslide for Theresa May's Conservatives; it ended in a hung parliament.

It was not just the predictions that were wrong. So was the insider-experts' playbook on how to win an election. Hillary Clinton's campaign strongly outspent Donald Trump's, airing three times as many adverts overall, including twice as many in the final two weeks (Motta, 2016). Mainstream media, although lukewarm about Clinton, came out strongly against Trump (Carlson, 2016). Trump made no attempt to seize the 'centre ground', offended numerous voter groups, was completely gaffe-prone, regularly caught out lying, led a completely divided party, had no political background and few campaign professionals to call on (Rennie Short, 2016). Jeremy Corbyn almost pulled off an unlikely victory in 2017 with few funds or professional advisers, virtually no media support, and most of his parliamentary party trying to force his resignation. They, along with 'outsiders' across Europe (Richards, 2017), were succeeding almost by rejecting the wisdom and practices of electoral professionals.

So too, for many there have been pronounced policy failures among the legions of technocrats and experts, of the kind relied upon by centrist, professional parties. These parties, in addition to moving closer to big funders and campaign professionals, also put great faith in the advice and expertise of some, key, highly paid professions: lawyers, accountants, entrepreneurs and academics. They were enthralled by neoclassical economics, as well as policies associated with globalization, open borders and multi-culturalism.

However, what party leaders failed to understand was that such professionals are rarely neutral technocrats finding their way to scientific-like truths and facts. They could still pursue their own personal interests or those of their profession or wealthy employer. And they were far from infallible. Thus, the economic experts in the wealthier economies failed to predict or explain the great financial crisis and what followed (Keen, 2011; Engelen et al., 2011; Earle et al., 2016). They tended to overlook continuing industrial decline, wage stagnation, housing crises and worsening employment conditions. They rarely seemed concerned that inequality was continuing to grow or that large regions were being impoverished. Such trends, which were recorded before the crash, were then exacerbated significantly following it (Crouch, 2011; Piketty, 2014; Streeck, 2017; Chapter 9, this volume). As Rennie Short (2016) explained, both left and right developed blind faith in policies that did little for many ordinary people.

In fact, in several analyses, the outcomes of the 2016 elections were seen as a conscious rebellion against wealthy political elites of all political persuasions (Muller, 2016; Rennie Short, 2016; Frank, 2016). Frank (2016), Barnett (2017) and Luce (2017) each argue that centre-left parties, such as the Democrats and New Labour, lost touch with and alienated chunks of their core working-class base. Analysis of demographic data in the US and UK reveals correlations between voting preferences and economic circumstances. Those areas which voted for Trump or Brexit most strongly were usually the same ones which had been 'left behind', suffering economic decline for decades. Trump and Brexit supporters were more likely to be from lower socio-economic classes, have less formal education, be in low-paid occupations or unemployed, have fewer assets and poorer housing, and be in greater personal debt; i.e., many had historically been more likely to support the Democrats or Labour. Similar such correlations were noted among those disaffected voters now switching their support to alternative parties in European states too (Conti et al., 2018). As Dennis Muller (2016: 17) put it:

> millions of ordinary people, particularly in the Anglophone democracies, have been left behind by globalization, and sacrificed on the altar of neoclassical economics ... voters in those circumstances know only one big truth: their living standards, share of the cake, and place in society are imperilled or reduced.

The rebellion was not just against politicians but also against the larger networks of business, media and other elites which seemed so connected to centrist, professional parties (Frank, 2016; Lewis and Carlson, 2016; Barnett, 2017; Flinders, 2017; Luce, 2017). For Carlson (2016; see also Lewis and Carlson, 2016), Davis (2018) and others, political reporters had become far too much a part of the establishments of Washington and Westminster. They have continued to prop up traditional parties while marginalizing newer parties and voices outside the political centre. The widespread collapse of local news media has only accentuated the sense of national journalists being too detached from the wider regions. Elite media were seen as speaking for elites not for ordinary people.

Thus, for many, politicians, the media, the wealthy and experts, were all wrapped up together. They had shared interests and had each profited from the political status quo that had developed over decades. So, when Leavers dismissed experts when challenged about the implications of leaving the EU, or Donald Trump made up his own 'alternative facts' or condemned critiques of him as 'fake news', many voters agreed with them. Those who directly opposed their 'political establishments', even if a billionaire (Trump) or an experienced political insider (Macron, López Obrador), gained widespread support.

If many centrist, professional-electoral parties are struggling to maintain power, is there a new' party model taking their place? For Crouch (2004), Silvio Berlusconi's Forza Italia party in Italy offered the alternative blueprint for new, emerging parties of the twenty-first century. This party developed without any 'organic' party membership or extended organizational structure being created. It led through an amalgamation of media and corporate elites.

Jumping forward the blueprint applies well to many of the new populist parties and their leaders (see accounts in Judis, 2016; Mudde and Rovira Kaltwasser, 2017). Additional elements are worth noting too. One of these is being able to exploit the current dynamics of mediatization. As politics becomes ever more mediatized (see Chapter 6) so newer parties have found media influence can bypass the need for extensive, well-funded party machines. Even when mainstream media is hostile, as is the case with Trump or Corbyn, newer parties can now progress, managing to either ride extensive negative coverage or by working social media networks.

Which leads to a second common element, which is that most alternative parties have 'strong', charismatic leaders. It would be hard to imagine UKIP's rise without Nigel Farage, the Dutch Party for Freedom minus Geert Wilders, En Marche! existing independently of Emmanuel Macron, or the Republican surge without Donald Trump. They crave the limelight and are more concerned to promote a cult of personality, and strong ideas and beliefs rather than take a neutral, mass appeal line. In this they are happy to make erratic proposals, voice extreme opinions and offend voter groups, if they can appeal to core sets of supporters and those generally disenchanted with the status quo.

Third, even if connected to parts of the establishment, their message is inherently anti-establishment, the personnel and institutions of the status quo. They ask for power on the basis they will challenge existing sclerotic or corrupt power. Such opposition encompasses both national government institutions and international ones such as the European Union or United Nations. They continue to cooperate with certain factions of the establishment in the media, the corporate sector, the bureaucracy and political party system. As long as they can ally with certain elite support networks, have enough financial means and good media exposure, they can afford to jettison the rest.

Fourth, they are highly flexible entities, organizationally and ideologically. Rather like the new social movements that have flourished in the digital age (see Chapter 8), they can emerge rapidly, pulling together and organizing supporters and communication operations in months. They are unencumbered by the machinery of traditional parties, the need to develop local operations, consult with members, or practise any form of wider policy dialogue. So too, instead of detailed policy analysis and larger visions they can offer vague appeals and issue statements that can chime with the events and feelings of the moment. In effect, unlike traditional parties, including professional-electoral ones, they can dispense with those democratic processes that slow organizations down. They combine the public profiles and autocratic organizational tendencies of authoritarian leaders with the flexibility and immediacy of the digital and fashion-led age.

Conclusion

Traditional parties, whether more centrist or ideological, in two-party or multi-party systems, are struggling to remain coherent, relevant and effective. As suggested here, part of the problem comes down to their inability to cope with fragmented, fast-moving media environments and diverse sets of voters and ideological concerns. Wider socio-economic and technological changes have made stable, top-down party management a very difficult task. Real democracy is too slow-moving to counter the changes brought by ICT-enhanced turbo capitalism. Real democratic organizations cannot keep pace with non-democratic corporations, international financial flows, instant fashions and social media; each of which are utilized by many newer parties.

Part of the problem is also linked to the protracted dominance in many nations of the centrist professional-electoral party. Such parties sacrificed supporters and members in the process of widening their appeal and becoming effective electoral machines. In addition to moving too close to campaign experts and wealthy funders, they became over-reliant on the 'experts' in policy-making, law, economics and other fields. Such reliance ignored the specialist, self-interested and non-neutral nature of such professions. Such experts, like the political classes they served, had also become too detached from the lives and experiences of the majority far away from the political centres of London, Washington, Paris and Berlin. Technocracies may be rational but all too often they also become detached and rigged.

Unfortunately, the current alternative models of populist parties do not inspire much hope either. Their radical alternatives offer even less in the way of democratic accountability and dialogue. For Mudde and Rovira Kaltwasser (2017: 116) 'populism has essentially become an illiberal democratic response to undemocratic liberalism'. They offer short fixes, 'bread and circuses' and easy targets of blame, but few detailed policy answers or longer-term visions. They seem little more stable than fleeting protest movements. Their challenge to the sclerotic and rigged political and media systems they critique is a necessary step, but 'creative destruction' does not offer clear answers.

Thus, neither option of rational rigged or radical irrational parties presents positive models. Does that mean party-based democracy is doomed? Political representation and governance is still party-based, but if such parties are neither coherent nor stable, then democracy itself is imperilled (see van Biezen and Poguntke, 2014; Chiaramonte and Emanuele, 2017; Hershey, 2017). To continue, either party-based systems need to be radically overhauled or democracies need to develop forms of governance with other types of organization and structure.

5

Political Reporting and the Future of (Fake) News

This chapter looks at conventional, legacy news reporting and the production of political coverage. For millennials, such a topic almost seems irrelevant as they increasingly gain their news from non-traditional sources. But, traditional news journalism remains fundamentally important to politics. For the political classes – politicians, bureaucrats and commentators – legacy news, particularly newspapers, remain closely read and influential. For voters, despite the clear rise of online alternatives, television coverage is still the main form of news used by citizens to evaluate parties and their leaders (Ofcom, 2017; Pew, 2017; Hansard, 2018). Even though individuals increasingly receive news via social media, much of the core material derives from professional news operations.

The discussion here revolves around two issues. One is news's function in sustaining the shared communicative spaces of the public sphere; spaces that are vital to multiple forms of public communication essential to democracies. The second focuses on the veracity or otherwise of news content. In the current climate, longer-term questions about 'facts' and 'truth-telling' are being revisited as claims and counter-claims about 'fake' news proliferate.

The chapter explores these issues through three sections. The first introduces established debates between liberal pluralists and critical political economists. For the former, news, although flawed, functions well enough through a mix of pluralist sources, professional values and practices. The duel threats, posed by aggressive political leaders and fabricated content, are seen to pose new threats to its integrity. For the latter, however, ongoing political, business and military influences have meant news historically favours powerful elite interests. In effect news, to a degree, has always been 'fake'.

The second section offers a third, alternative explanation for distortion, bias and fakery. Building on a mix of critical sociology and political economy accounts, this views news production as being influenced above all by the organizational and commercial needs of news operations. These have meant that news production, if not exactly fake, has always been compromised by its reliance on external sources, corner-cutting and pseudo methods for producing expert, balanced reporting.

As the third section argues, these issues have become more significant as the commercial and organizational methods that have sustained journalism for a century have broken down. The business model had been faltering for decades before the arrival of the internet caused havoc. In addition to wrecking traditional revenue sources, the new online ecology has reconfigured production practices, undermined credibility and fragmented audiences. The industry's responses, such as competing for advertising clicks or becoming more entertainment-oriented, have not alleviated these problems. In effect, the political public-sphere is becoming increasingly market-based at the same time as the market for news is collapsing.

Liberal Pluralist and Critical Political Economy Analyses of News

The liberal pluralist perspective ('liberal' meaning centre-ground not left-leaning) comes from a mix of former journalists' accounts and media sociologists (Lichtenberg, 2000; Zellizer, 2004; Deuze, 2007; Schudson, 2008, 2011; McNair, 2009). These sketch out an account linking professional journalism to public sphere principles, truth-seeking and democracy. Thus, trained reporters attempt to provide pluralist balance in their objective fact-driven copy. As such, they both hold the powerful to account as well as providing a forum for public debate.

Professional, Anglo-American style journalism is held up as the 'ideal' model of good modern practice. It developed over time, through market mechanisms, education, professional bodies and codes of practice (Chalaby, 1996). It is a model being increasingly adopted across democracies regardless of historical antecedents (Hallin and Mancini, 2011; Worlds of Journalism, 2016). This ideal image is reproduced in popular culture and in journalist biographies and fictional accounts, from Superman to Watergate. Such reporting has uncovered a range of corporate and political malpractices, from mass bribery at FIFA and manipulated VW car emissions, to Iran-Contra and the Panama Papers. In each case journalists have either uncovered corruption or worked closely with whistleblowers, such as Edward Snowden and Wikileaks, to publicize stories. In less stable countries, or authoritarian regimes, there are many courageous reporters risking their lives on a daily basis to investigate and hold power to account.

Few clear-thinking reporters or media sociologists would claim that coverage is truly objective or news media an entirely true reflection of societal interests. But, they would support the case that good journalism has over time developed the values and practices that are most likely to achieve such aims. It does so for a number of reasons, beginning with the 'occupational ideology' of the profession (see discussion in Schudson and Anderson, 2009). This includes a set of values around serving the public, objectivity, accuracy, impartiality, autonomy and truth-seeking. Such norms are passed on through specialist education and professional associations. Periodic surveys of journalists worldwide (e.g., Worlds of Journalism, 2012–16), do reveal that journalism is increasingly staffed by graduates with such professional education.

The ideals of 'public journalism' are then reproduced through the practices and procedures inculcated into reporters via the newsroom (Galtung and Ruge, 1965; Tunstall, 1971; Gans, 1979; Tiffen, 1989; Glasser, 1999). Organizational hierarchies and news beats direct journalists towards newsworthy topics and key sources that reflect wider public interests. Working with peers and editors helps identify the 'news values' that guide story selection. Journalists internalize such professional norms and operating procedures by being subject to a succession of subtle sticks and carrots: 'big' story allocation, story acceptance and priority placing, more autonomy, and promotion up the editorial hierarchy.

Reporters may not be experts nor be able to supply all sides of a balanced debate or argument. But, they learn ways to reproduce this by other means. Thus, expert and authoritative sources are sought out to provide facts and explanatory comment. Pluralist principles are central to achieving balanced, neutral news, meaning opposition parties are reported alongside governments, unions and pressure groups next to corporations, and so on. More than that, professional and market ideals ensure pluralism is reproduced on other scales: in terms of multiple types of media format and platform; in terms of highbrow and lowbrow publications and broadcasts and a mix of left and right media outlets. The *Sun* and *Telegraph* sit alongside the *Mirror* and *Guardian*, *Fox News* competes with *CNN*, *Breitbart* with the *Huffington Post*.

In many of these same studies of news production these processes, tools and cultures can occasionally lead to unreflective or erratic news coverage. News-gathering resources are frequently a problem. However, the news ecology in its entirety does well enough. The adoption of professional techniques, codes, norms and practices works to ensure mistakes and instances of bias are minimized or evened out. As journalists are fond of pointing out, the fact that they are an 'unlovable' (Schudson, 2008) profession, attacked from multiple sides, is also evidence they are doing a good job.

From this perspective, recent developments such as aggressive politicians and fake news on social media, are new direct challenges to professional journalism. New populist leaders, such as Donald Trump, Viktor Orban and Rodrigo Duterte, respond to their media critics with intimidation and 'fake news' condemnations. Such an approach both undermines reporters as well as leaving them unsure as to how to respond. Meanwhile, social media networks openly challenge their story agendas and frames. They also disseminate alternative fabricated stories with impunity and no professional accountability. For respectable, truth-seeking journalists, who have operated in legacy news operations for decades, these twin developments are an existential threat to their profession.

In stark contrast comes the work of critical political economists (Herman and Chomsky, 2002; Curran, 2011; Bagdikian, 2014; Fuchs and Mosco, 2017). For them, the inaccuracies and omissions of journalism do not follow some random path. They are shaped by the influences of powerful interests in society, such as corporate, political and military groups (or classes) and institutions. Coverage systematically favours such groups and their norms and values over others. Hence, news in its entirety conveys a 'fake' picture of society; one that advances the acounts of those who control the 'refeudalized public sphere'. Their classic starting point is Marx and Engels's (1846):

> The ideas of the ruling class are in every epoch the ruling ideas ... The class which has the means of material production at its disposal, has control at the same time over the means of mental production.

For much of the last two centuries, mass produced and disseminated news media has acted as the main form of mental production.

A wide-ranging critical literature has identified a number of 'top-down influences' (Curran, 2002) or 'filters' (Herman and Chomsky, 2002) through which content is shaped by the powerful. For Herman and Chomsky, five filters – ownership, advertising, sourcing, flak and anti-communism – redirect objective news reporters and organizations towards creating something more propagandistic or 'fake'.

Starting with the first filter of ownership, the main proprietors of news operations are governments and large corporations. Such organizations, whatever the professional ethos of their journalist employees, ultimately serve the interests and values of their political and business masters. Accordingly, reporters can be hired, fired, and guided in their newsgathering and choice of news agendas. That may lead to a failure to investigate certain corporations and political allies or more overt promotion of policies, parties and businesses.

Large media businesses are driven by the profit motive as well as their own political interests. They are answerable to a mix of super-rich 'moguls', executive shareholders and corporate board members. Owners, such as Michael Bloomberg in the US, Silvio Berlusconi in Italy, Carlos Slim in Mexico, the Barclay Brothers in the UK, and Rupert Murdoch, clearly have their own political agendas and wider influence. That influence has grown as fewer, larger media conglomerates have come to dominate the sector. Currently, just a handful of media conglomerates now own the majority of all forms of news, entertainment and information media in the US (Bagdikian, 2014). The same is true in many other nations. In turn, such news operations have greater power, first, over the shaping of general public discourse, and second, over politicians desperate to gain positive media exposure.

Advertising is the second filter. Big corporate advertisers can apply overt, direct pressure to media owners on certain news topics deemed sensitive to their interests (Thompson, 2000; Thussu, 2008; Curran, 2011). On a less overt level, advertising also shapes news content by promoting certain news stories, formats and citizen interests over others. Wealthier, larger, older mainstream audiences are catered to more than poorer, younger, specialist ones (Curran and Seaton, 2018). A need to appeal to, and entice audiences, also leads news-gatherers to focus more on stories of conflict, human interest, celebrity, sensationalism and scandal.

Powerful and well-resourced elites are also able to exert their influence as key news sources. Reporters naturally seek out those at the top of government and business as they are of public interest and regularly feature in news stories. They are also a frequent source of story-relevant information. Thus, media access to prominent politicians and legislative spaces (Kurtz, 1998; Barnett and Gaber, 2001), and military leaders and zones (Tumber and Palmer, 2004; Thussu and Freedman, 2012), can all be granted or withdrawn accordingly. As suppliers of information, sources can 'spin' the material they present. The fourth filter is 'flak'. Employed media managers may apply public pressure to journalists, undermining their accounts or credibility; something that today's aggressive, populist leaders do on a regular basis.

Last but not least comes the filter of anti-communism. In this respect, a larger critique of the communist threat pervaded general coverage of foreign affairs and security matters. Such a filter may not have been so applicable in the years following the Cold War but has now returned again with Vladimir Putin. In between, many have broadly interpreted the filter to relate to alternative perceived threats to Western capitalism or democracy. Recent examples here have been the threats posed by terrorism, immigration, the Middle East, and China.

In addition, political economists argue that top political journalists have themselves become part of the ruling elite. In the UK, US and elsewhere, reporters work in offices based on parliamentary and presidential sites (Davis, 2010a; Bennett, 2016). Demographically, both professions are dominated by middle-aged, well-educated males from wealthier backgrounds (NTO/Skillset, 2002; CRE, 2005). In Britain, 43% of national newspaper columnists have had a private education and 47% were educated at Oxbridge universities (CSM, 2014). In regular surveys of 'trust', journalists and politicians usually hover together near the bottom (Ipsos-MORI). Former journalists become media managers for politicians or actual politicians. Finally, it is political and business leaders that have come to dominate the news, becoming the key, often only, sources that reporters talk to about politics and the economy (Davis, 2010a; Manning, 2013; Bennett, 2016; Berry, 2016).

For each of these reasons, the rich and powerful are far more likely to set news agendas and story frames. Thus, the 'propaganda model' (Herman and Chomsky, 2002) has a powerful case to make; especially so in times of war or national crisis. In the US, this plays out in hostile coverage from mainstream media towards: political outsiders like Trump or Sanders, progressive policies such as tax rises or the introduction of an affordable healthcare system, and countries which challenge US power. In the UK, news coverage has been consistently more favourable to the Conservative Party from a clear majority of newspapers over many decades and elections. Such papers have also been highly critical of the EU over many years and came out very strongly in favour of a Leave Vote during the 2016 Referendum on EU membership. An analysis (Loughborough, 2016) of news content found that, adjusted for circulation, 82% of biased coverage supported Brexit. Thus, for critics, journalism has always been subjected to direct elite pressures. Most news may not be entirely 'fake', but, it still serves up a very partial, elite-serving account of the world.

The Organization of News as a Business

So far, the discussion has identified two different perspectives which frame analysis and evaluation of news media. The chapter now offers a third perspective that explains the causes of news distortion and the potential for fakery that exists in the professional production process itself. This account sits between the micro-level liberal analysis of journalists at work and the macro-level socio-economic analysis of political economists. Instead, the framework develops at the mezzo-level of the institution and field (see Benson, 2004). This emphasizes the roles of the news organization and industry competition. Here, the main influence on news output relates to the organization of news as a commodity, as it is managed by competing commercial corporations.

From this point of view, a lot of ordinary news work does not have much to do with public sphere ideals nor with powerful elites exerting their control. Rather, it is about the need to produce and distribute a new mass-market product, using an erratic and unreliable source of raw material, on a daily basis. This is aimed at a fickle, fast-changing, sceptical and gradually declining consumer market. This has been the case for several decades. Consequently, news organizations are constantly adapting and looking for new efficiencies to maintain their output under increasingly challenging conditions. So, yes, high ideals and external political and economic influences are part of the mix. But, so are the influences and needs of the news organization and the professional field of journalism. These in themselves create systematic distortions in news outputs.

To start, news almost by definition is what is unpredictable and immediate. It is raw, unprocessed, unknown events and actions that are then selected, interpreted and reshaped into news. This is the service offered by news organizations to consumers. The promise is to pick what is of most interest (or 'newsworthy') to publics and deliver a story in an intelligible and eye-catching way: the disaster, the policy, the corruption, the sports result, and so on. The promise also includes presenting the new product in a recognizable format at a regular time for consumption. Papers, broadcasters and websites are expected to offer something that fills a minimum space every 24 hours according to a recognizable house style. So, news is branded as *BBC News* news, *Der Spiegel* news, *Huffington Post* news, the *Chinese People's Daily* news or *Fox News* news. That output has to continue with the same resources regardless of how much newsworthy 'news' there is on any given day.

All of this puts news organizations and their reporters in an almost impossible position. On the one hand, their product is sold on the basis that it is up-to-date, informative, enlightening, expert, objective and trusted. On the other, the very conditions of production make those things extremely hard to attain. The harsh reality is that reporters do not have the necessary resources of time, money and knowledge required to fulfil such professional expectations. Quite simply, they can't be expert and informed on the large range of topics they cover. They don't have the time to become expert, find expert and objective sources, understand all sides and complexities, and so on. The presentation of professional and authoritative autonomy is, in part, a confidence trick of the industry itself.

To function, the journalist profession has adopted a number of institutional and professional practices. Some of these are purely about making organizations function efficiently, in the same way a modern factory is configured to produce commodities. Some are individual news-gathering practices which have become proxies for achieving 'balance' or 'expertise'. Some simply come down to doing things on the cheap.

To produce news efficiently, production is highly organized around tight editorial hierarchies, linked sets of deadlines, clear beats and routines, and established news sources (see classic studies of Tunstall, 1971; Gans, 1979; Fishman, 1980). In this respect, many modern news rooms have come to fit the Weberian/Fordist model of hierarchical, rationalized production that is associated with large bureaucracies (Weber, 1948) or factories. Everyone, from top to bottom, has a position with identified skill sets and tasks. Even the most senior reporters or star columnists have their positions and output expectations within the operation.

To deal with the unreliable supply of raw source material, news producers have developed content that is less time dependent. Some of that may be coverage of more predictable 'diary events' like top sporting events, PMQs (Prime Ministers Questions) or high-society weddings. Some of this is not hard news per se but is presented as such. This includes 'features' on people and topics of interest, from gardening to celebrity and political profiles, which can be published any time. Then there are commentaries or op-ed pieces with flexible time-slots and no new source material to collect. (see Franklin, 2005; Allan, 2010). Such soft and non-news now makes up the majority of content in newspapers.

Similarly, the professional, fourth estate directives of reporters have, in many ways, come to be achieved more symbolically than substantively. As Schudson and Anderson (2009: 96) observe: 'the process of journalistic legitimization is primarily a rhetorical one ... established as much by the *representation* of knowledge as the actual possession of knowledge.' Many daily practices are no more than short-cuts or proxy substitutes for what is required. This can be observed in the routines of professional news gathering. These work to produce seemingly objective, authoritative, balanced and informed news despite the fact that journalists have only limited resources and knowledge of their story area.

So, reporters aim at balanced reporting by taking opinions from opposed individuals, regardless of whether those individuals are properly representative of the story (see Allan et al., 2000). Global warming sceptics are reported on a par with climate change scientists even though the vast majority of scientific evidence and opinion warns about human-caused climate change. Correspondents seek out those in positions of authority or labelled 'expert' to make up for their own lack of expertise (Hall et al., 1978; Herbst, 1998; Stauber and Rampton, 2003; Schudson and Anderson, 2009). Opinions are used in place of facts and difficult to find data. Conveying the opinions of 'experts' replaces their own expert analysis. They go to similar sources to also determine what 'public opinion' is and what 'public interest concerns' are. Fourth estate values, which critically hold the powerful to account, have come to be represented by personal conflicts and scandals rather than real evaluations of policy and personal competency. It's far easier for journalists to present the personal than research and understand the policy.

Over decades, with more time and resource constraints, organizations have begun gravitating towards cheaper areas of news production, such as commentary and features, rather than real-time reporting. Foreign news bureaux have been wound down. Investigative reporting, which demands resources and specialist knowledge, has declined considerably (Davies, 2008). Complex, detailed topics, or topics where sources are hard to access, are avoided. Long-term evolving stories, like environmental or welfare issues, are by-passed unless a clear crisis arises. Real investigations of policy, finance and banking, climate change, poverty and energy issues, all of great importance to citizens, have become all too absent. Instead, non-complex, cheap, human interest and celebrity stories, scandals and gossip, have all become staples.

Perhaps most importantly, there is a continual search for cheaper sources of story material. All media companies subscribe to newswire services which gather and package up news from elsewhere. Large quantities of press and video releases arrive daily at the desks of reporters. The temptation is to take all this external supply and quickly repackage it into the right format with minimal effort. Such materials are what Oscar Gandy (1982) called 'information subsidies' and they have become an integral part of the journalist profession. Gandy and other classic studies of reporting (e.g., Sigal, 1973; Fishman, 1980) all observed that, as journalist resources became stretched, so dependency on external source supplies rose.

The digital age has offered multiple new cheap sources of news subsidy (Fenton, 2009). In the world of multi-platform news organizations and multi-tasking, the same copy can be reformatted and reused in multiple outputs (Braun, 2015). Online news has enabled journalists to continuously monitor rival content, then cut and paste a story with minimal adjustment into their own outputs. Controversial tweets and blogs of public figures can be quickly used to construct a story. Phone hacking in the UK, which became widely used before being exposed and prosecuted was, in effect, a far cheaper way of finding regular news scoops than traditional, time-consuming and costly forms of investigative news gathering

All these organizational and personal practices have consequences for the shape and integrity of news content. They have produced various systematic biases that erode the public sphere and impede fuller, more deliberate forms of democracy. Personal scandals and controversial political statements are reported far more than policy failures, political and corporate incompetence. A commitment to balance supports the publication of endless 'spin' and fabricated opinions. Certain elite sources dominate coverage because they are seen as authoritative and expert. Those organizations and individuals that offer a regular supply of news information subsidies are overly reported. Everything and everyone else struggles to be reported.

Thus, news reporting is prone to reproducing power imbalances and distortions in society because of the very practices, ideals and routines of professional journalism itself (Hallin, 1994; Thompson, 2000; Fenton, 2009). They have developed to make up for the fact that journalists do not have the necessary resources of time, money and knowledge, required to fulfil professional expectations. But, relying too much on outside forms of news supply, lacking the time to understand and test sources and information, artificially aiming to achieve balance and authority, each increases the possibility that content will be compromised. There is a fine line between news produced on the cheap and using professional fakery, and news that is actually fake. The danger is, as news reporters come under greater pressure, so that line becomes far too easy to cross.

The Breakdown of the News Business Model and the Future of (Fake) News?

The inside picture of how news is really produced is vital to an understanding of what is happening to the profession now. In the space of a decade a slowly declining industry has tipped dramatically into freefall. Few big legacy-media players have found innovative solutions that enable them to keep producing public service journalism while also remaining profitable. In fact, the most common outcome has been poorer quality, hollowed-out news, disinterested and untrusting audiences, and more financial losses.

The dominant issue has been declining revenues leading to ever-increasing resource constraints being imposed on reporters. The trends and responses were set from the 1970s to the early 2000s in the US, UK and Europe. Competition kept growing, spreading the audience and advertising pot ever thinner. Output demands on individual journalists grew too as papers and broadcasters produced more content to entice a larger audience. Each new technology propelled both trends faster. In an effort to remain profitable, news organizations raised prices above inflation, cut editorial staff, and enforced various cost-cutting measures (see Franklin, 1997; Davis, 2002; Kovach et al., 2004; Davies, 2008; Pew, 2009a; Freedman, 2009).

Regular surveys of journalists (NUJ, Pew, Worlds of Journalism) all noted the worsening conditions of the profession. More output was demanded per reporter. In the UK, Tunstall (1996) estimated that, between the 1960s and 1990s individual output had at least doubled. Just over a decade later, Davies (2008) concluded that journalists were now having to fill three times as much news space as they did in the 1980s. In the US, Kovach et al. (2004: 28) recorded between 1985 and 2004, an increase in story output of 30% per reporter. In these accounts modern news production had become 'McDonaldized' (Franklin, 2005), with its outputs best described as 'Churnalism' (Davies, 2008).

The resource issue turned into a full-blown crisis following the financial crash of 2007–8. The news industry was hit by a perfect storm of factors as slow declines suddenly reached harsh tipping points (Anderson et al., 2015; Pew, 2016a; Davis, 2017a). Between 2007 and 2009 newspaper markets declined in all OECD countries, by up to 30% in the worst cases (OECD, 2010). By 2012, much of the industry in the US and Europe was struggling to survive, with many print and broadcasting organizations collapsing or on the verge of bankruptcy. In the UK, the top eight national daily newspapers, lost almost 35% of sales between 2010 and 2016. That was on top of the 26% of sales lost the previous decade (Ofcom, 2017; ABC, 2017). In 2016 alone, they lost 13% of their advertising.

In the US, between 2005 and 2016 (Reuters, 2017), newspaper advertising revenue dropped from $49.4 to $18.3 billion (63%), and full-time employees from 68,610 to 41,400 (40%). TV news fared better financially despite continuing to lose viewers over the same period. Cable news lost 27.7% of viewers in the seven years up to 2015 (Pew, 2017). In 2015 alone, Pew (2016a) recorded a loss of news advertising revenues of 8% and a 10% drop in full-time newsroom employees. While advertising was migrating online it was not going to online news sites as newspapers gained $1 in online advertising for every $5 lost in print advertising (Pew, 2012). Google, Facebook and a handful of tech companies now get more than 80% of that income but do little to support actual news operations.

Many news organizations, such as the *New York Times* and *Guardian* have attempted to set up alternative subscription systems to survive. Several small new public interest operations, such as ProPublica or the Bureau of Investigative Journalism have also emerged. Unfortunately, to date, these alternative funding models and digital news players have yet to prove financially sustainable, or to make up for the gaps left by the declining legacy news sector (Benson, 2017). In the online era, very few are willing to pay for their news. According to the Reuters Institute (2017) survey of thirty-six nations, only 14% of people did pay for their online news in the last year.

A second key issue is that news organizations' response has been to rely more heavily on external information subsidies. These include increased use of news wire services, user-generated content and social media sources. Subsidies have also come from the rising public relations industry, which has expanded tremendously to fill increased demand. In the UK, the sector grew 11-fold in real terms just in the last two decades of the twentieth century (Miller and Dinan, 2000). In the US, by 2008 there were four times as many PR specialists employed as media editorial staff (McChesney and Nichols, 2010). PR practitioner numbers had grown to 258,000 by 2010 with a projected rise to 316,000 by 2020 (US Labor Bureau, 2010). Their employment has spread beyond governments, parties and large corporations. A range of public institutions, interest groups and medium-sized businesses now deploy their practices and personnel in attempts to intervene in politics and public discourse. An important part of their impact has been in generating 'expert' and 'scientific' research for correspondents (Davis, 2002; Stauber and Rampton, 2002; Miller and Dinan, 2008; Cave and Rowell, 2014). Without specific expertise, generalist journalists end up reproducing such outputs uncritically.

It is difficult to determine exactly what percentage of news is made up of subsidies such as news wire content or PR material, but a few studies give some indication. Lewis et al.'s UK study (2008) recorded that 49% of national press stories were either entirely or mainly dependent on news wire agency copy. In Australia, one study found 50% of government news releases were reproduced 'virtually verbatim', and between a half and two thirds of news stories in three national papers came from PR material (Turner et al., 2000: 42). In the UK, Lewis et al.'s study (2008) found that 19% of national press stories and 17% of broadcasts were entirely or mainly reproduced PR material. In the US, McChesney and Nichols (2010) estimated that 40–50% of newspaper stories began life as press releases, while only 14% originated from reporters. A majority of journalists surveyed in the fifteen countries in Table 5.1 believed that PR was having a strong influence on their profession.

The third key issue is the increasing influence of the digital eco system on legacy journalism practices (Pew, 2016a; Ofcom, 2017; Reuters, 2017). The obvious impact has been on declining news revenues. Less obviously, but no less important for the profession, is the loss of control over news agendas, news cycles and news distribution (Anderson et al., 2015). Since consumers increasingly come to news through social media, news aggregators or google searches, reporters have become increasingly powerless to shape and monetize their own outputs. Vargo and Guo's (2017) recent data suggests that partisan online news sites now set agendas more frequently than the *New York Times* or *Washington Post*. Reuters' (2017) survey of thirty-six countries found that 54% of people prefer to get news via algorithms in social media, next to 44% who actively seek out established online news sites.

That in turn, has further impacted on reporting practices as legacy news media attempt to compete with their fast-moving but less accountable online rivals (Lasorsa et al., 2012; Braun, 2015; Graves, 2016; Elvestad and Phillips, 2018). Established operations are less rigorous about fact-checking, verifying sources or ensuring objectivity norms. As Elvested and Phillips (2018) note, traditional news stories and headlines are increasingly selected to capture traffic on their online versions. For Braun (2015: 5) the new question for reporters is: 'how do journalists get non-journalists to distribute their messages?'

As Table 5.1 shows, all such trends go far beyond the US and UK. The 'Worlds of Journalism' survey, covers fifteen of the sixteen sample countries discussed in earlier chapters: **A**rgentina, **A**ustralia, **Br**azil, **Ch**ile, **G**ermany, **H**ong Kong, **H**ungary, **In**dia, **It**aly, **J**apan, **S**outh Africa, **Sw**eden, **T**urkey, the **UK** and the **USA**. The survey generally throws up very similar results when it comes to noting trends about competition, increased working hours, declining resources, the influences and impacts of social media and public relations, and the consequences for journalism in terms of declining ethical standards, increased pressure to sensationalize news and declining journalist credibility.

As the new news eco-system has emerged so the professional norms and practices of reporters have become ever more unsustainable. The legacy news that is left still attempts to offer the pretence of authoritative autonomous journalism but, below the surface, it is anything but. Instead, coverage is increasingly watered-down, under-researched, more poorly sourced and checked, cannibalistic, rehashed, sensationalist and highly dependent on PR materials. It is also more composed of non-news. The cracks are now there for seasoned news consumers to see. In 2016, Pew (2016a) reported on the 'tectonic shifts' taking place in the industry. Davis (2017a) wondered about the 'death of public knowledge'. Anderson et al. (2015: 3) concluded that we had entered an era of 'post-industrial journalism' in which:

Table 5.1: Worlds of Journalism Survey Data 2012–2016

	Ar	Au	Br	Ch	Ge	HK	Hu	In	It	Ja	SA	Sw	Tu	UK	US
Competition Rise %[1]	+48.2	+55.3	+56.3	+36.9	+88.4	+47	+74.2	+90.9	+68	+58.7	+75.1	+74.4	+39.2	+60.3	+61.9
Av Wk Hrs Incr/Decr[2]	+68	+75	+68.8	+55.6	+72.1	+62.2	+77.1	+74.1	+59.2	+46.8	+64.1	+55.5	+64.8	+79.8	+69.9
Social Med Influence[3]	+91.9	+99.2	+96.5	+75	+94.1	+78.3	+91.8	+76.7	+95.2	+86.8	+99.3	+95.7	+100	+97.8	+90.4
PR Influence[4]	+47	+58.1	+36.7	+6.3	+51.6	+25.1	+57.1	+61.8	+46.4	+41.5	+41.5	+50.4	+32.7	+54.6	-7.8
Ethical Standards[5]	-12.4	-25	+1.5	-4.3	-32.7	-20.8	-27	+14	-47.4	+45.7	+4.5	-14	-66.1	+20.6	-28.1
Pressure Sensational[6]	+50.5	+49.6	+57.5	+31.4	+53.8	+41.7	+77.3	+55.7	+65.9	+29.1	+67.8	+57.9	+41.5	+41.8	+8.3
Journalist Credibility[7]	-41.9	-47.1	-32.2	+0.9	-54.8	-25.5	-32.3	+24.5	-74.7	-43.2	-23.6	-34.8	-68	-57.3	-40.7

Percentage of journalists saying …
1. competition is increasing minus those of those saying not.
2. their average working hours had increased minus those saying not.
3. social media is having a strong influence on journalism minus those saying it's having a weak influence.
4. that public relations is having a strong influence on journalism minus those saying a weak influence.
5. that ethical standards have got stronger minus those saying they have got weaker.
6. pressure to sensationalize news is getting stronger minus those who say weaker.
7. journalist credibility is increasing minus those saying it's decreasing.

there is no such thing as the news industry anymore. There used to be one, held together by the usual things that hold an industry together ... Those conditions no longer hold true.

Such is the decline in the veracity of the core news product, that there is a growing problem of public trust. That includes in mainstream, legacy news producers. Despite the emergence of a new news subsector of fact-checkers, to scrutinize political statements and their coverage (Graves, 2016) trust levels remain low. The Reuters (2017) global survey found that only 43% of people trust 'most media most of the time'. A US poll (Pew, 2016b) found that 23% of Americans, knowingly or unknowingly, had shared a fake news story. 32% said they often spotted fake news online and 51% said they had read news that was at least partially 'inaccurate'. Newman and Fletcher's (2017) nine-country study found that 67% of people did not trust news because it was full of 'bias, spin and agendas'. The research found that citizens did not identify a clear separation of 'fake' and 'real' news, but instead, saw news on a sliding scale. Even if not 'fake', it was increasingly classed as 'poor', 'satire', 'advertising', full of 'propaganda' or simply contained 'false' elements. Substantial majorities of journalists surveyed in all but two of the fifteen nations (Chile, India) in Table 5.1, thought the credibility of their profession was decreasing.

Under these circumstances, when Donald Trump or Benjamin Netanyahu reject reporting as 'fake news', much of their audience is all too ready to believe them.

Conclusion

In effect, the autonomy and professionalism of journalism has been eroded by the strong impacts of market forces and the new digital news ecosystem. This has forced a growing reporter dependency on those who control the new platforms, alternative suppliers of information subsidies and the promotional professions in general. It has also made even legacy journalism into a more sensationalist and less reliable source of political coverage. That in turn, leaves news open to the charges of being 'fake news', even when that term is used by unscrupulous populist politicians.

To the public it is presented the same way. But, behind the production process, it is clear that the product itself increasingly relies on cutting many corners, using questionable practices and relying on partial and self-interested sources, all of which are prepared to say and do whatever it takes to gain news access. If all this continues, either we won't have newspapers and news broadcasters, or what they produce will no longer be 'news' as it was traditionally conceived.

Instead, news is coming to resemble watered-down pub coke, fake Lacoste T-shirts or Rolex watches. Each of these may look like the real thing but they are made with incredibly cheap and unreliable materials. They taste bad or quickly fall apart soon after purchase. The same has happened to news. It may look like news but it isn't.

6
Media–Source Relations, Mediatization and Populist Politics

This chapter looks at the changing dynamics of politician–journalist and party–media relations. The majority of political news content derives from these interactions. Likewise, media considerations can have a strong influence on political agendas and policy debates. Thus, these relationships also have implications for public understanding and the proper functioning of democratic public spheres.

The chapter is in three parts. The first introduces the topic of media–source relations exploring the various ways it has been framed in democratic political communication. The section then presents two opposing positions taken on relations. Part two follows with an exploration of a third, more-recent paradigm, focusing on the ways politicians and parties have become subject to 'media logic' or 'mediatization'. From this perspective reporters do not simply report the political arena, they are part of it; and political decision-making is as influenced by media considerations as by party objectives.

Part three makes the point that, with recent developments in both media and politics, each of these perspectives now needs to be rethought. As political parties and legacy media become more fractured and less central to the public sphere, notions of managed media, pluralist balance or mediatized politics make less sense. Instead, as the chapter concludes, media–source relations have become reconfigured on both sides by populism and entertainment culture; a media ecology that new populist parties are better suited to operate in.

Media–Source Relations

Simply put, a large proportion of political news coverage comes out
of direct and indirect exchanges between sources and journalists.
Periodically, reporters develop a story through independent investigation. However, most content derives from daily exchanges between
the two sides, via either formal press conferences and press releases
or informal meetings, emails and social media.

Much of the relationship is formalized and systematized
through reporting beats. News media and large institutions are
drawn together by their 'bureaucratic affinity' (Fishman, 1980).
Correspondents seeks regular news story material and governments and big organizations frequently supply that. Over time,
multiple news beats and institutionalized exchanges have developed
around crime and policing, education and health, the military and
national defence, industrial relations and so on (Ericson et al.,
1989; Schlesinger and Tumber, 1994; Manning, 2000; Franklin
and Carlson, 2010).

The most developed and reported beats centre on national
polities where political sources (politicians, parties, spin doctors) and
journalists interact intensely on a daily basis. In many established
democracies the relationship has become entirely institutionalized.
In the White House, Capitol Hill and Westminster, journalists have
on-site offices and broadcasting spaces. They share social facilities
such as bars with politicians. There are regular, organized media
conferences, briefings and press releases. Many specialist political
correspondents are there longer than the average elected politician
(see early accounts in Hess, 1984; Tiffen, 1989; Tunstall, 1996;
Barnett and Gaber, 2001).

In classic descriptions of the media–source relationship, both
sides need each other and develop a professional association based
on exchange. Politicians need positive publicity and journalists need
high-level access and story information. What is clear is that the two
groups have competing objectives. Journalists attempt to maintain
their autonomy as they seek to critically report and hold powerful
politicians and governments to account. For their part, politicians
attempt to manage reporters and media to present themselves in the
most favourable light. In Herbert Gans's (1979: 117) *Deciding What's
News*, he equated relations to an ongoing 'tug of war' or 'tango dance'
in which journalists and politicians jostle for the upper hand with
neither gaining overall control:

The source-journalist relationship is therefore a tug of war: while sources attempt to 'manage' the news, putting the best light on themselves, journalists concurrently 'manage' the sources in order to extract the information they want.

However, in many practitioner and media sociology accounts, it becomes clear there is also a great deal of cooperation as well as conflict. In the democracies of Southern Europe, there has been a history of 'party-press parallelism' (Chalaby, 1998; Hallin and Mancini, 2004). Patron-based or 'clientalist' relationships have also been recorded in hybrid democracies such as Mexico and Russia (Benavides, 2000; Roudakova, 2008). Even in the US, cross-profession coalitions of correspondents and politicians can develop around specific agendas and campaigns (Protess et al., 1991; Baumgartner and Jones, 1993).

Scholars looking at media–source relations tend to investigate two particular questions with a bearing on democratic communication. These I term the 'adversarial-exchange' and 'pluralist-source conflict' debates (Davis, 2010a). The adversarial-exchange paradigm focuses on power relations between the two sides. It asks do correspondents have sufficient independence and autonomy from politicians to report news critically and objectively? The pluralist-source conflict debate looks at the issue of plurality. Do reporters offer a strong balance of sources and perspectives from across the political spectrum when constructing stories?

For a mix of liberal media sociologists (Schlesinger and Tumber, 1994; Zellizer, 2004; Schudson, 2008; Esser, 2008; McNair, 2009) and journalists the answer to both questions, with some qualifications, is yes. Much of this comes down to the practices, economic considerations and professional norms of the journalist profession. Although sources may initially supply information, journalists take over in terms of following, developing and writing the story (Reich, 2006; Stromback and Nord, 2006). As Esser (2008) noted, the presentation of broadcast journalist reports in France, Britain, Germany and the US, mean that journalist narrations outweigh political voices by three to one. News values and the need to attract consumers means that reporters will not simply act as passive respondents to political and other leaders (Schudson, 2008). Long gone are the days when correspondents reverently covered the speeches and political affairs of leading statespersons.

Instead, recent decades have been characterized by a steady rise of negative and adversarial reporting (Hallin, 1994; Esser, 2008; Wolf,

2018) as well as career-ending scandals (Pilger, 2005; Greenwald, 2014; Davies, 2015). Despite the financial struggles of the sector, there has been a steady stream of investigative exposes, including: Wikileaks, the Snowden Files, FIFA corruption, the Panama Papers, the Paradise Papers, UK MPs' expenses and the German VW car company's 'Emissionsgate'. Jacob Zuma, Silvio Berlusconi, Nicolas Sarkozy, Park Geun-hye, Hillary Clinton and Benjamin Netanyahu are some of the world leaders who have had their careers curtailed by such revelations.

On a more day-to-day basis, others emphasize a sense of pluralist source opinion being reproduced in coverage. Political elites may be dominant figures in news but standard reporting practices mean that journalists make sure to collect a range of conflicting views. In turn, politicians struggle to dictate media agendas for long and new perspectives emerge. In the UK, Schlesinger and Tumber's (1994) study of crime reporting revealed the high levels of conflict occurring between different elite sources. The legitimacy and ability to dominate agendas and story frames by such figures fell as public discourse became more contested.

In the US, Hallin (1994), Bennett (1990) and Entman (2004), have developed a larger theoretical framework around notions of elite pluralist conflict and reporting. Using the example of coverage of the US–Vietnam War, Hallin (1994) argued that stories and their interpretations fell into one of three categories: 'consensus', 'legitimate controversy' or 'illegitimate political activity'. Political coverage of the war initially took place within one of the first two categories. However, as the conflict progressed, elite contestation developed. This led to more 'illegitimate' or radical sources and opinions coming to be reported, ultimately resulting in pressure for a US withdrawal. Bennett's 'indexing hypothesis' (1990), using the example of US foreign policy in Nicaragua, theorized that when political elites were in broad consensus on an issue, then coverage reflected that. Reporters rarely looked beyond the political centre for critical comment. However, when this broke down, correspondents again began presenting a wider spectrum of views and alternative voices.

Clearly, at the present time, there is widespread political elite conflict, both between and within parties (see Chapter 4). This suggests that the ability of powerful sources to dominate reporters and maintain their authority is likely to be considerably weakened. Consequently, the potential for new political leaders and challenging ideas to emerge has been enhanced.

In contrast, for various reasons, critical media sociologists argue that journalists lack autonomy, and that reporting is still not sufficiently pluralist. Not only are political sources more in control of the tango dance more of the time, that control continues to grow. As several studies have shown, in many periods and places (Philo, 1995; Darras, 2005; Reich, 2006; Lewis et al., 2008; Tiffen et al., 2014), it is political sources that instigate the large majority of stories. They, as 'primary definers' (Hall et al., 1978) set the reporting agendas and initial story frames for 'secondary definer' journalists to respond to. As journalism becomes more dependent on external 'information subsidies' (Gandy, 1982), it is governments and large corporations which have been best positioned to supply those subsidies. They are the largest patrons of the public relations industry (Davis, 2002; Lewis et al., 2008; McChesney and Nichols, 2010). In difficult circumstances, such as during social unrest, war and terrorist threats, they have the necessary resources to produce wide-ranging propaganda outputs (Rampton and Stauber, 2006; Dinan and Miller, 2007; Sussman, 2011; Thussu and Freedman, 2012).

Having fostered such dependence, established governments and parties are then able to control journalist access. Individual access to war zones or parliaments, to news conferences, press releases and senior figures, can all be offered or withdrawn (see Kurtz, 1998; Barnett and Gaber, 2001; Franklin, 2004; Woodward, 2006). At this same personal level, political sources can spin journalists or subject them to 'flak', pressuring them and their editors to produce favourable copy. A current strategy of populist politicians like Donald Trump, Benjamin Netanyahu, Nigel Farage and others, has been to directly attack individual reporters and their publications. Such lines go even further in more limited democracies like Turkey, Poland and Mexico, where the rates of journalist deaths and detentions is rising (RSF, 2016). Under these circumstances, it has become increasingly difficult for reporters to assert their autonomy while also maintaining their access and own legitimacy.

As critics also argue, even when elites are in conflict, pluralist sourcing remains limited. Research consistently reveals that elite sources continues to dominate most areas of news reporting in most countries and time periods (GUMG, 1976; Hall et al., 1978; Herman and Chomsky, 1988; Stromback and Nord, 2006; Franklin and Carlson, 2010). They are the most covered and cited individuals. That and typical reporting styles mean that they are automatically allotted a higher level of legitimacy and authority than non-political sources and journalists themselves. It is extremely rare that a study finds otherwise. What is frequently missing is the views of others outside the political arena: interest groups, trade unions, front line soldiers, ordinary employees and consumers, among others. What is also missing is the voices of those who live and work beyond the metropolitan centres where elite national politicians and journalists operate.

What follows is that politics and issues like economics or education, become understood and reported within ideologically narrow spaces. Agendas and interpretive frames are limited. Too much that is regarded as 'legitimate controversy' beyond the political centre is treated as 'illegitimate political activity' within it. The current popular backlash against out-of-touch cosmopolitan political-media elites in many countries is testimony to this (Frank, 2016; Barnett, 2017).

Media Logic, Mediation and Mediatization

In recent years, the media–source relationship has also been explored on a less conscious, socio-cultural level. Accounts here stress the wider influences of 'media logic' or 'mediatization' on politicians, parties and governments. At times these can be quite abstract and vague in their discussions (see critique by Deacon and Stanyer, 2014). One thing that they do agree on though is that politicians are not managing media so much as being subjected to mediatization.

There are stronger and weaker conceptualizations of how mediatization operates. Various authors have taken the first approach, inferring that modern media in its various manifestations is an all-pervasive force. Over time it reshapes everything. As Krotz (2007) puts it, 'mediatization' is no less than a 'meta-process', as powerful a force of social change as globalization or commercialization. In this vein, it was Marshall McLuhan (1964) who first declared that 'the medium is the message'. Each new form of mass communication does not merely convey messages but also shapes communication itself. Years later, Altheide and Snow (1979; Altheide, 2004) coined the term 'media logic'. They argued that media production had its own autonomous logic of operation, driven by news cycles, news values, news beats and so on. Such 'media logic' came to impose itself on politicians and parties. That led to parties packaging policies as newsworthy stories, timing news releases for media deadlines, or presenting leaders as attractive personalities. For Meyer (2002), media increasingly 'colonizes' politics with such logics. Politics, in turn, becomes dominated by an 'iron triangle' of politicians, pollsters and media executives, who together conceive problem definitions and policy solutions in media-oriented terms.

Mazzoleni and Schulz (1999; Mazzoleni, 2014) and Stromback (2008; Stromback and Esser, 2014), follow a similar line. They see a historical transition whereby 'political logic' becomes slowly subjugated to 'media logic'. Stromback's schema defines a four-stage transition. In the first stage media becomes an increasingly important source of information for society and polities. Stage two describes media becoming a more autonomous entity but still subjugated to the political. By stage three media is in the ascendancy and by stage four, its logic entirely pervades politics and governance. Politicians and parties, in turn, adapt their approaches to policy-making and even their base ideologies. They become passive respondents, enthralled by media, doing whatever necessary to capture media attention.

There is an alternative, more nuanced conceptualization that is is less technologically determinist in its approach to 'mediation'. Influenced by work on 'uses and gratifications' theory (Katz et al., 1973–4) and audience studies (Morley, 1992), it sees both media and sources adapting to each other in a more interactive, 'co-determining' and reflexive way. Such authors (Thompson, 1995; Davis, 2007b; Livingstone, 2009; Lundby, 2009) ask: how do individuals actively use media and communications? In the case of politics, how do politicians and political institutions inadvertently alter their behaviours, relations and discursive practices to engage with news media? Much recent literature on the topic has taken this more interactive, co-constitutive and reflexive approach to how media and political logics combine (Davis, 2010a; Lander, 2013; Hepp et al., 2015). Wolfsfeld (2011), for example, offers a Politics-Media-Politics (PMP) model in which politics and media take turns to influence agendas. Van Aelst and Walgrave (2017) and their contributors, debate the characteristics of a dynamic model of interaction in their 'information and arenas' paradigm.

Whether one takes a hard, determinist or more co-constitutive line, the issue still comes down to one of society and politics being reshaped, in part by interacting with media. For practical purposes, the question has now become how exactly is mediatized politics manifested and can that be clearly recorded?

One way is through looking at the changing shape of news content. Studies show reporting has steadily drifted away from depth coverage of speeches and parliamentary debates and is increasingly constructed of soundbite summaries. Hallin's (1994) study of US political broadcast reporting in the post-war era observes this shift. In the 1950s it was common to have lengthy speeches and debates reported in full. By the 1990s, reports allowed politicians just over ten seconds to make a case. Esser's (2008) study of the 2000s recorded that average times had dropped to seventeen seconds in the UK, 10.8 seconds in Germany and 8.8 seconds in the US. Accordingly, politicians have adapted and now pepper speeches and interviews with short, pithy soundbites, knowing that these will be the ones picked up in the main news broadcasts: 'Either you are with us or with the terrorists' (George Bush), 'Tough on crime, tough on the causes of crime' (Tony Blair), 'It's time for change' (Barack Obama), 'Make America great again' (Donald Trump), 'Strong and Stable' (Theresa May).

Similar longer-term trends have also been recorded in changing types of news story during election periods. Since the 1970s, election coverage has become dominated by a mix of personality-driven, negative and 'horse-race' content (Hallin, 1994; Blumler and Gurevitch, 1995; Franklin, 2004). Thus, the most common news story during any election is now one that focuses on polls and who is winning and where. Actual policy discussions, even of leading issues for voters, get relatively small levels of copy. In the 2015 UK election (Loughborough, 2015), 45.9% of broadcast coverage and 44.5% of newspaper stories were driven by horse-race themes. The economy, one of the two most important issues for voters, was discussed in 8.1% of broadcast and 10.5% of newsprint pieces. The NHS, the other top issue for the electorate, was only covered in 3.5% of stories. In the 2016 US election (Patterson, 2016), news coverage was dominated by horse-race topics and negative controversies. Horse-race accounts made up 42% of the total, controversies 17% and policy positions just 10%.

Another indication of mediatization can be gauged by observing the changing behaviours and practices of politicians. In a key study, Davis (2007a; 2009) interviewed and observed some sixty UK politicians, investigating how they both consumed media and interacted with journalists. He found British MPs to be generally media-obsessed consuming, on average, five different news sources each day; a mix of newspapers, broadcasters and websites. Twenty-four-hour news channels and/or news website feeds were a constant background presence in their offices. UK politicians were also likely to possess media expertise. Some four fifth had either taken media training courses or had had prior professional experience in journalism or public relations. All three main party leaders in the 2015 UK election – Ed Miliband, Nick Clegg and David Cameron – had had stints in these professions. Consequently, many appeared to have an extensive knowledge of 'news values', news routines, individual publications and journalists. Lastly, politicians had very high levels of contact with political journalists. Two thirds talked to reporters at least once each day, while some senior ministers might have ten to twenty such engagements in a day.

With this heightened interaction with journalists and increased consumption of news, political thinking and behaviour are inevitably influenced in various ways. As Davis (2010b), concluded, journalist-politician relations not only set media agendas, but political ones too. They play an important part in the 'politics of politics' within parliaments themselves (see also Cook, 1998).

For one, news media and reporters have become a major source of information about the business of politics itself. So, stories contribute to the setting of daily parliamentary agendas (Baumgartner and Jones, 2014; Lengauer et al., 2014; Fawzi, 2017; Walgrave et al., 2017). In Sevenans's (2017) study of Belgian politics, such media information was 'decisive' in generating political activity for a quarter of politicians. Prominent news stories would become key issues and talking points for MPs, journalists and other parliamentarians. Politicians also gain information about how political agendas and power struggles are developing within a parliament by talking to seasoned journalists (Davis, 2009a; Kunelius and Reunanen, 2012; Baumgartner and Jones, 2014; Dindler, 2015).

For another, politics is often practised through media channels rather than directly. Party leaders increasingly make political choices with future news headlines in mind (Reich, 2006; Davis, 2007a; Wolfsfeld, 2011; Dindler, 2015). Policy and legislative agendas can be selected with likely media responses in mind; either encouraging more emotive newsworthy topics or avoiding more technically dull ones. Politicians leak information and plant stories in order to undermine opponents within their own parties. Media skills are a key consideration for parties when they select and promote their leaders (Stromback and Esser, 2014; Lengauer et al., 2014). In effect, journalist–source relations and the mediatization of politics generally, mean that such interactions have contributed to the 'social construction of politics' itself.

Populist Media Meets Populist Politics

There is now a major problem with each of the media–source

relations paradigms presented so far. That is that both news media and political parties have undergone substantial change over the last decade. On the one side, established parties are declining and fragmenting (see Chapter 4). They are being challenged by new parties, social media and very sceptical electorates. That makes media management by political sources an increasingly difficult task. On the other side, news media have also become fragmented, disrupted, multi-dimensional, unstable and untrusted, with news cycles being far less defined and news formats more diverse (see Chapter 5). Thus, it seems increasingly problematic to develop a strong mediatization paradigm based on powerful, autonomous news media influencing all else.

In the chaotic and anarchic public sphere emerging, neither politicians nor news journalists and stable media appear to be dominant. Politicians still attempt to manage media, and politics is mediatized in various ways, but media–source relations is also subject to another growing influence: populism. In an effort to survive, both the political and media fields have gravitated towards mass culture, entertainment and populism.

Currently, populist politics appears to be offering a substantial challenge to democracies everywhere. The term itself is ambiguous and controversial, having different histories and associations globally, a variety of causes and ideological links, and all too often simply being a term to denounce one's opponents (see definitions in Judis, 2016; Mudde and Rovira Kaltwasser, 2017). The reasons for the current wave of populist challenge are varied. As Chapter 4 explains, economic arguments make a lot of sense. There are clear parallels between the 1930s, 1970s and last decade, when economic shocks were followed by the rise of more extreme parties. Alternatively, there is also a case to be made against globalization and multi-culturalism, seen by many as causes of social, economic and cultural disruption. This has also spurred the rise of nationalism and a hate of the 'other' by right-wing populists.

Without denying that such factors have driven the new wave of populism, this section now explores the topic through the dynamic of media–source relations and mediatization. Both news media and politics have always had populist tendencies, with periods when populism was quite pronounced. In both sectors one can see recent historical trends have also led them towards populism. As such, there is an additional explanation to be found in political communication for the rise of anti-democratic populism (see Aalberg et al., 2018).

For over a century, critics have periodically lamented times when serious news has seemed to drift towards tabloid content and 'yellow journalism' (Williams, 1997; Campbell, 2003). A further wave of such accounts emerged in the last decades of the twentieth century (Postman, 1985; Dahlgren and Sparks, 1992; Franklin, 1997; Delli Carpini and Williams, 2001; Thussu, 2008). These noted that, as news sales and advertising slowly declined, and competition intensified, news producers had joined a 'race to the bottom' to recapture consumers. Gossip, scandal, scare stories and human-interest pieces became more common, as journalism began turning to the entertainment world for inspiration. In the US, Postman (1985) declared that 'we were amusing ourselves to death'. In the UK, Franklin (1997: 4) labelled the new news content 'newszak' or 'bonk journalism'. Thussu (2008) traced such developments on a world-wide scale as news became 'global infotainment' or was subjected to 'Bollywoodization' in India. Even war coverage became reconfigured through the infotainment lens. As Franklin summed it up (1997: 4):

> Journalism's editorial priorities have changed. Entertainment has superseded the provision of information; human interest has supplanted the public interest ... journalists are more concerned to report stories which interest the public than stories which are in the public interest.

A key component of this tabloidization has been an increased focus on celebrity as a means of drawing consumers (McLachlin and Golding, 2000; Turner et al., 2000; Evans and Hesmondhalgh, 2005). Celebrity news, as a percentage of magazine and newspaper content, has steadily shifted up in Australia, the US and UK. Such has been the demand that media companies have begun creating their own celebrities or 'celetoids' (Rojek, 2001; Turner, 2009). This coverage has included presenting politicians as celebrities as well as reporting celebrities who publicly support politicians and political causes (Marshall, 1997; West and Orman, 2003; Wheeler, 2014).

Accordingly, political news coverage has tilted towards profiling and evaluating the personalities of leaders (Hall Jamieson, 1996; Franklin, 2004). In most European and US elections of recent decades, a disproportionate amount of copy has been devoted to presidential candidates and leaders at the expense of other politicians (Scammell, 2014). For example, in the 2017 UK election, the two party leaders, Theresa May and Jeremy Corbyn, accounted for 56.8% of all coverage of individual politicians. News content includes regular poll ratings of party leaders and comparative measures of their personal traits. It is Trump versus Clinton, May compared to Corbyn, or Emmanuel Macron against Marine Le Pen.

Such trends have been exacerbated by the extreme economic circumstances encountered by the news industry in the last decade (see Chapter 5). News producers are losing audiences and advertising share to both entertainment media and the online world. Their responses have often been to try and compete with both to claw back income. So, they are venturing ever further into celebrity and tabloid territory. They are also producing more extreme headlines to draw online click-bait traffic (Braun, 2015; Graves, 2016; Reuters, 2017; Elvestad and Phillips, 2018). There is an even stronger focus on personalities, party splits and negative or extreme news in politics. Even serious news sites now mix standard news stories with celebrity features, trivia and eye-catching bizarre events.

Politics has followed a parallel trajectory towards an increased emphasis on personality politics and populist appeal. Several studies have documented the overlaps that have emerged between politics, popular culture and celebrity (West and Orman, 2003; Corner and Pels, 2003; Street, 2003; van Zoonen, 2005). As West and Orman (2003) reveal, many successful US political careers have played on the cultural resonances associated with family dynasties. These include the Kennedys, the Clintons and the Bushes in the US, as well as the Trudeaus, the Calderons and the Churchills elsewhere. Such individuals have an advantage in terms of drawing media exposure and public recognition at an early stage. In addition, public figures from outside politics have used their fame to run for office. Vaclav Havel, Imran Khan, Arnold Schwarzenegger, and Ronald Reagan, have each succeeded in transferring their 'symbolic capital' from the field of entertainment to that of politics. Thus, when Donald Trump stood for the Republican nomination after fourteen seasons of *The Apprentice*, he was more recognized than his multiple Republican opponents. 92% of registered Republicans knew him, while only 81% recognized Jeb Bush and 66% Ted Cruz (Lawrence and Boydstun, 2017: 51).

From the 1980s onwards, professionalized parties recognized the importance of selling leaders. Charismatic leadership was no longer left to chance as personal image management became a core component of communication strategy. Parties conducted private polls and focus groups to test public images and guide presentations (West and Orman, 2003; Corner and Pels, 2003; Stanyer, 2007; Davis, 2010b). They aimed to personalize political images and cultivate a sense of public intimacy, so imitating the 'para-social relationships' (Horton and Wohl, 1956) of the entertainment world (Stanyer, 2013; Holtz Bacha et al., 2014; McGregor et al., 2016). Thus, leading politicians began appearing more frequently on light entertainment chat shows and comedy programmes like *Saturday Night Live* or *Have I Got News for You*. During elections, political adverts and campaign material both played on these appealing personal traits while also attacking the personalities of opponents. Insider accounts of Tony Blair, George W. Bush, Gerhard Schröder, Nicolas Sarkozy, and David Cameron, have argued that each rose on the basis of their TV-friendly personalities rather than their policies.

Thus, parties put less stock on traditional policy debates and appeals to informed voters. Instead they chose to promote individual personalities, party brands and popular causes to the wider electorate. Consequently, as Corner and Pels (2003) argued, politics had become as much attuned to aesthetics, fashions and style as to ideologies and policies. This has contributed to a new form of populist 'media democracy'. For Lawrence and Boydstun (2017: 39): 'politics today is increasingly saturated with entertainment platforms and values, creating unprecedented opportunities for unconventional political actors to enter and succeed in politics'.

Consequently, it is no surprise that studies frequently show publics evaluating and voting for parties on the basis of which party leaders have more appealing personalities. Lees's (2005) study of polls at the 2002 German election, found that people preferred Edmund Stoiber's policies but voted in greater numbers for Gerhard Schröder because of his more favourable 'character traits'. In the 2000 US election, polls recorded that Al Gore reflected the policy preferences of more of the wider electorate on four of seven key policy issues (Knuckey and Lees-Marshment, 2005). However, Bush was ahead in four out of seven key character traits. That Bush won suggests that personality trumped policy. The same results were recorded in the 2004 election where Kerry, despite being ahead on more policy positions, lost out to Bush's more appealing personality traits (Kenski and Kenski, 2009).

These duel developments have had consequences that have boosted the rise of populist leaders and parties. They have undermined traditional parties, media and institutions while also creating an environment in which alternatives can thrive.

So, for one, there has developed a growing chasm between the private sphere of institutions and real politics, and the symbolic and populist space of the public sphere (Bennett and Entman, 2001; John Corner, 2003; Davis, 2017a). Real, substantive politics has become less transparent while symbolic pseudo politics has become what publics see. Actual party positions, policy development and political decision-making is more obscure and unaccountable. Instead, politics and its reporting is about grand gestures, phrases and symbolism, with few details. The hyperbole from all sides never becomes a reality.

Second, selling politics and news like passing fashions, and leaders like celebrities, is likely to bring greater instability (Davis, 2018). Both the fashion and celebrity worlds are in constant flux and driven by rapid turnover and change. They promote a repetitive cycle of instant gratification and rejection. Tony Blair and George W. Bush, two such personality politicians, both had some of the most positive and most negative poll ratings of any post-war prime minister or president. Bush went from 90% approval and 6% disapproval, in September 2001, to 25% approval and 71% disapproval in October 2008 (Gallup, 2008). In 2008, Barack Obama won a landslide vote winning the Presidency, Congress and Senate for the Democrats. Two years later the Democrats had some of their biggest losses for over half a century. Electoral volatility has been a key feature of recent elections in the UK (2016, 2017), the US (2016), France (2017) and the Netherlands (2017), and elsewhere. In a six-week election period in 2017, Theresa May dropped 44% in her personal approval ratings. Emmanuel Macron's approval ratings declined from 66%, just after his election in May 2017, to just 31% eighteen months later.

In effect, the 'populist turn' in both media and politics has contributed to the marked decline of trust and faith in both professions. The longer the same public faces remain on screens and fail to deliver, the stronger the distrust. If politicians will say anything to gain media exposure, regardless of the realities experienced by many ordinary people, and if journalists will cover anything that gets them more readers and viewers regardless of the 'facts' or experiences of their readers, cynicism will inevitably grow. So, we have entered a time of 'post-truth politics', 'fake news' and discredited 'experts', where all sides become damned as a self-serving cosmopolitan elite.

Under such circumstances one can see that the current mediated political environment is more conducive to the new type of populist party, charismatic leader and firebrand commentator. Such figures do not need policies or details when emotions and feelings predominate the public sphere. They are not encumbered by traditions or ideologies, or the checks and balances of professional media and party organizations. And they benefit from not being one of those establishment figures which have dominated news screens and papers for years.

Thus, have arisen more populist parties and movements, from the Tea Party, Front National and True Finns on the right, to the Occupy Wall Street movement, Syriza and Podemos on the left. So too, comes the rise of anti-establishment, populist leaders such as: Sarah Palin and Donald Trump, Nigel Farage and Boris Johnson, Marine Le Pen and Geert Wilders, Benjamin Netanyahu and Beppe Grillo, Shinzo Abe and Narendra Modi. So too, there now seem to be more similarities than differences between these party leaders, operating in democracies, and those in more authoritarian states, such as Xi Jinping, Recip Erdogan and Vladimir Putin.

Conclusion

Media–source relations has played a central part in public communication in democracies for many decades; far more so than the casual observer would know. Journalist and politician exchanges and relations became fully institutionalized over a long period. Together they came to set news and political agendas, promote and undermine parties and leaders, have a strong influence on public perceptions, and became a core component of the politics of politics itself. For many, in both media and politics, it is now difficult to see things conducted in any other way.

However, it is also clear that this ecology is neither optimal for democracies nor sustainable. As the two sides have become more inter-twined so they have co-created disconnected political bubbles. Many see them as all part of one self-serving, out-of-touch elite and, as Chapter 7 reveals, are turning to other forms of participation and types of media. More than that, they have lost their duopolistic position of control over public communication. Both sides are fractured, conflicted, polarized, and distrusted. They may still sit at *the official centre* of national polities but that no longer guarantees being at *the centre* of either politics or media. And trying to emulate their rivals, on social media, in the entertainment world, and in extreme, populist parties, is a high-risk strategy with no obvious indication of success.

Part III
Interest Groups and Citizens

7
Citizens, Media Effects and Public Participation

This chapter looks at citizens and political communication. It is split into two discussions. The first explores the subject of participation and engagement, focusing on the problem of public disconnect from formal politics. The second reviews the evolving paradigms of media effects research.

The first discussion investigates the 'crisis' of public engagement. It sets out two contrasting positions on democratic participation and related explanations for the crisis. For those who support a 'liberal' limited, rational choice model of representative democracy, public disengagement is not rational and is blamed on individual and cultural failings. Alternatively, for those advocating greater 'republican', participatory forms of democracy, the failure is more institutional than public. Citizens can be quite rational in their rejection of formal politics but are no less politically engaged or interested in public affairs. They have just turned to alternative forms of engagement. Governments and parties need to be more receptive to those.

The second discussion turns to the question of media effects. Research here has progressed through several cycles, moving between stronger and weaker models of media use and influence. As with debates about participation and crisis, alternative positions relate to base assumptions about individuals, their behaviours and relationships to media. Those who assume subjects are passive and malleable, and look for powerful strong media effects, are usually disappointed. Others who develop more complex and nuanced accounts of subjects and indirect, subtle and long-term effects, have more success. But, as the discussion concludes, the new fragmented, multi-media environment and prosumer culture of social media are forcing researchers to go back to the drawing board.

Citizenship, Rationality and the Crisis of Formal Participation

Theoretically and practically, public participation and engagement is regarded as a prerequisite for healthy democracy and is essential for government legitimacy to be maintained. Where this breaks down, state authority is weakened, potentially moving nations towards crisis. Such crises have been increasingly common across the globe recently (see Chapter 3), from Greece and Iceland to Mexico and Brazil.

Put like this, healthy democracies should encourage participation. The problem is that there is not a clear consensus on what political participation is or what its limits should be.

In debates about how modern, representative democracy best operates, there have developed quite contrasting views of citizenship participation (see overviews in Dahlgren, 2009; Couldry et al., 2010). At one pole exist advocates of 'liberal' limited, rational choice models of representative democracy. The thrust of this position, as publicly set-out by Walter Lippman (1922), is that general publics are too ignorant or distracted to engage with the complexities of national politics. Of necessity, public affairs should be left to politicians and experts who are able to critically engage with the issues. Politicians are kept accountable by informed journalists and by being forced to periodically compete for office (Schumpeter, 1942). Robert Dahl (1961, 1989), among others, offered detailed accounts of how modern representative democracies or polyarchies did and should operate.

At the other pole sit supporters of greater 'republican', participatory democracy, such as John Dewey (1927). For Dewey, as he challenged Lippmann, healthy democracy encourages individuals to participate in public affairs at various levels. Political institutions and media should be configured towards promotion of greater participation. Others followed in this line (MacPherson, 1965; Fishkin, 1992; Dryzak, 2002), drawing out the ways and means by which democracies could be more inclusive. As Crouch (2004) explained, democratic political systems vary in their encouragement towards more 'minimal', 'representative' or 'maximal' and 'direct' forms of participation. Like many left critics, he supports more 'maximal' versions but recognizes that more minimal forms are the more likely to develop as democracies age.

This conceptual split also informs differing accounts of the 'crisis' of citizenship participation. For those whose democratic framework is based on a limited, rational choice model of democracy, crisis questions come down to the decline of formal forms of participation through political parties and state institutions. Over the space of half a century, key measures of formal participation, from voting and joining parties to trust in institutions, has been steadily declining (see Chapter 3). From this position, since democracies have been positive for most people, the rational response of citizens should be more not less participation. Accordingly, their framing of the 'crisis' looks to inadequacies among the public rather than to the failings of institutions. They offer what Hay (2007) terms 'demand-side' explanations, focusing on citizens, as opposed to 'supply-side' accounts that question political organizations. Putting it a little crudely, their varied explanations are that non-participating citizens are variously: too spoilt, too ignorant, too lazy or too individualistic to engage.

Starting with Inglehart (1977, 1990, 1997), his thesis, in effect, amounts to stating that citizens in wealthy capitalist democracies are simply too spoilt. Such democracies have produced more literate and critical citizens. As their material needs are less a concern they have adopted 'postmaterialist' values, leaving them with disparaging attitudes towards authority and the state. In fact, their reluctance to vote and their critical outlook are more signs of healthy prosperity than of democracy's failings. A related line on citizenship failure is about ignorance and over-expectation. In the 1970s, discussion on the 'overloaded state' (see Crozier et al., 1975; Buchanan and Wagner, 1977) argued that governments had over-extended themselves. This led to public expectation being heightened to a level beyond what was reasonable. Both Dalton (2004) and Norris (2000, 2002) have, at times, supported both lines about pampered publics and unrealistic demands. Such attitudes show that people, quite simply, do not comprehend the complexities of modern politics and institutions.

For others, the problem is laziness. For Hibbings and Theiss-Morse (2002) in the US, and the Hansard Society (2009) in the UK, although citizens felt strongly about politics, only a small number were willing to become involved (see also Webb, 2007). Most people want influence without the commitments of actual participation. For Putnam (1993, 1995, 2000, 2002) the issue is that modern citizens have become more isolated and individualistic more generally. His studies of local society in the US and Italy, recorded a decline in local, social forms of participation, be it for political or leisure purposes. Hence people bowled alone rather than joined bowling leagues. Modernization, suburbanization and electronic entertainment all contributed to citizens doing things on their own and their loss of 'social capital'. Without such interactions, trust eroded on multiple levels, including in relation to national political institutions.

Despite their differences, each of these studies focused on the citizen and public culture as the root causes of disengagement. In so doing, they let political and media institutions off the hook. As earlier chapters on parties, governments and news media (4, 5 and 6) suggest, these core organizations of democracy have gone through substantial change. They are as likely if not more so to have contributed to declines in formal participation. That is not to say publics and culture are blameless. For whatever reasons, most citizens do not want to participate in politics most of the time. But, it is to argue that modern political institutions are a cause of disconnect too.

At which point, one sensible response is to investigate more thoroughly why publics are or are not participating, how they view institutions, and experience participation first-hand. As Dahlgren (2009) argues, all too often, the sociology and culture of real citizens has been missing from traditional political science accounts of engagement. Instead of asking why citizens are irrational or deficient because of their lack of formal participation, sociologists have questioned what it is about political institutions that have led publics to lose faith in them. Rather than treat citizens as a surveyed mass to be divided into demographic blocks, they have taken more qualitative and depth approaches. Such research reveals not just which demographic groups participate but why they do?

A number of such studies in the UK have revealed the many rational reasons why citizens choose to disengage from formal politics (Pattie et al., 2003, 2004; Power, 2006; Couldry et al., 2010; Hansard annual audits). These mixed methods projects, drawing on diaries, focus groups and interviews as well as surveys, explored participation from a citizen's perspective. Pattie et al. (2004) developed a 'general incentives' model, arguing that combinations of incentives are key to promoting or discouraging citizen engagement. They then applied the incentives model to a number of other arguments, such as the rational choice model and Putnam's social capital perspective. Couldry et al. (2010) got a range of individuals to keep personal diaries of their media consumption and responses, as well as exploring group media interactions through focus groups.

One obvious conclusion from this work is that the choice of many citizens to not participate in formal politics is quite rational. They are no less interested in politics but have just loss faith in the political system; to the extent that voting seems pointless. Pattie et al. (2004) found that 28% of respondents believed that 'my vote makes no difference' and 55% thought that they had 'no say in what government does'. The Hansard Society's (2018) annual audits of political engagement in the UK have recorded the percentage of people satisfied with their system of government has steadily declined since they began surveys in 2004. In 2018, only 29% were satisfied with the British system and only 34% felt a sense of being 'able to bring about political change'. Among eighteen to twenty-four-year-olds, only 21% thought government allowed ordinary people to get involved in politics and just 16% thought the same about political parties. In the US (Pew, 2018), only 35% surveyed had a favourable view of the federal government and 61% said 'significant changes' were needed in the 'fundamental design and structure of American government'. Similar results have been recorded in multiple countries in the World Values Survey (see Chapter 3). Clearly, if large swathes of the population feel that way about their governments and parties, the incentives for voting or engaging via formal politics are going to be low.

Another conclusion is that democracies are prone to generating both virtuous and vicious circles of participation. In other words, some groups are continually incentivized to engage while others are not. In general, those most likely to participate are those who are better educated, wealthier, in high-status occupations, older, male, (in Western democracies) white, and living in more prosperous regions. In the UK, Hansard (2015) recorded that 71% of those earning over £35,000 per year were 'certain to vote', but only 48% of those earning less than £35,000; 58% of those from higher classes were certain versus 40% of those from lower ones; 52% of whites were set against 33% of BME citizens; 63% of homeowners were compared with 37% of renters. Hansard also observed (2018) that 75% of over 65s were certain to vote against 44% of eighteen to twenty-four-year-olds; 41% of those living in London and 37% of those in the south-east of England were 'satisfied' with the system of government versus 23% of those in Wales and 14% in Scotland.

Similar disparities have been recorded in surveys across the EU and US. Armingeon and Schadel (2015) found clear correlations over an extended period between voting, wealth and education levels, in eight Western European nations. In the US, Pew (2018) documented clear correlations, between wealth, age, education and race, on the one hand, and political knowledge, engagement and satisfaction with the US system of government, on the other. For example, 46% of those aged eighteen to twenty-nine years talked about politics daily or weekly versus 62% of over 65s. Forty-five per cent of those with a post-graduate level of education scored highly on their 'civic knowledge of politics', against 12% of those leaving education after high school. Higher engagers are also more likely to have associational/professional memberships, to read broadsheet newspapers or watch high-brow news programmes. They are both more informed and more confident about their knowledge.

The bigger picture is that those who tend to do well out of contemporary capitalist democracies are also more likely to be engaged. They have a bigger stake and more incentives. Those who do less well, in terms of income and status – the poor, ethnic minorities, the young, women, less educated – are all less likely to participate. In many cases, the gaps in participation are growing over time (see Armingeon and Schadel, 2015). In effect, at one end there is a group of very incentivized and engaged 'winners' and, at the other, a significant group with far smaller stakes who are turning away altogether. Thus, Bennett and Iyengar (2010) noted that, hidden within the data on political polarization in the US, there was a growing number of disinteresteds who no longer engaged with either mainstream media or politics. Similarly, Couldry et al. (2010) found that some 28% of those they surveyed had minimal interest in 'hard' news and political affairs.

Arguably, such trends are likely to have been exacerbated by the practices of electoral-professional parties and their advisers. If certain groups are less likely to vote in elections, then hardened campaigners are less likely to allocate precious funds and attention to them.

These demographic differences in participation were significant for the two shock election results in the UK and US in 2016. Analysis of voters for the EU Referendum showed that the young and ethnic minorities strongly supported staying in the EU. However, although 64% of under twenty-fours did vote, 90% of over sixty-fives voted and a clear majority of this demographic wanted to leave. It was a similar story with the young and ethnic minority vote for Hillary Clinton. Such groups had been temporarily inspired to come out in larger numbers during the Obama elections of 2008 and 2012 but were not so motivated in 2016.

Alternative Forms of Participation

Another response to 'demand-side' arguments about falling participation is to look at how actual citizens chose to engage. Publics may
vote and join parties less but that does not mean they are simply
apathetic and inactive. In fact, several studies have found people,
including those who avoid party politics, to be very interested in
political affairs and engaged in other activities (Pattie et al., 2004;
Couldry et al., 2010; Hansard, 2018). Fifteen years of Hansard
audits (2018) have recorded a steady increase in political knowledge,
interest and participation practices, even as faith in government and
parties has been decreasing.

Once again, for critical scholars more oriented to social and
cultural studies of citizenship, political participation is regarded as
an endeavour that goes beyond formal politics (see, for example,
Crouch, 2004; Dahlgren, 2009; Couldry et al., 2010). Healthy
engagement is not simply reducible to periodically selecting one's
representatives or doing politics through parties. Their views have
far more in common with 'republican', participatory visions of
democracy, with an emphasis on strong 'civic culture' informed
by 'civic education' and 'civic literacy'. In healthy political systems
the facilitation of a strong civil society promotes participation as an
objective in itself.

In all democracies, civil society participation has evolved in many
ways. In most cases the civil organizations and networks involved
have increased over time. Most obviously, this is recorded in the
rising numbers of interest groups and people with paid memberships to such groups (see Chapter 8). In addition, large numbers
of citizens temporarily join social movements, go on marches and
demonstrations, or take industrial action as part of a trade union.
There are many other lesser forms of participation too, including
making donations, attending political meetings, signing petitions,
boycotting companies, writing letters or emails to politicians and
newspapers, and producing political blogs and tweets.

In fact, such upward trends in civil society involvement have
continued in many mature democracies regardless of the declines in
formal political participation. Table 7.1 takes the sixteen countries
used for comparison in earlier chapters (**Ar**gentina, **Au**stralia, **Br**azil,
Chile, Germany, Hong Kong, Hungary, In**d**ia, Italy, **J**apan, **Po**land,
South **A**frica, **Sw**eden, **Tu**rkey, the **UK** and the **USA**). The first
two rows, taken from IDEA (Institute for Democracy and Electoral

Table 7.1: Comparing Political Participation

	Ar	Au	Br	Ch	Ge	HK	Hu	In	It	Ja	Po	SA	Sw	Tu	UK	US
1. Elec Particip Sc [1]	.81	.79	.75	.46	.66	-	.63	.70	.68	.52	.49	.54	.83	.84	.60	.33
2. Civil Soc Partic Sc [2]	.76	.84	.77	.70	.91	-	.56	.65	.70	.64	.66	.73	.90	.54	.83	.92
3. Particp Score [3]	6.1	7.8	6.1	4.4	8.3	5.6	4.4	7.2	7.2	6.1	6.1	8.3	8.3	5.0	8.3	7.2
4. Joined Strike %[4]	85	45	52	84	43	28	-	-	-	12	14	78	18	79	-	26
5. Attend Demo %	90	51	76	87	38	81	-	-	-	25	32	79	33	76	-	54
6. Signed Petition %	82	72	63	83	68	88	-	-	-	53	64	76	64	86	-	68

1. IDEA (2017) Electoral Participation Score, 2015
2. IDEA (2017) Civil Society Participation Index Score, 2015
3. Economist Intelligence Unit, political participation score, out of 10, 2017
4. World Values Survey, joined strikes at least once recently % in 6th wave (2010–14)
5. World Values Survey, attended peaceful demonstration at least once recently % in 6th wave (2010–14)
6. World Values Survey, signed petition at least once recently % in 6th wave (2010–14)

Assistance), show electoral participation and civil society participation measures. IDEA has comparison data for these figures going back to 1975. In the older, wealthier democracies (e.g., Australia, Germany, Italy, Japan, Sweden, UK, US), countries have recorded drops in voter turnout over several decades. In contrast, their civil society participation levels have stayed the same or increased. The 2015 figures for each have surpassed those for electoral participation. In other words, there is a good case to make that recorded indicators of political apathy apply more to parties and governments than to politics in general.

Looking at specific forms of action in the UK, Hansard (2018) found that over a twelve-month period: 23% of the UK public had donated to charities/NGOs, 24% had signed petitions, 10% had boycotted a product or company, 6% had taken part in a public consultation and 5% in a campaign. Eighty-eight per cent said they would engage in these or related activities if they felt strongly on an issue. In a similar period in the US, Pew (2018) found that: 29% had expressed their campaign support on social media, 23% had contacted an elected official, 14% had made contributions to a campaign and 11% had attended a political rally or event. Rows four, five and six in Table 7.1, taken from the World Values Survey (2010–14), record the percentages of three types of participation. Japan and Poland score very low on joining strikes and attending peaceful demonstrations while Chile and Argentina score highly here. Hong Kong and Turkey score highest when it comes to signing petitions while Japan again scores low here.

Alternative forms of participation have expanded significantly with the rise of digital, online media. If traditional political institutions and news media have operated limited communication channels and been too exclusionary, new digital developments have promised much (see Chapter 10). For one, new media has offered many new opportunities for citizens to engage more directly with political parties and governments (Bimber, 2003; Gillmor, 2004; Chadwick, 2006; Coleman and Blumler, 2009). State institutions now make publicly available detailed information on parliamentary processes. They manage online public consultations and facilitate e-petitions. Parties can now consult more with ordinary members, raise funds, disseminate alternative political news and information, and organize local activities.

Second, the new digital ecology can enhance participation through alternative forms of political organization and network. Thus, traditional interest groups, such as Amnesty or Greenpeace, were early adopters of new ICTs for their campaigns (Downing, 2001; Rheingold, 2002; Curran and Couldry, 2003). Since then, new kinds of campaign group and mobilization strategies have been made possible by the new communication environment itself (Castells, 2012; Gerbaudo, 2012; Bennett and Segerberg, 2013). These varied from online-only groups, like MoveOn, Hollaback and 38 Degrees, to anti-capitalist and anti-state protests like Occupy and those of the Arab Spring.

Lastly, new ICTS have added to the ways and means citizens can participate. Vissers and Stolle's (2014) survey of Canadian students recorded increased and alternative forms of online participation in comparison to offline forms: 50.2% had posted opinions on social and political issues on their Facebook pages in the previous six months, with 10.1% doing this often. 22.5% had joined the Facebook pages of a political group and 21.7% had contacted a political or government official online in the same period. These figures were significantly higher than for the equivalent offline activities.

Although the digital world has helped to increase participation, questions remain about whether it has had a significant impact on formal politics. Leaving aside criticisms of 'clicktivism' or 'slacktivism' (Morozov, 2012; Fuchs, 2014), studies suggest that the digital is only likely to be reinforcing those virtual and vicious circles of participation that exist off-line. Initial research found that those most likely to use the web for political participation were, above all, those with an existing history of participation (Dahlberg, 2001; Polat, 2005; Curran and Witschge, 2009). This was the same whether individuals were professional political participants or ordinary, engaged citizens. The finding has been repeated in varied research projects in multiple countries since (Dimitrova et al., 2014; Vissers and Stolle, 2014; Vaccari et al., 2015; van Aelst et al., 2017). As Dimitrova et al. (2014: 110) concluded:

> the use of different forms of digital media, controlling for other factors, has little impact on political knowledge. As in the era before the internet, what matters more for political learning is political interest, prior political knowledge, and attention to politics in traditional media formats.

In addition, if anything, cyber forms of activism and participation have been no more successful at achieving larger political goals than traditional offline forms. Local, participatory sites have struggled to operate in the long term while interest groups have not been able to maintain higher levels of deliberation and engagement with their members (Dahlgren, 2005; Wikland, 2005; Kavada, 2015). Most of the large-scale new social movements of the last decade, have failed to retain coherence and direction, usually ending up being either repressed, marginalized or extinct. Their impact on mainstream politics and institutions has been limited (Fenton, 2016a; Coleman, 2017: 22). As Coleman states, 'connective action may be good at mobilizing radical inputs, but it offers no mechanism for translating them into outputs'. Thus, in many ways, alternative forms of participation and communication have left many constituent groups in society as frustrated and disillusioned with formal politics as ever.

In conclusion, there are several explanations for why citizens are voting or joining parties less, and for why they are ever-less trusting of government. Although some of these can be put down to say political apathy or individualism, they can also be linked to the failings of democratic institutions. People, especially those who gain relatively little from capitalist democracies, do not vote or join parties because they see little point. That does not mean they are any less interested, engaged or 'rational'. They have simply chosen other forms of organization, types of participation and alternative communication platforms. They are part of a wider civic culture of engagement; something that is positive for democracy.

The key question is whether formal political parties and state institutions are able to adapt; to listen and respond properly to these alternatives. At this point, the evidence suggests that they are not. Their default response is to bunker down in their established centres and networks rather than open up. In which case, the sense of crisis will only increase as traditional political players continue to lose public trust, and citizens look either to more democratic but powerless substitutes, or to more anti-democratic parties and leaders that challenge the status quo (see Chapter 8).

Media Effects and Influences: From Strong to Limited to Strong Again

After nearly a century of media effects research the question of whether media has a strong or weak effect on publics remains inconclusive. Separating media from other variables of social influence and proving causality have always been notoriously difficult. The field has reinvented itself and its agenda several times (for overviews see McQuail, 2010; Perse and Lambe, 2017). Debates and consensus have shifted and re-shifted as media technologies and audience habits change, or researchers reconceptualize the problem and developed new methods.

At the risk of over-simplification, there have been four broad, overlapping stages of effects research; each of which is relayed in this chapter. These are marked by a mix of historical periods and academic paradigm shifts. In the first phase, coinciding with the arrival of mass broadcasting in the interwar period, media was associated with strong effects. In the second phase, for much of the latter half of the twentieth century, a consensus developed around limited media effects. In the third period, research became more nuanced, focusing on a series of lesser effects which, cumulatively, resulted in a sense of strong media influence. It might now be argued, with the increasing hegemony of digital, networked media, we have entered into a fourth phase with, as yet, no clear consensus.

The strong effects position developed in the 1920s and 1930s in Europe and the US. At that time, political turmoil, combined with fears about broadcast media's impact on the ignorant masses, propelled assumptions about powerful media influence. In Europe, the emerging Communist, Fascist and Nazi regimes made ample use of the new technology to spread propaganda. In the US, there were similar documented examples of media-inspired mass responses (Lippman, 1922; Lasswell, 1927). The supreme example of this was Orson Welles's radio broadcast of War of the Worlds in 1938 (Cantril et al., 1940). The story, about an alien invasion, was told in such a realistic way, that many listeners believed it to be real. Mass panic followed across parts of California (although the degree of panic is disputed). Together, these developments supported the seemingly common-sense notion that media could have a strong effect on public beliefs and behaviours.

Consequently, political and commercial interest in the potential power of media increased; an interest that continued to develop amid the tensions between the Soviet Union and West in the early Cold War years. Large amounts of funding were generated in the US for further research. Studies explored a range of topics from voting behaviour to increased violence (Lazarsfeld et al., 1944; Bandura and Walters 1963). The base assumption was that the public generally, and vulnerable constituent groups such as children in particular, would be strongly affected. In all cases, media was likened to a 'magic bullet' or 'hypodermic needle' that, if deployed correctly, could trigger strong, mass responses.

Accordingly, research attempted to demonstrate this. In the post-war period thousands of studies were conducted by a mix of psychologists, sociologists and mass communication specialists. The studies varied but were premised on a two stage, cause and effect model. Experiments were designed to isolate media as the independent variable. Media stimuli were then presented to individuals and their personal cognitions or behaviours recorded.

One common method involved social surveys. In 1950s America, television was slowly rolled out across the nation taking a few years before blanket coverage was established. Effects scholars used this to compare inhabitants in cities with and without TV. (Himmelweit et al.,1958; Hennigan et al., 1982). The same logic was in evidence with opinion surveys taking place before, during and after elections. Another common approach used experimental models in psychology labs. Subjects were shown bits of media, sometimes especially constructed, and then asked a series of questions or simply secretly observed. In one notorious series of 'bobo doll' experiments, children were shown images of adult aggression and then left in a room with a doll to see if they imitated what they had seen (Bandura et al., 1961)

Unfortunately, repeated attempts to reproduce strong effects failed in the large majority of studies. Results only showed small correlations. Most people, most of the time, did not become more violent as a result of viewing violence. The tiny group that did, already had a propensity to violence. It was the same with political beliefs and voting behaviour. Those most politically engaged, who followed politics most in the news, were also the ones most set in their beliefs. They would not be dissuaded. Those without strong political views, who were more open to persuasion, avoided news generally. Thus, most people, most of the time, did not change their minds about parties or switch their votes. Typical, was a series of studies in the 1940s by Paul Lazarsfeld that looked at Democrat and Republican supporters in Erie County in the US. After extensive research, their frustrated conclusion was (Lazarsfeld et al., 1944: 95):

> The real doubters – the open-minded voters who make a sincere attempt to weigh the issues and the candidates ... exist mainly in deferential campaign propaganda ... in the movies and in the minds of some political idealists. In real life, these are few indeed.

For lack of evidence, the strong effects paradigm came to be marginalized within the field by the 1960s. It has always had advocates outside it though and periodically resurfaces in one form or another.

Critical political economists (Miller, 1994; Herman and Chomsky, 2002; Thussu and Freedman, 2012) frequently link public confusion about international conflicts to state-instigated propaganda efforts through mass media. For example, in the lead up to the second Gulf War with Iraq in 2003, the Bush and Blair administrations erroneously argued that Iraq had both had a role in 9/11 and had a secret stockpile of 'weapons of mass destruction'. In January of that year, 68% of the US public believed the first statement. Three years later, some 60% of Republican voters still thought the second (PIPA, 2006). Evidence has never been found for either proposition. Politicians and campaigners have also continued to voice their concerns over strong media influences. With each new technological wave of media, most recently the internet, very similar assumptions and concerns about strong media effects are voiced. The online world, as with other media before it, is associated with marked increases in anti-social behaviours, violence, eating disorders, games addictions and so on.

But as far as mainstream effects researchers were concerned, media magic bullets or hypodermic needles did not exist. Instead, they found their way to a new 'limited media effects' consensus. This directed the second phase of research in the field which focused on identifying and exploring more limited levels of influence. One such effect was 'reinforcement' (Klapper, 1960; Schramm et al., 1961). A classic example of reinforcement involved the televised Nixon–Kennedy presidential debates of 1960. In post-debate surveys, Democrats believed that their candidate Kennedy had done better and, vice versa, Republicans thought the same about Nixon. This reinforcement effect has been recorded in a number of elections since. It is also relevant to recent discussions about increased polarization and social media use over the last decade (see below).

A key shift during this phase was the turn to 'uses and gratifications' (Rosengren, 1973; Blumler and Katz, 1974). Instead of assuming people were affected by media, the starting point was that individuals used media for particular purposes. Various empirical studies have explored this idea subsequently. A parallel body of 'audience studies' work in the UK, investigated how audiences consumed news and popular culture (Morley, 1980; Ang, 1985; Radway, 1987). They argued that media content was polysemic; that is, it always contained many meanings beyond that intended by producers. Each media text also had to contend with multiple, conflicted other texts. As with US studies, researchers turned to observing how people actively consumed media, for pleasure, for reinforcement, and for identity construction. Both bodies of work had a similar impact on the effects tradition, in that the focus became more about individual media uses rather than media effects on people.

Such developments encouraged political communication scholars to downplay media's impact on elections. For most election periods in the US and UK, the overall swing between parties was not more than 3–4%. Little seemed to have changed since Lazarsfeld's studies. In which case, voters were likely to have already made up their minds on the basis of other factors.

For many, preferences were better explained by 'socialization theory'. Most people did not follow politics that closely and relied on guidance from interactions with close family and friends. This made sense, especially when many families, communities and states voted the same way for generations. For others, the most powerful determining factor on elections was the state of the economy. If the economy was doing well, the incumbent party was likely to be re-elected and, if not, deposed by the challenger. Thus, the maxim of Bill Clinton's successful 1992 campaign was: 'It's the economy stupid!' Arguably, economic factors have played an important role in several elections taking place in the wake of the 2007–8 financial crisis. In both the Brexit Referendum and Trump election of 2016, voting patterns were very much tallied with class and poverty. Those in poorer areas were far more likely to vote for a big change, as represented by either leaving the EU or electing a political outsider to the Presidency.

In the later decades of the twentieth century, a third phase of effects works emerged, pushing the field back slowly towards notions of strong effects. For such researchers, the trick has been to dispense with the original two-stage effects model, and to start asking subtler questions about how media might be influential in less overt ways. Instead of looking for powerful and immediate effects, they have focused on longer-term, smaller but cumulative effects, as well as on less direct and conscious impacts. In effect, they have reframed the question. They have also come to consider people as reflexive individuals rather than unthinking masses who react like chemicals in a scientific experiment.

One approach has been to consider the impact of minor media effects over a longer time period. Partisan reinforcement is one such example. While seen as 'limited', over time it can have quite a strong, cumulative effect. Opinions and more extreme interpretations can harden. Mild biases and predispositions can become stronger. In this vein, Gerbner's 'cultivation analysis' (Gerbner et al., 1986) compared heavy television watchers with light ones. Regular viewers had different impressions of issues and their importance, as well as of society and their role in it. For example, they had a rather distorted view of crime, believing instances were rather heavier and of a more serious nature than they were.

It has also been argued that cumulative media influences alter the way citizens relate to society and political affairs more generally. Noelle-Neumann's (1984) 'spiral of silence' theory, argued that individuals fear being isolated in their opinions and out of step with dominant ideas and values in society. As a consequence, they have a tendency to adhere to those prevailing views they see repeated regularly in media. 'Media (or Video) malaise theory' (Robinson, 1976; Ansolabehere and Iyengar, 1995; Capella and Jamieson, 1997) postulates that critical television coverage lowers public trust in politics and encourages disaffection generally. As US political news is mainly negative and critical, so citizens become disengaged and less motivated to vote. This can be a crucial election factor as getting out the vote becomes as important as gaining voter support on paper.

Researchers have also turned to looking at a series of alternative, more limited effects paradigms: agenda setting, priming and framing. The most prominent theory tested in recent decades has been 'agenda setting'. McCombs and Shaw (1972) argued that media's main effect was not telling people 'What to think' but telling them 'What they should think about'. Their work showed a strong correlation between frequently covered news topics and the issues that people thought were 'most important'. If the media chose to cover more stories on crime, immigration or terrorism, so people think that those are priority political issues. One obvious consequence of this is that more newsworthy issues are likely to gain greater coverage and public interest than less newsworthy ones. Another outcome is that politicians and parties who promote certain populist agendas get more publicity. Most mainstream news coverage of Donald Trump during the primaries and election period of 2016, although generally negative, did keep the public spotlight on him. He gained considerably more coverage than his Republican rivals. So, negative or not, people thought a lot about Donald Trump.

'Priming' is similar to agenda setting in that it triggers audiences to relate to particular events and issues (Berkowitz, 1984). In elections, media primes people to think about key issues as well as contextualizing those issues (Iyengar and Kinder, 1987). This can impact on voters as different parties and individuals are considered more adept on certain policy issues. Labour and the Democrats are considered to be better on policy areas like health, education and welfare.

Conservatives and Republicans are thought to be better at managing policing, defence and the economy. George Bush Senior had high approval ratings for his handling of the first Gulf War, the issue which most dominated news at the time. After the war, the media turned to focus on drug crime and the economy, which became primed issues in the months before the 1992 election. Bush was not considered adept on either and his high 70% ratings dropped steadily, leading him to eventually losing the election (Iyengar and Simon, 1993).

The 'framing' of issues and events is also important to how publics interpret politics and politicians. Framing research has developed out of different disciplinary traditions. In psychology, Kahneman et al.'s (1982) work on individual calculations of risk found that the framing of a decision altered how people evaluated risk, affecting their final decisions ('equivalence framing'). Gamson (1992) and Entman (1993), drawing on anthropological and sociological traditions, focused on the selection, salience and schema of media stories, which are then used to interpret events and issues ('emphasis framing'). Are public protestors reported according to the substance of their campaigns or by the conduct of their actions? Are acts of political violence conducted by 'terrorists' or 'freedom fighters'? Iyengar (1990) found that the way poverty was framed made a big difference to how viewers interpreted the issue and its solutions. When news reports focused on individuals, viewers saw the issue as one of individual responsibility, meaning those at the bottom were responsible for their conditions. When poverty was reported using social and economic data, the public thought that poverty was a wider problem of society that required political action.

In the last decade, the ways news media have selected, primed and framed stories around the economy, race, immigration and nationalism, have potentially influenced wider public concerns and interpretations of those issues. How the 2007–8 financial crisis and economic fallout that followed was framed in news coverage across Europe and the US was significant (see collection in Basu et al., 2018). Where media focused on inequality, the super-rich and financial wrong-doing, left-leaning movements and parties gained support. Where the story was about wasteful government spending, immigration and welfare scroungers, right-leaning groups and parties advanced.

Arguably, such coverage was likely to have had an impact on recent elections. In 2014, Ipsos-MORI (October 2014) surveyed publics in several countries, asking them to estimate how many Muslims, immigrants and unemployed there were as a percentage of the population. In every case, average estimates were far higher than reality. In the UK, the average respondent thought that Muslims made up 21% and Continental Europeans 15% of the population. The actual figure for both was 5%. Dixon and Williams's (2015) study of race and crime representation on US network and cable news found that African Americans were very underrepresented. Latinos were 'greatly overrepresented' as undocumented immigrants and Muslims were 'greatly overrepresented' as terrorists.

Clearly, misperceptions about immigration contributed to increased levels of nationalism and support for Brexit and Donald Trump in 2016. They have similarly contributed to the rise of nationalism and anti-globalization in various European elections (Germany, France, the Netherlands, Italy, Hungary and Sweden).

In effect, the dropping of assumptions about dumb publics and powerful direct media influences liberated the media effects tradition. Reassessing both enabled older, seemingly less significant effects to be revisited, and new, more nuanced ones to be explored. Cumulatively, this work suggested that media can have a quite powerful impact on beliefs and behaviours in a variety of ways. As Iyengar (1997: 216) came to conclude:

> research into the effects of mass communication has come full circle. Initial concern about the vulnerability of voters to propaganda campaigns gave way to findings of "minimal consequences". Effects research was rejuvenated by more limited priming paradigms. As these paradigms have matured, discussions of "massive consequences" have been revived.

Media Effects: Difficult Questions and a New Fourth Phase?

This century, the field has changed tack once again. Such has been the change to our mediated political environment, scholars have wondered if we can still talk about strong media effects without mass media (Chaffee and Metzger, 2001). News media are ever more fragmented and distrusted. Audiences are more dispersed and active too. Both trends suggest a return to limited effects or even the end of the field of research altogether. On the other hand, as I argue here, there is much to suggest that media can still be highly influential in various ways. The tradition just needs rethinking once again.

Several recent reviews of media effects research (e.g., Bennett and Iyengar, 2010; Cacciatore et al., 2016; Valkenburg et al., 2016; Perse and Lambe, 2017) all point out the obvious elephant in the room: *mass media* is fast becoming just *media*. Through the 1980s and 1990s, the big broadcasters in most countries lost their dominant hold of the audience as cable, satellite and other new technologies opened up a world of hundreds of channels. The story of the twenty-first century has been one of new digital platforms, providing numerous new news sites to be accessed from anywhere. The latest developments in social media have been more disruptive still. Not only have such shifts taken away major revenues from legacy media, they have transformed the relations between audiences, content producers and advertisers. Audiences increasingly produce their own content, share links with their self-selected networks, and become tracked and micro-targeted by advertisers and election campaigns. In just a decade, whether driven by new media industries or audiences, citizen-media relations have become more individualized and personalized.

At the same time, mainstream news media has not only lost market share, it has lost trust and its hegemonic agenda-setting role. Newman and Fletcher (2017) found that two thirds of people in their nine-nation study did not trust mainstream news. Reuters (2017) 36-country study recorded that more people got their news from social media than from actively visiting online legacy news sites. Vargo and Guo's (2017) study of intermedia agenda-setting revealed that online, partisan news sites set more news agendas than the once dominant *New York Times* and *Washington Post*.

The news media audience has also been transformed by the new environment. In addition to news consumption by algorithm and social media, individuals increasingly view news with split attentions and while multi-tasking; i.e., they watch two or more media at the same time. This poses new problems for scholars trying to measure media attention and influence (Valkenburg et al., 2016). Individuals or prosumers, especially the young, spend as much time creating content as consuming it; 'mass self-communication' (Castells, 2009) as opposed to mass communication. They choose to enter into self-selecting and polarized information networks and 'filter bubbles' (Pariser, 2011; Sunstein, 2018). As a consequence, many seasoned effects scholars have cast doubt on the future of their field or called for major rethinks (Chaffee and Metzger 2001; Bennett and Iyengar, 2010; Cacciatore et al., 2016).

Although each of these developments suggest the mass media effects tradition is becoming redundant, does that necessarily mean a return to limited effects or that the field is dead? I would argue not.

First, those at the centre of power in politics, business and media, still consume a wide range of legacy media and relate to it in everyday politics (Davis, 2009a; Stromback and Esser, 2014; van Aelst and Walgrave, 2017). Mediated agendas and frames remain very influential at this level. Journalists and politicians are all part of the same political and information networks. Even though politicians are sceptical about media they still behave as if it is very influential (see Chapter 5).

Second, news media, in all its forms, is still the main way that publics learn about politicians and parties, as well as many distanced and multifaceted policy areas. Social (socialization theory) and economic (the economy stupid) explanations for voting patterns now make rather less sense. If voters are more mobile and increasingly losing their natural political and class alignments, then socialization no longer seems to explain voting patterns. So too, many election outcomes are not dictated by economic matters, especially as non-traditional party issues like race and immigration come to the fore. Obama won re-election in 2012 in spite of a struggling economy and the UK voted for Brexit in spite of the dire warnings about what would happen to the economy. In many elections of the last half decade swings have been rather more than 3–4%, often reaching 10 or even 20% over an election period (see Chapter 4). Since most people's impressions of politicians are via media, this suggests a continuing media effect. The same argument holds true in relation to foreign affairs and complex issues like climate change. So it stands to reason that media can have a key role.

Third, there remains a high degree of overlap between news media of all varieties. All choose to cover and comment on major events and stories, such as elections, disasters, public scandals, major sporting events and so on. Alternative news sites, aggregators and disseminators, are heavily reliant on legacy news operations for core content (Reese et al., 2007; Benson, 2017). They may offer quite different opinions and emphases, but the topic areas are very similar. As Vargo and Guo's (2017: 17) innovative study of US intermedia agendas shows (see also Merez, 2011), there is a very high level of interdependence between all news sites (legacy, emergent and partisan) when it comes to news agendas: 'we found the network agendas of various media outlets to be highly interdependent, symbiotically networked and homogenous'.

Fourth, in the new digital networked news environment, 'partisan reinforcement' has become an increasingly powerful effect. The signs are that polarized opinion formation, between Labour and

Conservative, Democrat and Republican, Remainer and Brexiteer, is intensifying (Dunlap et al., 2016; Pew, 2017; Reuters, 2017; Naryana et al., 2018) across a number of issues. People are choosing to follow friends, networks, media, websites and stories they approve of, while avoiding those they do not. Social media algorithms and micro-targeted promotional messages and political information are exacerbating this. Together, this means powerful forms of partisan reinforcement for those interested in political affairs, or further exclusion altogether for those with lesser interests. Such trends have been explored variously with 'agenda melding' (Shaw et al., 1999), 'reinforcing spiral theory' (Slater, 2007), or 'preference-based reinforcement' (Cacciatore et al., 2016). The polarization of views to such a degree clearly has significant consequences for beliefs and practices in democracies.

Conclusion

As the first part of this chapter argued, publics are not less interested in politics, news and public affairs. They simply feel abandoned by the traditional institutions at their centre. The more that professional political centres struggle with policy complexity, powerful global forces and voter anger, they more they barricade themselves in, becoming more distant from their citizenry.

There are several responses to that. One has been apathy and making do. Another has been to turn to alternative forms of political organization, participation and communication. Dense civil society networks have grown. But, the centre has failed to adapt and to be receptive. On many issues, these are producing a split of two or more polarized camps, while a growing disengaged and disenchanted block are ignored on the periphery. A forceful opening up of the closed centre, political and economic decentralization and power-sharing, are essential responses.

As the second part argued, media effects have rarely been so crude and overpowering as to shift minds and behaviours instantly. But media influence on politics and publics has always been more funda-mental than any limited media effects paradigm suggested. Media and communication remain central to politics even as news media ecologies keep changing and individuals become more media-savvy and active. How and why media effects operate are subject to change too but they continue to exert influence. It is up to researchers to revise their paradigms and adapt their methods accordingly.

8

Organized Interests, Power and the Policy Process

This chapter explores an under-represented area in political communication textbooks: that of civil society, organized interests and the policy process. Over the last century, behind the world of formal political parties, mass media and stable institutions, has developed an extensive and more fluid mix of organized interests, digital media and policy networks. They range from large corporations and well-funded political lobbies to progressive interest groups and dynamic new social movements. As political parties and mainstream media falter, so opportunities have increased for them to intervene in political arenas and media spheres.

The literature here is extremely diverse and located as much in several sub-fields of sociology and media as in political science. The chapter tries to pull together this varied work by comparing and contrasting the resources and opportunities of powerful, insider organizations with weaker, resource-poor and outsider groups. The former support the status quo with its inequalities and disempowered citizen groups. The latter seek to challenge them and to reconnect wider public concerns and social justice to politics.

In critical accounts, large corporations and entrenched interests tend to have more influence more of the time. Whether it is connecting with government or media, they have more resources, opportunities and greater access. This translates to greater public authority and legitimacy as well as power over agenda-setting, frame-making and policy outcomes. It is why neoliberalism has triumphed, why sexual and racial inequality persist, and why insufficient attention is being devoted to pressing environmental issues. For optimists however, despite set-backs, professionalized interest groups have harnessed alternative resources and strategies to good effect. Immediate goals may often fail but longer-term ones, such as shifts in political culture, party policies and institutional behaviours, have been achieved.

The chapter is in four parts. The first sketches out this alternative political communication environment, offering a framework for analysing and comparing different organized interests. The second and third parts review established debates between pluralists and critical scholars in relation to politics, policy-making, media and communication. Equality and environmental issue agendas are used as examples. The final part revisits the discussion in light of recent developments: the rise of fast-evolving, tech-savvy new social movements and the expansion of highly influential and expensive intermediary professions. It concludes that these twin trends combined are creating a growing divide between public, visible politics and private, opaque policy and regulation.

Political Communication in Civil Society

There are many reasons to look at political communication beyond the formal-institutional world of parties, governments, media and elections. First, the state and political parties do not operate in a social vacuum but emerge and develop policies in response to wider organized interests and public opinion. Second, as earlier chapters show, the traditional organizations and media of politics have lost legitimacy, support and power in society. Finally, it is clear that the number and type of organized interests have grown rapidly in recent decades. Their opportunities for intervention have increased too. Thus, there exists a parallel system of civil society organizations, networks and communication forms that impact on politics at all levels.

The range of literatures covering civil society comes from a diverse mix of sub-disciplines in sociology, political economy, critical media studies and, to a lesser extent, political science (see overviews in Beyers et al., 2008; Della Porta and Diani, 2015). Put together, this wide body of work makes it clear just how much organized interests have developed in the latter half of the twentieth century. The number of such organizations not only increased rapidly, so did their level of professionalism and range of communication strategies.

On the one hand, through the twentieth century businesses became much more aware of the need to be politically proactive; to manage their public image, develop lobbying strategies, intervene in public debates and leverage their political access (Marchand, 1998; Mirowski and Plehwe, 2009; Mizruchi, 2013). On the other, a range of non-corporate interest groups emerged to put their own cases (Amoore, 2005; Jordan and Moloney, 2007; Beyers et al., 2008). These challengers took up the causes of workers and consumers, racial and gender inequality, the environment and animal welfare, and more. Many of these, such as Amnesty, BRAC or the Danish Refugee Council, became established transnational organizations with extensive resources and memberships. The numbers of such INGOs (international non-governmental organizations) increased from 22,200 in 1990 to 56,000 in 2010 (Kaldor et al., 2012). Alongside these flourished social movements, think-tanks, charities and others (Davis, 2013; Della Porta and Diani, 2015; van der Heijden, 2016).

A key feature of this alternative political communication ecology is its professionalization (Cutlip et al., 2000). This spreads across public and private, left and right, small and large organizations, with the same consultancies happy to offer their services to all sides. By the 1980s, the corporate sector in the US and UK was funding an extensive industry of PR and public affairs specialists to influence state legislation, regulation and budgets (Miller and Dinan, 2008; Baumgartner et al., 2009; Ferguson, 2012). Unions, charities and others, followed a similar path as the professional communication sector expanded (Deacon, 1996; Davis, 2002; Sireau, 2009; Cronin, 2018). Thus, many organizations in civil society have come to compete within a 'public relations democracy' (Davis, 2002).

At the same time organized interests were expanding, traditional and formal institutions were losing public connection, trust and influence (Putnam, 2000; Hay, 2007; Mair, 2013; Chapter 4, this volume). Parties lost their once-large memberships and loyal supporter bases. Governments lost trust. News media have struggled to manage as revenues and consumers dropped substantially and competition intensified across multiple media (Anderson et al., 2015; Davis, 2017b; Reuters, 2017; Chapter 5, this volume). Trust in their content, even among the most established legacy producers, has also continued to decline.

Each of these trends combined have changed the landscape of political communication. How should this alternative political communication environment be analysed and what are the core questions to be asked?

The framework set out here draws from these varied sub-disciplines but focuses on two questions: what types of organized interest are most able to gain access, set agendas, and determine issue frames, and, what kinds and combinations of resources enable them to do so? Whether talking about the private political spaces of government, the varied policy-networks around them, or the mass mediated public sphere, political communication still involves conflict and competition between different interests for information control. In that competition, certain interests are advantaged by having access to particular resources and so prevail more often. Usually, it is those who have more in society and represent the status quo (corporate interests, elites, older wealthy white males), succeeding over those who have less and challenge it (unions, critical interest groups and social movements, other demographic constituents).

Such a framework pulls together the literatures of several related sub-disciplines. It connects to the classic debates about power, access and decision-making in politics between pluralists and critical elite and Marxist scholars (see overviews in Clegg, 1989; Held, 2006). For critics, differences in resources and access mean certain interests regularly gain more influence over decision-making at political centres. For pluralists, although such things are unevenly distributed, they are still dispersed and fragmented enough to ensure that no one powerful interest can dominate for long (polyarchy) (Dahl, 1961). Similar exchanges take place between pluralists and political economists in regard to resources, media access and representation (see Curran, 2002; Chapter 5, this volume). The framework also links to two common research agendas in the interest group literature: 'political opportunity structures' and 'resource mobilization'. For some, access and influence is governed by the state of 'political opportunity structures' (Kreisi, 1991; Tarrow, 1994; Gamson and Meyer, 1996). These relate to the openness of government, natural political alignments between politicians and outside interests, and the level of conflict between political leaders. Some interest groups are 'insiders', close to government, or 'outsiders', on the distant periphery of the political process (Grant, 1978).

In the 'resource mobilization' literature (McCarthy and Zald, 1977; Jenkins, 1983) organized interests harness a combination of resources to campaign and achieve their goals, with some being evidently 'resource-rich' and some 'resource-poor' (Goldenberg, 1975). The most obvious of these resources are economic, human and organizational. They also can include cultural (beliefs, values and identity) and symbolic resources (legitimacy, public sympathy, celebrity) (see Cable, 2016; Edwards and Kane, 2016). In each of these discussions, interests and their influence are related to their access and possession of varied resources, with some types being more clearly advantaged than others. In summary, the resources involved are: *access, economic, human, organizational, cultural* and *symbolic.*

These resources have a bearing on the modes of communication and strategies adopted by different organized interests as they attempt to influence their various audiences: politicians and civil servants, journalists and publics, members and supporters (see table in Davis, 2007a: 136). These run from private, exclusive forms of routine access to government, to mass and digital media-oriented campaigns to violent and illegal acts.

Powerful, insider groups, corporations and individuals, with large economic resources and symbolic authority, are most likely to use private, routine or institutionalized communication forms (Marsh and Rhodes, 1992; Marsh, 1998). They may have formal representation on a committee or advisory board, or simply arrange personal meetings with ministers and civil servants. A greater range of groups and institutions will resort to lobbying, producing advocacy documents and other written submissions. Any business association, medium-sized corporation, trade union or public interest group, with established human and financial resources, will use such methods. Going down the scale, organized interests will also submit formal submissions to state departments and parliamentary committees or may be called to give evidence in person.

Using mass media and going public is another strategy. Organized interests produce newsworthy material and cultivate journalist contacts to gain useful coverage for a cause or to undermine rivals. They may also link up with public figures or celebrities to generate news interest. Raising public awareness puts pressure on politicians to respond. Alternatively, interests of all kinds now use new ICTs to develop a variety of political networks, to organize and to disseminate information (Castells, 1997, 2015). These may be elite networks of politicians, bureaucrats, lobbyists and others linked to 'policy communities'. They may be interest groups and social movements using the web to cohere, organize and mobilize their members (Gerbaudo, 2012; Bennett and Segerberg, 2013). All kinds of group or organization may make use of mass and alternative media to influence both publics and decision-makers. However, they are more likely to be utilized by moderately resourced interests with less direct political access.

At the more radical end, usually deployed by resource-poor, outsider groups, campaigns can engage in public protests, boycotts and stunts that draw media coverage. More extreme still, they can resort to acts of civil disobedience, illegal acts, violence or terrorism to both gain public attention and put pressure on those in power.

Organized Interests in Politics and Policy-Making: The Equality Agenda

To return to the questions posed above: what kinds of organized interests dominate politics and policy-making, and what combination of resources allow them to do so? While pluralists, acknowledge the advantages of certain groups, they contend that none prevail in the long-term. For critics, however, deficiencies are systematic and cumulative. They are continually reproduced at the political centre. This explains why the agendas and policies of particular elites, white (in the West) males and large corporations continue to win out.

In basic pluralist political theory (see overviews in Dunleavy and O'Leary, 1987; Held, 2006), which still dominates in many politics departments, the state is envisioned as a neutral arbiter balancing competing societal interests. Classic liberal pluralists, such as Truman (1951) and Dahl (1961), argued that the exercise of power is fragmented and non-cumulative. It is shared and fought over by various competing groups in society. Although power and resources are not spread evenly across societies, they are dispersed and continually contested. That means no single group can take and maintain control for too long. In Dahl's famous study of governance, or polyarchy, in New Haven (1961), he found that powerful groups were more advantaged but that none continued to maintain power. Thus, leadership was subject to renewal, and substantial changes were enforced over time.

Go back to the time of Dahl's original account and things have changed substantially in relation to a range of equal rights; go back a century and they are unrecognizable. Organized interests, oriented around the civil rights movement, trade unions, women's suffrage and feminism, and the LGBTQ movement, have won a number of individual campaigns over a protracted period. In most mature democracies, the general public are substantially better off than they once were. Extensive welfare state structures have developed to ensure much higher mean levels of education, healthcare, home ownership and life expectancy. The rights of racial minorities, women and the LGBTQ community have all been recognized and enforced by law. Each is much better represented in parliaments and corporate boardrooms. Wider cultures and attitudes have shifted. As Kaldor et al. (2012: 2) state:

> Contemporary society is far more conscious of environmental and human rights and the importance of gender equality, and far more inclusive in terms of race, language, religion or sexual orientation than in the 1950s and 1960s.

Surveying the current socio-political balance of power in mature democracies, the potential for organized outside interests to continue bringing about progressive change appears strong. Part of this relates to a growing sense of fracture and conflict across several leadership spheres, from politics and business to media and culture (Naim, 2013). As Chapter 4 documented, established political parties are increasingly fragmented. They are either riven by internal splits, breaking into multiple new parties, or haemorrhaging votes and parliamentary seats. In advanced economies, there have emerged clear divides between old-fashioned industrial forms of capitalism, financialization or finance-led capitalism, and the new type of 'platform capitalism' (Palley, 2013; Srnicek, 2016). This has set up conflicts between industrialists, financiers and hi-tech entrepreneurs, each promoting alternative regulatory visions to decision-makers. Business leaders are far more conflicted and atomized when it comes to working together (Mizruchi, 2013; Useem, 2015). Individual leaders now have a far more precarious existence as the time they spend at the top diminishes each decade (Freeland, 2012; Elliott, 2014; Davis, 2018). Chapter 5 similarly revealed that the gatekeeping function of traditional mass media has declined as income has plummeted and the media environment has been reconfigured by multiple digital alternatives (Anderson et al., 2015; Reuters, 2017).

Such divisions are now continually reflected in many nations. Brexit negotiations have shown the dramatic tensions and differences that now affect British elites over notions of free trade, economic management and migration. There are very similar conflicts in and around Trump's White House and Washington, in relation to these same issues as well as defence and international affairs. The same is clear across many European nations as older, establishment leaders are challenged by radically different ones from both left and right.

In the space that has opened up, interest groups have flourished. Part of this has been through connecting to and reshaping formal political institutions. On the one hand, NGOs have gained in substance and memberships. A large number are officially recognized by governments and international bodies such as the UN or EU (Kaldor et al., 2012; van der Heijden, 2016). On the other, they have infiltrated and transformed political parties. Single-issue protest movements, such as the 15-M movement in Spain, have become fully fledged parties competing for parliamentary seats. Others, such as the right-leaning Tea Party in the US or left-leaning Momentum in the UK, have worked within established parties, pushing policy developments in new directions. Social movement campaigners and practices have been taken on by Bernie Sanders and Jeremy Corbyn with these parties drawing large numbers of new members (Bode and Dalrymple, 2016; Chadwick and Stromer-Galley, 2016).

However, critical scholars can also make a strong case that the organized interests of the status quo have reasserted themselves in recent decades. The equality agenda has faltered as change has slowed or even been reversed since the 1970s. Particular individuals, demographics and corporate organized interests continue to do extremely well. Wealthy, middle-aged white males of a certain background keep profiting and holding positions of power, while women, ethnic minorities, those from poorer backgrounds and the young, do less well or remain very under-represented at the top. Such trends reflect an inherent 'mobilization of bias' (Schattsneider, 1961), which has halted the path of progressive change. The only question is how does this operate? Three broad critical perspectives are offered here.

One is presented by (post) Marxists, from Miliband (1969) and Poulantzas (1975) to Crouch (2011) and Streeck (2017). For them, the state never has been and never will be a neutral arbiter balancing competing interests but, instead, acquiesces to the demands of the capitalist class. Governments see themselves as being dependent on the owners of capital and big business for their own long-term survival. Capitalism brings investment, employment and tax revenues. So even without overt corporate pressure, political leaders try to entice big corporations with favourable tax and regulatory regimes (Lindblom, 1977; Offe, 1984; Cerny et al., 2005). This may continue even as capitalism becomes a direct threat to democracies themselves (Streeck, 2014). In effect, the corporate classes are empowered by their extensive economic and symbolic resources, both of which give them superior access to the political centre.

A second approach comes from work on power and decision-making (see overviews in Clegg, 1989; Lukes, 2005). This critical literature has looked at agenda-setting and decision-making at the top. Bachrach and Baratz (1962) argued that there were two dimensions or 'faces of power' in operation. The powerful not only made the final decisions they also decided what made it onto the political agenda. Outsiders and resource-poor interests rarely accessed and influenced either of these stages. Later, Lukes (2005) argued that there was a 'third dimension' of power in operation. This was cultural or ideological. Wider publics did not always know what was in their own best interests as powerful organizations worked to keep pressing issues out of the public arena. So, it has been with pollution, cigarettes, unhealthy food, the slashing of health and education budgets, unequal pay between genders and races, and, of course, global warming. Thus, the powerful use their stronger access, human and cultural resources to affect decisions and influence public knowledge and debate.

A third approach focuses on cooperative and self-serving elites as they work together to further their mutual interests. In classic studies of elites (Mills, 1956; Domhoff, 1967; Useem, 1984), those at the top of business, politics and other powerful institutions, are connected through a number of social, cultural and organizational mechanisms. They come from similar wealthy families, go to the same exclusive schools and top universities, then join the same elite clubs and sit on interconnected boards of corporations and public bodies. In each case the social networks marginalize or exclude poorer classes as well as women and ethnic minorities. There are several modern accounts of how such elite social and cultural networks operate, influencing society and politics more widely (Khan, 2011; Freeland, 2012; Wedel, 2014; Jones, 2014). In these contemporary studies, the socio-cultural mechanisms that unite elites have evolved, but they still enable powerful interests and certain demographics to tilt political decision-making and policy in their favour. So, once again, superior social, cultural and economic resources bring enhanced access and influence over politics.

Whichever critical paradigm is favoured, it is clear that inequality has continued to rise through four decades of uninterrupted neoliberal politics and policy (see Chapter 9). This has been particularly strong in the US, UK and other liberal market economies. It has also had a strong effect in other nations and systems, from Sweden and Germany to China and Russia. Since the late 1970s, such policy regimes have favoured large corporations, international finance and the super-rich, at the expense of trade unions, welfare state systems and consumers. Trends include: rising economic inequality; reduced direct tax burdens on companies and the wealthy with increased indirect tax burdens on everyone else; restricted trade union rights, longer working hours and creeping casualization of the workforce; cuts in welfare state and infrastructure spending; wage stagnation and growing private and national debts; ever-rising pay of corporate leaders, tax evasion and avoidance by multi-national companies (see Stiglitz, 2010; Wilkinson and Pickett, 2010; Shaxson, 2011; Dorling, 2014; Streeck, 2014). Such things have continued whether states were led by centre-left parties (Democrats, Labour, Social Democrats) or centre right ones (Republicans, Conservatives, Christian Democrats).

Equality has faltered in other ways too. Women and ethnic minorities are better represented on the boards of companies and in parliaments but very few countries come close to having the balances and diversity that exists in wider society (IPU, 2017). Just taking the UK example, in the 2010–15 parliament, 22% of MPs were women and 4% were ethnic minority. In 2016, just 14% of executive board members of financial institutions and seven percent of the chief executives of the UK's top companies were women (Chinwala, 2016). Many religions still refuse to allow women to take senior positions while many nations still deny LGBTQ rights. The high-profile *Black Lives Matter* and *#MeToo* movements reflect the continuing problems of institutional racism and sexual harassment. The arrival of President Trump has only set back each of these causes, with more tax cuts for the rich and his clear personal hostility towards women, abortion rights, immigrants and ethnic minorities.

Organized Interests and Media: The Environmental Agenda

Similar issues of plurality, resources, access and power have been explored by media sociologists in relation to organized interests and news influence. Here, there is overwhelming evidence that media access and representation is entirely skewed towards powerful organized interests and individuals, with a distinctly white, middle-aged male bias. On this point, the literature is very consistent across nations and periods. Almost all surveys of news content reveal that powerful sources, be they from government institutions or the corporate sector, have a more dominant presence in mainstream news. They are the most cited sources, the most covered in news stories and tend to provide the biggest supply of press releases and other newsworthy material (Bennett, 1990; Philo, 1995; Tiffen et al., 2014; Knowles et al., 2017).

Thus, the question is not who dominates but why do such sources dominate news agendas and story frames? Political economy explanations, tied to media ownership and advertising are discussed in Chapter 5. An alternative perspective, linked to interest group access and resources (resource mobilization) is offered here. This looks at disparities in organizational, economic, and symbolic resources.

Starting with the organizational, large institutions, be they public or corporate, have a 'bureaucratic affinity' (Fishman, 1980) with media organizations. News-making has traditionally been managed through set news beats and routines. Journalists go to physical locations, cultivate close individual contacts (sources) and receive regular newsworthy information from these. Such practices obviously favour large, media-oriented institutions. These offer spaces for journalists to work in, information officers to talk to, press releases, social media feeds and other material (Tiffen, 1989; Ericson et al., 1989; Schlesinger and Tumber, 1994). Conversely, interest groups and unions are rarely part of an established beat while social movements are not stable entities with set physical locations and regular infor-mation outputs. Many interest group causes, such as global warming or tax evasion, can be complex and long-term issues. They require depth understanding and do not easily conform to human interest and deadline-driven news media requirements.

A second resource advantage is economic. Governments and large businesses have considerable economic means for obtaining media coverage. They are by far the largest employers of public relations and advertising. They have extensive communication operations, with impressive budgets and staff numbers, and can inundate media with news-ready material on a daily basis. The largest multina-tionals spend hundreds of millions each year on their promotional activities, including on 'advocacy advertising' (Miller and Dinan, 2008; Sussman, 2011). Even well-funded interest groups cannot hope to compete with these budgets, let alone smaller, resource-poor ones. Miller (1994) and Herman and Chomsky (2002 [1988]) offer two classic examples of states out-communicating their oppositions on military conflicts in the UK and US respectively. In each case governments had hundreds of times the outputs and personnel of their challengers.

Symbolic resources are a third factor separating powerful and weaker organized interests. Hall et al.'s (1978) work explained that journalists, in their search for 'objective' and 'authoritative' inter-viewees, automatically seek out established figures and organizations. Such subjects tend to be those in positions of power and influence, in recognized positions of authority, and are understood to have rare expertise or experience. Such perceptions are only enhanced by news coverage. Thus such individuals (and institutions) become 'primary definers' of news while journalists and everyone else are reduced to being 'secondary definers' (see also Bennett's 'indexing theory', 1990).

For smaller interest groups, unions and social movements, with less legitimacy and profile, gaining similar levels of media exposure is problematic and risky (Gitlin, 1980; Clarke, 2001; Sireau, 2009). They are often confronted by an awkward dilemma: 'command attention' by doing something radical and 'newsworthy', or, try to be authoritative and 'secure legitimacy' but risk gaining little coverage (Cracknell, 1993; Cable, 2016; Edwards and Kane, 2016). In trying to get into the news, they may be co-opted by news producers and news values. This means that celebrity leaders, human interest stories and confused campaign objectives may dominate content rather than actual campaign goals, messages and serious analysis.

However, weaker, more peripheral organized interests in society have adapted to find ways of compensating for their resource disadvantages. Starting with the organizational, professionalization has achieved much to enable weaker, progressive interests to compete. Studies of environmental movement campaigns (Anderson, 1997; de Jong, 2005; Hansen, 2010; Cable, 2016) and other protest groups (Davis, 2013; Cronin, 2018; Wright, 2018) have documented their advocacy and media strategies. These include becoming part of policy networks, growing their research departments, and making links with sympathetic lawyers, scientists and other experts. They also involve in-house media-training, building up a set of journalist contacts and the frequent production of news releases and newsworthy reports. Such practices have enabled these organizations to become regular information subsidy suppliers to news makers. Thus, NGOs like Friends of the Earth and the WWF (World Wide Fund for Nature), have worked to establish their credentials as legitimate public experts and commentators on policy issues, both for government departments and news journalists.

Economic resource deficits are either not so important or can be compensated for in several ways. Baumgartner et al. (2009), who tracked organized interest campaigns over 98 policy issues over a four-year period, found that economic resources were a decisive factor in only 5% of cases. Not all promotional activity requires extensive resources. Advertising may incur large costs but, as poorer interests have realized, if journalists can be lured to a story, news coverage is free. The basic technical communication costs (broadband connections and camera-equipped mobile phones) for organizing and publicizing activities are relatively cheap. Websites, videos and social media campaigns can be produced and spread across large networks with relatively little expertise and cost (Gerbaudo, 2012; Bennett and Segerberg, 2013). Most importantly, resource-poor groups can make up for their lack of finance with their extensive use of human resources. Unions, interest groups and social movements have large numbers of motivated volunteer members who are willing to work for free on campaigns (Davis, 2002).

Social and symbolic differences in media are not so clear cut now. Political and business heads are in frequent conflict. Journalists are more likely to produce critical stories of politicians and large corporations (Davis, 2002). Repeated surveys show very low levels of trust of such institutions and leaders (Ipsos-Mori, Pew); rather lower than scientists, educators, charities and public service professionals. At the same time, interest groups have learnt to use the symbolic resources or capital of others. They increasingly team up with celebrities, politicians, academics and scientists to present and promote campaigns on their behalf (Davis, 2002; Sireau, 2009; Cronin, 2018). Thus, smaller, resource-poor groups may never gain 'primary definer' status, but they are able to utilize that of others. In effect, their ability to achieve 'proxy media access' negates their need for extensive symbolic resources.

All this applies to environmental campaign groups. Their list of successes gets longer each year and includes: achieving lead-free petrol, better food standards, the removal of CFCs in fridges and aerosols, growing government investment in renewable energy and electric cars, tighter regulations on transport emissions, home and corporate recycling initiatives, and moves to end the use of single-use plastics. Environmental concerns are far more recognized than they once were by political parties and governments. Dozens of nations now have established Green parties and most of those have a number of elected representatives at local and national levels.

However, for many, despite the many warnings of impending environmental disaster, national and international responses to problems remain far too slow (Klein, 2015; Monbiot, 2017). A key battleground here has been around the threat of global warming. On this point there is a strong scientific consensus. Studies show that between 90 and 100% of scientists agree that human-made climate change is occurring and that global efforts are imperative to limit temperature rises in the coming decades. In many studies the figure is as high as 97% (see Cook et al., 2016). Yet, state progress has been far too slow here to avert damaging temperature hikes. The interest group sector here has continually struggled to influence news discourse and governments as powerfully resourced business and political leaders have obstructed their efforts.

For decades, established climate scientists and environmental groups, such as Greenpeace and Friends of the Earth, have failed to gain consistent mainstream news coverage. A 1990s survey by Hansen (1993) found that only 6% of news sources for environmental reporting came from such groups. A Reuters study (Painter, 2009) of the international climate conference in Copenhagen, found that only 12% of people cited there were actual scientists. The figure was the same for the 2015 Paris climate change conference. Outside of natural disasters and international conferences, environmentalists gain relatively little coverage. The issues are complex and long term, with difficult to assess risks and costs, with technical rather than human-interest story lines.

Meanwhile, the corporate-funded anti-climate change movement has thrown extensive resources into undermining the idea that scientific consensus on the issue exists. Led by fossil fuel companies such as Exxon Mobil and Koch Industries, huge sums have been spent in lobbying and public relations activities. They have set up a number of corporate coalitions, funded think tanks and 'astro-turf' (fake grass-roots organizations) to discredit all opposition. Between 1998 and 2005, Exxon Mobile gave $16 million to 43 different think tanks to write sceptical reports (UCS, 2007). Between 2002 and 2010, a corporate network of billionaires, facilitated by the Koch brothers, channelled $118 million towards 102 organized interest groups to discredit the science of climate change (Goldenberg, 2013). These misinformation campaigns, as well as casting doubt on the science, accused campaigners of hyperbole, and argued that the economy and jobs were threatened by any new regulations.

Ultimately, corporations have been successful in nullifying public concern and more active state regulation, especially in fossil-fuel dependent nations such as the US, Canada and Australia (see McCright et al., 2015; Dunlap et al., 2016). In these states as well as much of continental Europe, doubts about global warming, especially among pro-business parties, have set in. These trends have been most pronounced in the US. In the 1970s, Republicans and Democrats were not far apart in their acceptance of the issue, but much higher levels of scepticism have been registered in Republican circles in recent decades. In 1997, 37% of Republican voters thought global warming was exaggerated in the news but, by 2016, 59% thought so. By 2016 only 47% of Republican voters thought there was scientific consensus on the issue, while 82% of Democrats did. Perhaps more importantly, anti-climate campaigns and coverage resulted in fewer people thinking it to be a pressing issue. In a Pew (2012) poll, out of 21 political issues, the US public put it at number 21. In 2016, only 37% of the general public and 18% of Republican voters 'personally worried a great deal' about it (figures in Dunlap et al., 2016).

By 2016, 90% of Democrats had pro environmental regulation voting records against 10% of Republicans. President Trump was one of many Republicans to deny that the climate change problem existed. Accordingly, one of his first acts in power was to withdraw the US from the Paris Agreement on climate change. He has also cut funding for climate research and monitoring bodies, and rolled back Obama-era regulations since.

Organized Interests After 2011: The Growing Gap Between Public and Private

In the last decade organized interests followed two, quite different communication pathways. On the one hand, dynamic new social movements sprung up to challenge the status quo. Their campaigns were highly visible, making extensive use of social media networks and generating wide media coverage. They made significant impacts on public discourse but, ultimately, many failed to achieve the substantial political changes they hoped for. On the other hand, establishment interests became more entrenched and quietly successful at maintaining their interests. They exploited their private networks and employed expert intermediaries to work the political system out of public view. The cumulative result was great disappointment for progressive causes and movements on the left; something that right-wing populist alternatives have since been able to exploit.

In the wake of the 2007–8 financial crisis and global economic recession that followed, a number of new protest movements sprung up everywhere. Many of these were concerned with inequality, exploitation and repression. Despite bad economic times for most, transnational corporations and financiers appeared to be more powerful and wealthier than ever. Inequality spiked upward and the gap between the super-rich and rest expanded (Piketty, 2014; Streeck, 2017). Even international bodies, such as Davos, the UN and OECD, acknowledged that the global capitalist system was no longer stable or fair. Media attacks on bankers, the financial sector and over-paid CEOs were common. In Iceland, public outcry turned into the 'pots and pans revolution' (2009–11) which led to the resignation of the government, and trial and imprisonment of several corporate leaders.

2011 was the year, much like 1968, when large-scale protest exploded in multiple countries (Gerbaudo, 2012; Mason, 2012; Bennett and Segerberg, 2013). The anti-capitalist Indignados sprung up in Spain. The OWS (Occupy Wall Street) movement appeared in New York, spurring hundreds of related protests in over eighty other countries (Gitlin, 2011; Tormey, 2012). They attacked financiers and 'the 1%'. In the US, these protests dominated news coverage for much of the Autumn (Pew News Coverage Index).

Violent anti-government protests also took place in Tunisia, Syria, Libya and Yemen. The symbol of the 'Arab Spring' was Tarir Square in Egypt, where Hosni Mubarak's government was eventually forced out (Howard et al., 2011; Eltantawy and Wiest, 2011). Similar activist movements have since appeared in the shape of the Greek anti austerity movement, Gezi Park in Turkey, Movimento de Junho in Brazil, the Umbrella Revolution in Hong Kong, Nuit Debout in France, and Yo Soy 132 in Mexico (Castells, 2015; Gerbaudo, 2017). As Della Porta and Diani (2015: 9) noted, after decades of relative neglect, it was time 'to bring classes, capitalism and the like back into social movement studies'.

So too, have come a series of high-profile campaigns around race and gender equality, that began in the US and then spread internationally. In 2013, the *Black Lives Matter* campaign took off. This focused on institutional racism, police brutality and high African-American homicide rates. It has continued to gather pace since, linking with allied campaigns abroad. In 2017, multiple allegations of sexual assault by the film producer Harvey Weinstein led to the mass #*Me Too* movement. What began as a critique of sexual harassment in Hollywood soon spread to become an international campaign taking in politics, media and the corporate sector.

All of these movements gathered together supporters and participants in the tens or hundreds of thousands and, in some cases, millions. Although they took place in different countries and circumstances they shared several features. Each appeared incredibly rapidly, drawing large numbers of people to key locations or online campaign sites. The terms 'viral', 'contagion' and 'swarm' are typical in accounts. Each rejected rigid, centralized, top-down hierarchies with fixed leaders and representatives. Each lacked clear manifestos or detailed policy proposals, beyond demands for change at the top. Each was also critical and distrustful of mainstream media reporting.

Instead they encouraged flatter, horizontal structures, with deliberation and direct democratic participation a must. Each made extensive use of the digital, online media environment, using social networking applications to organize, engage and publicize. They appealed to 'the personal' and 'the cultural' concerns of their members and operated with fluid and flexible affiliations to established political interests. Despite their lack of media strategy and official spokespersons they drew extensive media coverage and significant public support. Gitlin's (2011) description of OWS is equally applicable to other movements: 'horizontal democracy is spunky, polymorphic, energetic, theatrical, scattered and droll … it tends to care about process more than results'.

Unfortunately, most of these movements died as quickly as they were born (some are ongoing). Mayor Bloomberg had OWS's Zuccotti Park camp in New York dismantled, as did city authorities elsewhere. Like the anti-globalization protests in the 1990s, or the anti-poverty initiatives of the 2000s, it has left little lasting imprint on public or political discourse. In Egypt, after three years of violence and coups, the military stepped in, strengthened its forces and pushed the country further towards authoritarian rule. Other movements of the Arab Spring experienced a similar outcome. The responses to opposition and attempted coups in Syria and Turkey have been brutal, military retaliations by Bashar al-Assad and Recep Erdogan respectively. Reviews of these movements (Castells, 2015; Gerbaudo, 2017) have since acknowledged the limitations and disappointing outcomes for each. As yet, the #BlackLivesMatter and #MeToo campaigns have outed several public figures but have yet to bring substantive changes to the institutional and corporate sectors they have challenged.

The very elements which caused each of these movements to burn so brightly were the same ones that saw them falter too. By refusing to develop clear proposals, objectives and leadership structures, and by retaining their distance from conventional media and political institutions, they limited their potential to effect institutional change. Despite being bigger and more dazzling than many such movements before them, most lacked stability and suffered a similar fate. As Gerbaudo (2017: 234) concluded: 'In almost all cases the powerful stayed in government and continued in much the same fashion as before.' Whether talking about Hollywood or Egyptian politics, US policing or the UK financial sector, entrenched elite and corporate interests have managed to weather the protests and to consolidate their power. How and why was this?

Some of the answers are to be found in the recent growing literature on new elites, the super-rich and corporate advocacy. These powerful interests have been able to deploy their extensive financial resources to maintain influence and control; pure money power in action. For one, as states have struggled with their economies following the economic crisis, so politicians have turned more to big business and finance for solutions (Lapavitsas, 2013; Davis and Walsh, 2016; Engelen, 2017). Governments have become reliant on financial centres to fund their huge debts and budget deficits. Politicians have worked hard to lure international businesses to their shores with promises of favourable tax and regulatory regimes. (Crouch, 2011; Freeland, 2012; Streeck, 2014). Ministers and bureaucrats have thus become more subservient in their policy-making in an effort to appease those same powerful interests.

Second, large quantities of capital have been used to purchase expert intermediary knowledge. Intermediary professions have always played an important role in evolving capitalist democracies (Abbott, 1988) but have become more important in recent decades. This is because the machinery of government and public institutions, such as central banks or industry regulators, has become ever more technical, legalistic and specialist. Such institutions now manage multiple complex units, operating in highly technical silos that senior officials at the top only partially understand (Tett, 2010; Engelen et al., 2011; Davis, 2018). Those outside interests with ample financial means thus turn to expert intermediaries to help them navigate and achieve their objectives. They are a highly paid 'super class' (Adonis and Pollard, 1997), usually on salaries that put them in the ranks of the top one or 0.1% themselves. Their services are only affordable to those with large pockets.

Such elite intermediaries work in public relations, lobbying, accountancy, economics, law, computing, planning and finance (Miller and Dinan, 2008; Ferguson, 2012; Cave and Rowell, 2014). They are employed in top organizations that work for both government and private corporations. In London, just a small handful of exclusive accountancy companies and law firms service the top companies as well as going on secondment to UK government departments (Wilks, 2015). A small number of top lobbyists, all with offices dotted around Westminster, are ready to go into action over privatizations, government contracts, new regulatory and tax proposals, and so on (Cave and Rowell, 2014).

Similar operations are in play around Washington, Brussels and most large European and Asian capitals (Hoedemann, 2007;

Baumgartner et al., 2009; Ferguson, 2012; Zetter, 2014; Laurens, 2017). A key component of such lobbies is 'the revolving door' between private companies and government departments. Former ministers and civil servants leave their departments to join the boards of powerful companies and, vice versa, top corporate directors are seconded to departments or follow career paths between both sides. Thus, top lobby firms directly employ and sell to clients an insider understanding of the 'rules of the game' or technical grasp of the latest regulatory directives or tax regimes (Shaxson, 2011; Bowman et al., 2014).

Third, such powerful corporations and individuals are highly mobile and flexible (Cave and Rowell, 2014; Wedel, 2014), enabling them to leverage their insider knowledge and networks. Leaders do not only employ floating intermediaries, they themselves straddle private and public institutions, alternating between government departments and corporations, and taking multiple board positions on both sides. Wedel refers to them as 'flexians' who glide around fluid 'flex nets' (flexible networks) of similar elites. The same Goldman Sachs banker can take a temporary post as a presidential adviser or Fed official, involved in the creation of new financial regulations, before going back to make use of this knowledge at Goldman Sachs. The same semi-retired general can be a paid board member of a multinational military contractor while also advising a senate committee of the imperatives of taking military action in the Middle East.

Modern corporate elites and the super-rich are also internationally mobile (Freeland, 2012; Birtchnell and Caletrio, 2014; Urry, 2014; Davis, 2018). They have office branches and networks of expert advisers in multiple countries. They spread their assets, investments and property across several jurisdictions. They buy and sell in one country, transit the proceeds through another, and park the profits in an off-shore tax haven elsewhere. Russian oligarchs and Chinese Communist Party leaders use their political access in their home nation to become billionaires, then move their wealth to asset managers in European and US financial centres. In 2010, 83% of large companies had off-shore accounts and an estimated $21 trillion was held in such tax havens (Urry, 2014). If a tax regime changes or a new hostile political leader comes in, they can up and go as they need, buying residency where required.

By all such means, powerful corporate lobbies and individuals have continually frustrated attempts to properly reregulate high finance or halt global tax evasion. They have also blocked more concerted efforts to restrict fossil fuel extraction, pushed for lighter employment and food regulations, promoted the arms trade and conflicts abroad. In effect, they have ensured the continuing hegemony of powerful organized interests and rich, elderly white males. Much of this has taken place, out of sight of a weakened national news media, remaining opaque and unaccountable.

Conclusion

The forces of the status quo have always had superior access to government and more resources at their disposal. Outsider interests with limited resources have always had to battle to achieve either political influence or media coverage. That has made substantial political change difficult to achieve in most democracies. Despite that, changes have come, either through temporary campaigns and clear legislative responses, or via long-term social and cultural shifts. These have been boosted as new parties and communication technologies have helped reconfigure the political landscape, enabling alternative ideas and voices to penetrate. The possibilities for reform have often been greatest in crisis times.

The great financial and economic crisis was just such an opportunity for progressive change. Unfortunately, it has not happened. The louder individuals and critical groups have protested the more those beneficiaries of the establishment have held on ever more tightly. Institutional politics has become both increasingly complex and calcified, in effect making it too unresponsive to alternative public movements and outcries. Ultimately, this disparity between citizens and public protest on the one hand, and elites and private control on the other, has contributed to general public disillusionment with formal politics and economic life. In such circumstances, the many failures of new social movements to produce substantial change, coupled with the failures and compromises of many liberal-left parties, has left gaping spaces. Into those have moved right-wing populist parties, often still tied to establishment interests but appealing with their own anti-elite and anti-institutional rhetoric.

Part IV
Challenges and Disruptions to Democracy

9

Economics, the Economy and Media

This chapter looks at economics and economic policy-making in relation to politics, media and political communication. It also touches on a number of related themes such as neoliberalism, austerity, inequality, the 1% and financialization. How economies have developed in recent decades has thrown up pressing challenges to nation states everywhere. The fallout from the great financial crash of 2007–8 has been especially disruptive. For many, this has contributed to a growing sense of social and economic uncertainty, and destabilized democracy itself.

For traditional scholars in political communication, the subject strays out of the discipline's boundaries. It is a complex and dull topic, with high level maths and jargon. Many social scientists, along with most of the general public (and a fair few politicians and journalists) glaze over when presented with its terms, models and numbers. Economics is technical rather than political and something best left to trained economists and technocrats. However, others would argue that it has always been as political as it is technocratic. Its perceived neutrality and complexity is why economists have become so influential in politics today, and why neoliberal policy regimes have been so successful.

There are several reasons why the discipline should look more closely at the subject. For one, it has become one of, if not the most important policy areas for parties. It has featured prominently in most election campaigns of recent decades, acting as a key area of policy distinction. Earle et al. (2016: 15) found that the term 'the economy' was rarely mentioned in UK party manifestos until the

1950s. That changed from the 1970s onwards. It appeared 59 times in the 2015 Conservative Party manifesto. Over the same period in the US, conventional campaign wisdom decided that it was the key issue that won elections. Thus, in 1992 Bill Clinton's successful presidential bid forcefully directed campaign staff to focus on 'the economy stupid!'

Second, opinion polls (Ipsos-MORI, Pew, WVS) often signal it as the top issue that voters think important. In the last World Values Survey (2010–14), 56% of respondents across the fifty-eight countries polled said 'a stable economy' was 'the most important' issue in politics and society. Third, while many traditionalists in the field avoid the subject, more critical scholars believe economic factors such as inequality can not be separated from discussions of democracy. In fact, for many, growing economic problems, such as inequality, wage stagnation and deindustrialization, have become a major cause of current instability for capitalist democracies (Crouch, 2011; Frank, 2016; Streeck, 2016; Luce, 2017). Indeed, such issues had a major influence on the 2016 votes for Brexit and Donald Trump, as well as in many unexpected election outcomes elsewhere.

As such, this chapter offers a critical introduction to the subject. It is in three parts. The first introduces the basic concepts and thinking behind neoclassical economics, the dominant approach to economics and policy since the late 1970s. This presents the discipline as an apolitical pseudo-science involving rational individuals, price mechanisms and market equilibrium. Part two critiques this account, drawing on a range of heterodox economists to argue that the subject is, in practice, as much about politics as economics. The final part explores how economics is conveyed in media and public discourse. It explains the growing disparity between 'the economy' described by politicians and the corporate sector and that actually experienced by ordinary people.

Economics as Science

For over a century neoclassical economics has provided the dominant analytical framework for conceiving of and assessing markets and wider economies. It distinguished itself as a separate discipline in the nineteenth century, becoming steadily more autonomous through the twentieth century. Its influence waned after the 1930s depression but it then returned stronger than ever in amid the economic crises of the 1970s. At that point it came to exert a growing influence on politics and policy-makers, both across national governments and international institutions (see Mirowski and Plehwe, 2009; Davies, 2014; Davis, 2017a).

Neoclassical economics contains a number of intellectual building blocks. Together, these have edged the discipline away from other social sciences and encouraged its presentation as a (pseudo) science. This process of separation began in the nineteenth century when it evolved to identify itself as an autonomous discipline. Before then, thinkers such as Adam Smith, John Stuart Mill, David Ricardo and Karl Marx were political economists who viewed economics as being intertwined with politics, philosophy and social thought. Their accounts of markets, individuals and value were wide-ranging and involved social and human relations and political institutions.

Over time, the newly emergent field began to distinguish itself from the other disciplines. So, Smith and Ricardo came to focus more on markets and market mechanisms. Markets were the means by which individual self-interests were reconciled in society. The 'marginal revolution', developed at the end of the nineteenth century by Menger, Jevons and Walras, similarly pinpointed the market as the means of true value determination via the mechanism of price. Marginalists argued that consumers were deemed capable of calculating the 'marginal utility' of one commodity over another and deciding the price they should pay accordingly. In this thinking, all other conceptions of value, labour, individual behaviour and social relations, as well as all external non-market influences were consciously bracketed out.

Over the twentieth century this sense of market autonomy became increasingly pronounced. Economics became an independent subject of research with its own university departments and sense of professional identity. Markets and economies were increasingly theorized and analysed through models and complex maths. Behind this growing complexity certain key foundations became central. They can be found in most core text books (e.g., Lipsey and Chrystal, 2015) and simple introductions (Conway, 2012; Chang, 2014). Together, they help present economics in scientific or pseudo-scientific terms.

One of these core assumptions is that anyone who enters into a market, to buy or sell anything, is regarded as a 'rational individual', or 'self-interested utility maximizer'. Market actors behave with clear logic and are able to make calculations about the true value of goods. Being self-interested they are then directed to getting the best price they can. In other words, they operate like an advanced computer, deploying perfect logic like Spock from Star Trek.

Second, market values are set by the 'price mechanism' as determined by 'supply and demand'. Market values can be located in goods, services and human labour. If there is more demand for something than supply – oil, top goal-scoring footballers, the latest Apple iphones, bitcoins – then prices go up. If there is more supply than demand – steel, casual delivery drivers, property in economically depressed towns, bitcoins (again) – then prices go down.

Third, this mix of self-interested, rational individuals, markets and prices, all combine to produce market equilibrium and stability. They also produce goods and services that are made in the most efficient ways and at the lowest costs because, if not, the competition does it better and cheaper. This is what Adam Smith called the 'invisible hand of the market'. The more markets are left to operate free from government and other outside interferences, and the more trading is as frictionless as possible, the more likely markets will run smoothly and find their long-run equilibria. They resemble magic boxes where everything is miraculously sorted out for all sides.

Government policy-makers and economists have built on these basic foundations as they developed a range of institutions, measurements and practices for regulating markets and economies. Central banks produce and circulate currencies and set interest rates. Competition authorities monitor markets and break up monopolies. Treasury departments operate key economic levers, such as a range of tax and interest rates. They move them up and down to keep inflation in check and encourage certain market behaviours: e.g., more investing, more saving, house-buying, less cigarette consumption, and so on. The overall aim is to increase or stabilize economic activity, bringing more jobs and taxes. Economic authorities also have a series of tools and measures to evaluate the health of an economy or market. These include things like GDP (Gross Domestic Product) growth rates, unemployment and inflation rates, productivity, balance of trade, currency values, stock market indices and so on.

The presentation of economic policy, by politicians and media, contributes to the sense of economics operating in pseudo-scientific ways. The terms and evaluation measurements are regularly relayed in public debates and media coverage. They are used to pronounce the health or otherwise of companies, markets and national economies. Such indicators are spoken about as if they have clear causal relationships and rules and exist independently of the rest of the world. The complexity of the maths and models deployed contributes to the sense of economics being an objective science as well as to the idea that only trained experts are able to understand it.

This form of thinking and application of economics emerged in the first few decades of the twentieth century before the 1930s depression hit. It then fell away as a new economic orthodoxy – Keynesianism – appeared to offer better solutions to the economic problems of the time. It was resuscitated again when Keynesianism faltered during the next economic crises of the 1970s. Its revival was promoted by a mix of economic and philosophical thinkers (Friedrich Hayek, Milton Friedman), think tanks and rising economics departments such as the Chicago School (see Mirowski and Plehwe, 2009; Davies, 2014). Governments in Chile (Augusto Pinochet, 1973), the UK (Margaret Thatcher, 1979) and the US (Ronald Reagan, 1980) each turned towards neoclassical economics to underpin their neoliberal political agendas. Economists, particularly Chicago School-trained ones, were absorbed into governments around the world, and policy more oriented towards neoclassical economic thinking.

This was initially driven by Anglo-American nations (US, UK, Australia, New Zealand and Ireland) which adopted a 'liberal market economy' (LME) approach. Many nations since then have followed to an extent, whatever their 'varieties of capitalism' (Coates, 2000; Hall and Soskice, 2001). Even more 'coordinated market economies' (CMEs), such as Japan, Germany and the Scandinavian nations, have adopted certain more free-market policies, as have authoritarian nations like Singapore and China.

Such 'Washington consensus' principles also came to dominate the policies and practices of international economic institutions, such as the International Monetary Fund (IMF) and World Bank. Whenever a nation needed economic assistance, these organizations would offer it but only if a set of larger free-market conditions were adopted. It was assumed that such policy changes would automatically improve a country's economy, bringing more jobs, growth and taxes. Thus, economic stability would be achieved and debts paid off. Such ideas were forcibly imposed on struggling countries prior to 2007, such as Argentina, Korea or Thailand (Krugman, 2008). They were also adopted for a range of European countries, such as Ireland and Greece, in the wake of the 2007–8 financial crash.

As government economic management has become more directed by neoclassical economics, so a range of other policy areas have been affected. Common trends have emerged across multiple nations over several decades. These include: widespread privatization of state-owned industries, reduced taxes and market deregulation, trade liberalization and the encouragement of foreign direct investment, inhibiting of trade union rights, reduced welfare spending, and the marketization or outsourcing of common state functions such as education and transport infrastructure. Since the 1970s, national economies have had their highs and lows but, essentially, neoclassical economic policies were deemed a success.

The shape of neoliberal economies was entirely transformed too. Widespread deindustrialization occurred as heavy industry and production became outsourced to poorer economies with cheaper labour. The service sector grew instead. Less obvious to many, was the growth of the financial services sector and financialization (Epstein, 2005; Krippner, 2011; Davis and Walsh, 2016). International financial institutions grew significantly, coming to manage larger amounts of capital, provide a greater percentage of corporate profits, and make a greater contribution to national GDP growth. In the UK case, bank assets grew, from being roughly half the value of GDP in the 1970s, to become five times the value of GDP in the 2000s. There were also big rises in the values of shares, bonds, currencies and other financial assets. Increasingly, these came to be owned primarily by large, international funds. Consequently, the financial sector increased its influence over governments and economies.

Then came the 2007–8 financial crisis (see accounts in Krugman, 2008; Cable, 2009; Elliott and Atkinson, 2009; Ferguson, 2012). This was as big, if not bigger, than the 1929 Wall Street Crash. It soon turned into a global economic crisis. Trillions of government dollars had to be pumped into the financial system to avoid widespread failure and economic meltdown. A mix of bank nationalization, Treasury bailouts and QE (quantitative easing or printing money), and ultra-low interest rates were deployed. This left many states with huge public debts, struggling economies and severe cut-backs in their government spending programmes. It also left many millions of individuals homeless and in debt. In the post-mortems which followed, multiple culprits were singled out: poor financial regulations, opaque and highly risky trading practices with complex financial products, ignorant and dishonest politicians, large international trading imbalances, and greedy bankers.

Whatever the diagnosis, and whoever was to blame, there have remained large question marks over neoclassical economics with its strong focus on autonomous market mechanisms. Mainstream economists neither saw the wider financial and economic crisis coming nor have they been able to explain what happened. Several heterodox economist critics (Quiggin, 2010; Chang, 2010; Crouch, 2011; Keen, 2011; Davies, 2014; Earle et al., 2016), have since questioned the foundations of the economics discipline. For all of them, many of the problems came from allowing purist market philosophies to over-ride policy-making in all sorts of areas, from financial deregulation to free trade. Part of that influence stemmed from the discipline's self-presentation as a 'science'. But, for critics like Steve Keen (2011: xiii): 'the so-called science of economics is a melange of myths that make the ancient Ptolemaic earth-centric view of the solar system look positively sophisticated in comparison.'

Despite the collapse, and in spite of its intellectual failings, neoclassical economics has survived so far. It continues to dominate policy responses, in Donald Trump's US, Brexit UK, Emmanuel Macron's France and elsewhere. That is that free markets, lower taxes, reduced state spending ('austerity economics'), privatization, bigger trade deals and deregulation are the solutions for improving national economies.

Economics as Politics

Critics of mainstream economics come in all shapes and forms. However, one thing that unites them is their insistence that economics is neither a science nor something that can be detached from politics and social relations. Economics and markets are not separate, autonomous mechanisms that operate according to scientific laws. People involved in economic activity are not purely rational beings, capable of knowing everything and able to calculate what is in their own best interests all of the time. Markets don't behave like chemical reactions and humans are not Vulcans. Economics is like other social sciences – there are lots of patterns but no iron laws.

Neoclassical economics, although the dominant form of economics in academia and politics, is but one strand of economic thought. There are many alternative 'heterodox' strands too. These offer more convincing explanations of why markets go wrong. They also put forward ideas and policies which may alleviate the negative outcomes of unfettered free-markets. They are a mix of *political economists* (e.g., Colin Crouch, Wolfgang Streeck), *neo-Keynesian economists* (e.g., Paul Krugman, Joseph Stiglitz), *economic historians* (e.g., Karl Polanyi, Charles Kindleberger), *behavioural economists* (e.g., Daniel Kahneman, Robert Shiller), *economic sociologists* (e.g., Mark Granovetter, Richard Swedberg), *environmental economists* (e.g., Tim

Jackson, Kate Raworth), *development economists* (e.g., Ha-Joon Chang, Amartya Sen), and many others besides. In their varied studies, market instabilities, bubbles and crashes, and irrational calculative behaviour, are considered to be regular rather than abnormal features. Their accounts look outside markets, to long-term historical market data, to wider socio-economic trends and relationships, and to social and psychological factors.

For many (not all) of these alternative thinkers, economics is always political. For Ha-Joon Chang (2010: 10): 'Economics is not a science like physics or chemistry, but a political exercise.' For Thomas Piketty (2014: 20): 'The history of the distribution of wealth has always been deeply political, and it cannot be reduced to purely economic mechanisms.' States, economies and markets are interdependent. States need strong economies to provide jobs for people and taxes for governments. The economy and markets need governments to make rules and regulations by which they can operate. These include laws to determine property ownership, contracts, corporate governance structures, criminal behaviour and so on. More than that, markets and economies are dependent on a series of things that states maintain, such as currencies, transport infrastructure, and an educated and able workforce.

So, democracies and capitalism need each other but they also have quite different objectives. Politicians address citizens and uphold democracy. Economists talk of consumers and producers and uphold markets and profits. And the big question for all governments is: how should states behave to best enable economies to flourish while also remaining healthy democracies?

It is not possible to cover the many alternative schools of economics. Rather the chapter will now briefly touch on two particular strands which have proved highly relevant to politics and political communication. In the UK and US, the most well-known alternative to neoclassical economics and neoliberalism is Keynesianism. John Maynard Keynes, a lifelong member of the British Liberal Party, came to prominence in the 1930s, when the world economy was trying to recover from the Wall Street Crash of 1929. Then, as now, a financial crash was followed by an extended recession, leaving fragile and unstable economies. In many ways, Keynes was not a conventional economist. His great work, *The General Theory of Employment, Interest and Money* (1936), broke with the accepted wisdom of neoclassical economics. It often drew on his real-world observations of markets and market actors and was virtually devoid of complex maths and models.

In the 1930s, as with 'austerity economics' after 2008, governments responded to their soaring debts by making extensive cuts in their expenditure. They tried to balance their books and keep spending under control. What happened, as has been happening in Greece, the UK and to varying degrees in other countries, was that economic growth remained stunted as money was sucked out of the economy. The more cuts were made, the less money there was to go around, the less companies invested in new businesses and the less individuals had to spend. This became a vicious circle of economic decline. Keynes's answer in the 1930s was to do the opposite with a 'demand management' approach. This involved more borrowing and spending in order to create employment through big state infrastructure projects. In theory, this would bring a 'multiplier effect', a more virtuous circle of employment, more taxes and spending and more jobs. Then, when the economy was thriving, states could pay off their debts and get their finances back in order.

Keynes's ideas worked and for the next few decades that's what governments did. They moved taxes up and down and invested in nationalized industries and infrastructure projects. Many economies thrived until the 1970s. Then it all went wrong as an oil crisis hit, the Bretton Woods international system of currency exchange collapsed, and a number of minor industrial and financial crises followed. Both inflation and unemployment got out of control while strong unions battled to keep wages high. Keynes's ideas were discredited. The UK government had to eventually be bailed out by the IMF in 1976. The IMF said then what it still says now – cut state spending, privatize national industries, balance the books. So, with the Keynesian orthodoxy rejected, the way was paved for the return of neoclassical economics once again.

Then, in the wake of the financial crash of 2007–8, Keynes ideas were temporarily back in vogue (Skidelski, 2010). Both Gordon Brown in the UK and Barack Obama in the US promoted Keynesian-type economic policies in trying to re-inflate their economies. Then, after 2010, the new UK Coalition government, along with the EU generally, went back to conventional neoclassical economics and the return to austerity cuts. The UK as well as many economies in Southern Europe have struggled to get going again since.

Another alternative view of economics, one that is rarely taught in economics departments, comes from (post) Marxist political economy. Before economics broke away from other social sciences, various writers were regarded as political economists. Karl Marx and his co-author and benefactor Friedrich Engels, wrote prolifically during the second part of the nineteenth century (1848, 1867). They saw capitalism, the main form of economic organization in Europe then and now, as but one alternative. Capitalism as they observed it, was creative and innovative but also destructive and socially destabilizing. Its system, both supported and was a consequence of a political system that favoured the wealthy owners and managers of the means of production. Owners' wealth came directly from their exploiting the labour of those they employed. The more workers were squeezed the more they profited. Although capitalism keeps adapting and reinventing itself, and modern states attempt to ameliorate the worst excesses of market economies, the system always returns to this default.

For modern political economists (Crouch, 2011; Harvey, 2007; Mirowski, 2009, 2014; Streeck, 2016), neoclassical economics, far from being a neutral technical field, is in fact another means of sustaining capitalist exploitation. It was and is part of the larger political framework of neoliberalism. As Mirowski (2009: 426), typically states, neoliberalism 'was an intricately structured long-term philosophical and political project ... a "thought collective", that slowly penetrated national institutions of economic management.' Neoliberalism's use of modern economics has produced unstable economies and huge levels of inequality and personal debt, not to mention unsustainable levels of waste and environmental degradation.

Inequality has been a growing by-product of the dominance of neoclassical economics since the late 1970s. The most common measure of inequality used is the Gini Coefficient, which looks at the gap between the top and bottom earners in a country. For much of the twentieth century the coefficient declined in mature democracies. This was especially so in the decades after the Second World War when taxes and state spending were high. Just as the Thatcher and Reagan administrations came to power the downward trend went into reverse. It began climbing substantially in the US, UK and other countries which had adopted neoliberal policies. Thomas Piketty's *Capital in the 21st Century* (2014) traces these shifts in capital distribution across twenty nations over more than a century. His study among others (Wilkinson and Pickett, 2010; Dorling, 2014; Streeck, 2016) reveals the steady rise in inequality and the wider social, economic and political consequences of that for societies.

This rise in inequality is directly linked to neoliberal economic policies, such as reducing top rates of income and corporation tax or weakening trade unions. On the one hand, this has left the poor getting poorer as levels of personal debt have increased, real wage incomes for those in the bottom half have stagnated or declined, and housing costs have gone up sharply. As public debt has grown, and welfare state programmes been cut back, so more of the population has experienced worsening health, education and other outcomes. On the other hand, incomes and assets have shifted towards the super-rich or 1% (or 0.001%), as global tax avoidance and evasion continues to grow each year (TJN, 2015). A smaller number of billionaires own more wealth and have more influence over politics, media and the economy. In 2010, Oxfam produced a report which calculated that the net worth of the wealthiest 388 people in the world, was equivalent to the bottom 50% or three and a half billion people in the world. Each year that wealthiest people figure has gone down. By January 2017, it had dropped to just eight individuals owning the equivalent to the bottom half of the world. Those individuals, with a combined net wealth of $426 billion, were Bill Gates, Warren Buffett, Jeff Bezos, Larry Ellison, Michael Bloomberg, Mark Zuckerberg, Carlos Slim and Amancio Ortega. Six of those eight built their empires on new information and communication technologies.

For heterodox economists of all kinds the financial crisis cannot be explained by neoclassical economics. For post-Keynesians, economic historians and behavioural economists (Minsky, 1982; Kindleberger and Alibar, 2011; Shiller, 2000; Akerlof and Shiller, 2009), financial markets do not move to positions of equilibrium; in fact, quite the reverse. They are inherently unstable and contain individuals who can be as irrational as anyone, especially in times of market crisis. The more financial market deregulation was guided by traditional economic thinking the more unstable the global financial system became. Market bubbles and crashes became more frequent and bigger. Deregulation enabled an unregulated shadow banking sector to grow into something that was larger than the visible, regulated banking sector. It also facilitated the growth of a multiplicity of risky, opaque financial products, such as the derivatives used in the subprime mortgage market, where the crisis began. In the decade leading up the 2008 collapse, the total derivatives market rose in value from $15 trillion to $600 trillion, or nearly twelve times total world output (Cable, 2009: 34). Since derivatives are constructed and valued according to estimates of future values of real assets, the market had somehow risen to irrationally high values.

For political economists the deregulation of financial markets was also explained by politics. Over years, the financial lobby in the UK and US grew substantially, as did the influence of financiers in government policy-making itself (Engelen et al., 2011; Krippner, 2011; Ferguson, 2012; Davis and Walsh, 2016). The sector spent billions in persuading legislators to remove the safeguards put in place after the Wall Street Crash in 1929. A number of key figures moved between Wall Street and the Federal Reserve, the City of London and the Treasury and Bank of England. They persuaded the authorities that: strong autonomous financial centres were great wealth creators and the best allocators of capital in the economy, and, staffed by rational experts who understood economies best and knew how to manage risk. The financial crisis and its consequences proved all this to be wrong.

The response of critical political economists, post-Keynesians and others to events has been the following since 2008: austerity and cuts are bad and have stopped a full economic recovery taking place; government spending measures, such as low interest rates, VAT cuts and large infrastructure building projects should be used to stimulate the economy; banking and finance need to be better regulated and made less risky with governments intervening more. They also look to other forms of capitalism where state–market relations are different. For example, in Germany and Scandinavia, there is more state intervention or social capitalism, and there are much closer links between unions, corporations, banks and regions.

Economics in Media and Political Discourse

This final part looks at how economics is covered in news media and public political discourse. 'Economic news' covers a variety of types of economically oriented news, such as government budgets, macro-economic shifts and policies, financial markets, company news, industrial relations and personal finance.

What is argued here is that, in the main, economic news has come to be dominated by a limited range of elite sources and interests in government, business and finance. This has had a strong bearing on how the economy, markets and government interventions are presented and interpreted. It has also influenced what is counted as 'economic news' and who is authorized to speak on the topic. The consequence is that economic coverage is now written primarily by and for a small number of government and corporate sources and large financial investors. It therefore has less and less meaning for ordinary citizens.

In earlier centuries, economic news and information originated to serve wealthy individuals seeking to invest in new enterprises and international trade. However, through the twentieth century, as news organizations expanded their audiences, so copy also came to include a wider range of subjects. One of these was trends in and debates about macroeconomic policy, as discussed by politicians, academics and business leaders. In Parsons' (1989) historical account of the financial press in the US and UK, the economists Keynes, Galbraith, Samuelson and Friedman all made their impact on policy-makers through their frequent interventions in the press. Thatcher-Reagan era economic policies were debated as much in the business news pages as in university economics departments. In effect, economic news was an area of 'legitimate controversy' (Hallin, 1994) that spilled across political and other news sections. Disparate elite sources not only disagreed with each other, they were often at odds with business news reporters (Jones, 1986; Lichter and Rothman, 1988; Smith, 1988).

A second area was personal finance news as it developed in the post-war period of economic affluence (Parsons, 1989; Tunstall, 1996). Increased home and share ownership, as well as state encouragement to buy privatized industry shares or to invest pensions in financial markets, all spurred public interest and financial advertising (Curran, 1978; Newman, 1984). A third area of economic reporting developed around industry and industrial relations. Much economic policy in the UK and across Europe related to the management of nationalized industries. Labour unions were far larger with news outlets having specialist correspondents to cover industrial relations (GUMG, 1980; Marchand, 1998; Manning, 1999). In fact, in the 1970s union leaders were considered to be 'primary definers' (Hall et al., 1978), often being cited rather more than business heads or government officials

From the 1970s onwards, as neoliberal policies were enacted, the economy changed. State industries were privatized, and governments withdrew generally from economic intervention. Large-scale deindustrialization took place. Unions shrunk considerably. The international financial sector grew substantially. As inequality increased, private shareholding declined.

Alongside big changes to politics and economics in the US and UK, came changes to their news industries too (see Chapter 5). Legacy news media experienced a steady decline in consumers and advertising as competition grew. Hard pressed journalists had to produce more copy with fewer resources and turned to news wire and public relations content to fill the gap (Davies, 2008; McChesney and Pickard, 2011). Such developments hit the economic and business news sections as hard as any other reporting area (Davis, 2002, 2011). The financial sector quickly moved in, becoming a major 'information subsidy' supplier for economic news, with extensive financial advertising and PR material, and a plethora of high-profile CEOs and analysts to offer economic commentary.

Consequently, economic news came to revolve more around the communicative exchanges of big finance, large corporations and government treasury departments (Parsons, 1989; Davis, 2002). Finance ministers, transnational corporations, City analysts and international financiers predominated over other kinds of news source (Kantola, 2006; Davis, 2007b; Starkman, 2014; Thompson, 2017). For example, Knowles et al.'s (2017) produced a longitudinal, tri-nation study of newspapers in the UK, US and Australia, looking at three periods from the late 1980s to the latter part of the financial crash in 2008. The study not only recorded the clear dominance of business sources, the disparity between this group and others grew over time. Economists working outside of the financial sector, such as in academia or unions, became marginalized (Wren-Lewis, 2018). Keynesians and other heterodox economists were excluded altogether. The new primary definers of economic news, from government to the City, were in broad agreement on the merits of neoclassical economic policy.

This resulted in a more reductive and less pluralistic account of 'the economy' which filtered out many public interest elements. Finance ministers now talked much more about finance, banking, share ownership and international investment (see Davis and Walsh, 2016). A greater quantity of news content focused on company share values, the ups and downs of financial market sectors, and other international investor concerns. As union power declined and strike activity dropped considerably, union reporting was scaled back and industrial correspondents became a thing of the past (Manning, 1999). Wider debates about national industry and macroeconomic policy became far less common. Coverage of regional economic issues declined or were pushed into other news sections.

In turn, this has encouraged the dominance of certain economic ideas which support the interests of international business and finance. First, business news content became increasingly critical of state interventions in economies while also advocating market-type policies. Proposals for more regulation, higher taxes, stronger consumer or trade union rights, came to be treated as both extreme and prehistoric (Hutton, 1996; Durham, 2007; Kantola, 2006). In global business coverage, international (often Western-based) investors were favoured over national governments and democratic processes. Bennett et al.'s (2004) and Ojala's (2017) studies of the reporting of the World Economic Forum, found that the dominant story frames strongly promoted the interests and policy positions of such financial elites over those of citizens and activists. Kantola's (2006) analysis of *Financial Times* content showed that its coverage of some thirty-two elections between 2000 and 2005, repeatedly backed candidates which supported pro-market reforms, and opposed those parties and voters which did not.

Second, accounts record how economic reporting repeatedly promoted the narratives and trading practices that drove many financial market bubbles. This was clear in the dot.com boom and then bust of 2000 (Cassidy, 2002; Davis, 2007b). The lead up to the 2007–8 financial crisis showed that few lessons had been learned in the interim. Throughout this period, a small minority of economic journalists managed to ask more difficult questions. But these alternative 'doomsayers' were marginalized and easily drowned out by the general wave of traditional, uncritical business coverage in the US (Schiffrin, 2011; Starkman, 2014), UK (Schifferes, 2011; Manning, 2013) and Europe (Mercille, 2014; Picard et al., 2014). In each case, news was far more likely to promote each new bull market sector.

Third, economic news has come to present national economies in terms of their international investment potential; something that has little to do with the economy experienced by most of the public. For example, many headlines look at macroeconomic indicators, each of which can be positively spun by governments or used to make international (usually financial) investment decisions. These include: shifts in stock market indices, currency movements, unemployment rates, GDP and inflation figures, productivity rates, and so on. Such aggregated data does not record the vast differences in incomes, regions, professions, demographics, costs of living, etc that exist across a nation. In fact, lots of factors that have a big influence on daily living conditions are brushed over. So, inflation measures exclude changes to housing costs and mortgage interest payments. Unemployment rates do not account for the rise in precarious, temporary and part-time employment.

In the immediate aftermath of the 2007–8 financial crisis, economic elite consensus temporarily broke down and that was reflected in news coverage in many countries (Aresse, 2018). Bankers were widely criticized and doubts about global capitalism and neoliberalism voiced loudly. Protest movements like Occupy Wall Street flourished (see Chapter 8). Keynesian economists such as Joseph

Stiglitz and Paul Krugman got rather more coverage. Banks were nationalized, attempts to re-regulate finance were made and states stepped back into various forms of economic management (see Berry, 2018; Basu, 2018).

However, once banks had been bailed out and the international financial system had stabilized, public political and media discourse returned to its default position and traditional sources. A round of enquiries and new regulations resulted in the financial sector being declared safe once again (Engelen et al., 2011). The anti-state, pro-market, pro tax cuts, and international investor line prevailed anew. Debt management, budget cuts and austerity economics became the norm, with other views marginalized once again (Schiffrin, 2011; Berry, 2016; Aresse, 2018). At this point, national news operations had become even weaker and so were left with fewer resources to investigate and challenge the economic austerity consensus.

In recent years, Treasury ministers, bankers and top CEOs have moved beyond 'economic crisis' talk, to suggest stability and/or recovery. They have trumpeted every positive macro indicator from rises in GDP and booming stock markets, to declining unemployment and reduced borrowing. However, for many people, the economic reality is very different. In several economies, average wage income remains stagnant and precarious, while housing, food and fuel costs are rising. Some regions and cities have flourished while others have declined. Youth unemployment has remained extremely high in certain states such as Greece, Italy and Spain.

Conclusion

The neoliberal experiment, begun four decades ago, continues to dominate economic policy-making and media coverage of the economy in the US, UK and many other nations. So too, neoclassical economics has managed to exclude rival strands of thought, bracket out non-economic considerations, and to maintain its distance from other social sciences. During previous world economic crises, in the 1930s and 1970s, existing orthodoxies were rejected and new economic ideas took hold. This was not the case following the financial collapse of 2007–8. Whether this was due to a lack of new ideas or the entrenchment of the economic establishment, far too little changed. Fundamental problems, from rising inequality to growing debts and unstable economies, continue.

2016 was the year large groups of citizens rebelled in the UK and US. Growing inequalities and huge differences in economic perception and experience became suddenly clear (they were already apparent in parts of Europe and outside the rich West). In the UK, in London, Scotland, Northern Ireland, and a few thriving cities, the majority voted Remain during the EU Referendum. Most economists (some 90%, see Wren-Lewis, 2018) and related 'experts', both in the UK and international institutions, strongly supported the Remain case too, declaring an economic catastrophe would follow a Leave vote.

Those more likely to vote Leave were mainly in struggling deindustrialized regions, less educated, and in poorer and more precarious employment (BBC, 2016; Barnett, 2017). The dire warnings of what would happen to the economy if the UK left seemed largely irrelevant to them, especially as they had personally experienced years of increasing hardship. When Michael Gove famously said 'people have had enough of experts' (meaning economists), many Leavers felt the same. Years of wage stagnation, job insecurity in the 'gig economy', rising housing costs and welfare state cuts, left many asking themselves why they should believe the economists, politicians, or news media quoting them?

So too, it was a similar story for the 2016 US presidential election, with those who were less educated and poorer, as well as those in the impoverished, deindustrialized regions of the country, voting for Trump (Frank, 2016; Pew, 2016c; Luce, 2017). Traditional working-class Democratic voters, as with centre-left parties in the UK and Europe, had lost faith in their parties. While their party leaders had been embracing mainstream economic thinking and media commentary, so they had appeared to lose touch with how this partial, mediated vision of 'the economy' was not the one experienced by most ordinary citizens.

10
Digital Media and Online Political Communication

This chapter looks at the impact of digital media on political communication. Digital developments have already been discussed throughout the book. What is offered here is more a sweeping overview of digital trends and an introduction to the competing conceptual frameworks used to interpret them.

For many readers digital media is no longer 'new' or different but just part of the mix. All politics and media are now a hybrid mix of old and new and there is no need for a chapter just on the digital. Arguably, such thinking is mistaken. For one, it is worth taking stock of the disruptive changes experienced just in the last half decade. A lot of studies have documented specific changes across politics and media but what, in aggregate, do these mean for contemporary democracy? For another, the field has encountered several past 'new media' ages and has developed contrasting approaches to the topic. It is worth asking whether these paradigms still hold good or are now in need of a fundamental rethink?

The chapter is in three parts. The first two focus on a classic if slightly simplistic fault line that has framed debate about new ICTs (Information and Communication Technologies). These debates, taking place between 'techno-optimists' and 'pessimists', have resurfaced with each new technology, and have returned once again in the digital age. Optimists have argued that the latest new wave can overcome the deficiencies that have corroded mature democracies. There are new possibilities to democratize formal politics, news and information, and to open up fresh spaces for interest groups and individual participation. Pessimists, however, have argued that such work was and remains too technologically determinist in nature. Long-standing social, economic and political influences and structures are enduring, and have a greater bearing on how new ICTs are adopted and used. As the new digital world has bedded in, so old problems have resurfaced for democracies. Like every new communication technology before, the promises have proved unrealizable in practice.

The third part looks at what has happened this decade while also re-evaluating these interpretive frameworks. On the one hand, it is clear that optimists have had something of a sobering reality check. ICTs are but one influence on political communication and, alone, were never going to return democracy to some mythical ideal past model. On the other, pessimists also have to recognize the disruptive power of the new digital, online world. Clear tipping points have been reached, threatening the very institutions and media that have facilitated democracies for the past century. Entirely new phenomena and configurations are emerging. Together, these have torn asunder what once passed for national public spheres, leaving something altogether polarized, fragmented and anarchic.

A Brave New World of Digital Democracy?

Periodically in history there is an important breakthrough in communication technology which has a profound influence on all aspects of society, including the sphere of politics and democracy. The printing press, the electric telegraph, the telephone, television and home computing are some obvious examples. The biggest such example of recent times is the World Wide Web with its global communication infrastructure. Parallel technological developments have enhanced its capabilities and driven a powerful new communication era. These include such things as: exponential rises in computing speed, power and storage; the digitalization of culture and communications, enabling convergence and transmission across multiple formats; wireless technologies, allowing mobile connections and exchanges anywhere where a signal can be passed; and the roll-out of commercial, social media and other platforms, linking billions directly across time and space.

As with all previous such leaps in technology, so a wide mix of entrepreneurs, politicians, journalists and scholars have attempted to simultaneously speculate on and interpret developments. In many cases, those techno-optimists have also driven activity and investment.

Entrepreneurs and commentators both indulge in futurism and try to profit from it, riding each new wave as it comes. Politicians laud its economic and democratic potential and redirect research money towards it.

In this respect, the field of political communication is little different. In the 1990s and early 2000s, a clear thesis developed around the potential of the internet to revive ailing democracies everywhere. The argument had three parts. First, the normative values at the heart of public sphere theory (Habermas, 1989) were not being met in modern political communication systems. This seemed clearly observable in relation to things like voter turnout, political party engagement and individual participation (see Chapter 3).

Second, the communicative failings of old mass media, governments and parties were deemed to be a major contributory factor. Early internet enthusiasts (Negroponte, 1995; Pavlik, 1996; Kahin and Wilson, 1997), set out the problem. Traditional media and politics were top-down, centralized and hierarchical in nature. This left those at the top having a large say in both media and political organizations while leaving the large mass at the base having virtually none. In part this was about power relations. In part it was also due to the technological limits and costs of traditional communication media, resulting in a restricted number of outlets and frequencies operating. As media conglomerates grew, and traditional parties dominated, so large portions of society were excluded. In authoritarian nations, such as China, Saudi Arabia or Russia, participation was even more limited with fewer individuals able to dominate mass communication.

Third, the web and other new ICTs offer a way forward on several grounds (Castells, 2001; Coleman and Gotz, 2001; Norris, 2002; Jenkins and Thorburn, 2004). The internet's architecture has produced a non-hierarchical, many-to-many form of communication infrastructure. Compared to old media, new media is relatively cheap, easily accessible and offers an infinite amount of spaces, channels and forums. It is also global and unrestricted by artificial time slots and deadlines. The new communications ecology is characterized by 'radical decentralization', and widely populated by 'user-contributors' or 'prosumers'. These can take advantage of 'convergence culture' to co-create and share 'spreadable media' over multiple networks and platforms.

Under such conditions, old forms of top-down and centralized control, in commerce, culture and politics, cannot be maintained. Endless possibilities exist for new voices, platforms and outputs to develop and make challenges. In terms of commerce, a 'new economy' would emerge with new entrants replacing aging, sclerotic conglomerates (Negroponte, 1995; Gates, 1996). Since the 1990s there have been several new waves of techno-optimism about Web 2.0, Web 3.0 and the 'internet of things' (not to mention Web 4.0 and 5.0), all of which promise 'a true paradigm shift' (Schmidt and Cohen, 2013; Rifkin, 2014).

For those focusing on politics and democracy, the expectation was of a large increase in participation (Bohman, 1996; Coleman and Gotz, 2001; Dryzak, 2002; Norris, 2002). New ICTS offered a return to the kinds of ideal, more participatory forms of democracy associated with ancient Athens or eighteenth-century European public spheres. These were characterized by greater citizen access and equality. As Gibson and McAllister (2015) put it more recently, ideally, digital media would bring 'equalization' rather than 'normalization' in politics. Such potential has subsequently been explored across a number of types of political organization and activity. Four particular areas are briefly discussed here: governance, political parties, interest groups and journalism/public communication.

Starting with government, several authors set out the norms and criteria by which new digital forms of governance could be created and evaluated (see Dahlberg, 2001; Dahlgren, 2005, 2013; Polat, 2005). These involve: inclusiveness of citizens, open agendas, pluralist balance, rational debate and information presentation, safeguards against state and powerful actor dominance, and reciprocity. A spate of US and UK studies and institutional initiatives subsequently explored the potential for online exchanges between citizens, officials and politicians. These initiated, documented and evaluated the emergence of a 'civic commons in cyberspace' with 'citizen panels', 'e-consultations' and 'e-deliberations'. In effect, the intention was to use new ICTs to recreate virtual forms of town-hall style democracy.

Some studies investigated this potential at the local level. So, for example, Dahlberg (2001) observed what was happening in the pioneering Minnesota E-Democracy project in the US. Wikland (2005) and Åström et al. (2013) looked at what took place with digital trials in Estonian, Swedish and Icelandic municipalities. Much was explored at the national level too (Bimber, 2003; Coleman, 2004; 2005; Gulati, 2004; Ward et al., 2005; Chadwick, 2006; Lusoli et al., 2006; Davis, 2007b). In the UK, the Hansard Society worked closely with Parliament (Ferguson, 2006) to set up a series of online forums to accompany select committee consultations. By the mid-2000s, thousands of research papers, previously only available to MPs, were being made publicly available, with up to fifteen meetings being simultaneously webcast at any one time. Politicians increasingly began using the web in their daily activities, for purposes of: political research, tabling parliamentary questions, circulating and commenting on discussion documents and motions, and to communicate extensively with politicians, voters and other interests. Such democratic experiments and documented changes in practice have continued in a wide variety of parliamentary settings since (Coleman and Blumler, 2009; Shane, 2011; Dai and Norton, 2013). One of the most far-reaching of these involved the use of social media during the collaborative rewriting of the Icelandic constitution in 2011 (Valtysson, 2014)

A second focus for researchers has been political parties. Studies asked if new ICTs could be useful in halting long-term declines in party membership while also boosting levels of activism (Ward et al., 2002; Rommele, 2003; Lusoli and Ward, 2003; Gillmor, 2004; Trippi, 2004; Davis, 2005). They documented a series of positive developments in fund-raising, organization and information dissemination among ordinary members. Linked to this was the rolling out of individual MP websites and email addresses. By 2004 (Lusoli and Ward, 2004) some 76% of UK politicians had developed individual websites. These shifts were noted to be particularly significant for smaller, less-resourced parties such as the Liberal Democrats in the UK. They also provided a breakthrough in US politics, enabling relatively peripheral and less-resourced candidates to campaign without relying on networks of wealthy donors and PACs. Thus emerged the Democratic candidate Howard Dean in the 2003–4 US primaries (Gillmor, 2004; Trippi, 2004), as well as Ron Paul and various Tea Party candidates for the Republicans in 2007–8. Overall, such uses indicated a levelling of the political campaign playing surface. Digital media could be used, to an extent, to bypass mainstream media and established party-funder circles.

Such trends and optimism seemed to come to full fruition with the successful election campaign of Barack Obama in 2008 (Pew, 2009a; Hendricks and Denton, 2010; Magleby, 2011; Stromer-Galley, 2014). The Obama team's extensive use of new media helped catapult the then junior Democratic Senator towards his party's nomination and eventual election victory. Obama's campaign allocated ninety people to its online activities, using websites and social media to fund-raise, organize and engage across the US. The *My.BarackObama.com* website registered millions of supporters and was used to organize

35,000 groups and 150,000 events. His Facebook page had 3.18 million supporters. 1,820 campaign videos were produced and posted on YouTube, to be viewed ninety million times. Such actions were instrumental in re-engaging the kind of young and ethnic minority voters who had lost interest in Washington politics. Sixty-six per cent of voters under thirty, and 69% of new voters, supported Obama in 2008 (figures in Hendricks and Denton, 2010: xii, 7–11).

Studies since then have further explored the use of such platforms for citizen party engagement, particularly among younger voters (Bode and Dalrymple, 2016; Loader et al., 2016; Weeks et al., 2017). In Spain, Podemos made extensive use of social media to burst onto the political scene in 2014. Just five months after inception it had gained over 200,000 members and one hundred circles, winning 1.25 million votes in its first election (Fenton, 2016a: 184). Scholars have also documented the adoption of social media and hybrid media strategies by traditional party campaigners (Stromer-Galley, 2014; Wells et al., 2016). In 2015–16, Bernie Sanders employed the veterans and digital methods of recent new social movements to mount a serious challenge to the established Democratic candidate Hillary Clinton (Chadwick and Stromer-Galley, 2016). For Wells et al. (2016), Donald Trump proved equally adept at gaining attention in both legacy and social media, thus generating an estimated $2 billion in free coverage. He succeeded despite the collective hostility of the powerful political-media nexus in Washington.

A third area of exploration has been interest groups, social movements and activism. Scholars tracked 'resource-poor' groups as they used new ICTs to generate funds, publicize campaigns, and organize and engage members, in their attempts to take on governments and corporations. In the internet's infancy, in the 1990s, a set of underdog groups achieved successes against far larger such opponents, using basic computers, video equipment, mobile phones and the web (Downing, 2001; Curran and Couldry, 2003). In Mexico, impoverished peasants in the Chiapas region formed the Zapatistas and took on the might of the Mexican government (Martinez-Torres, 2001). In the US, Anti-globalization protestors organized and widely promoted their protests at the 'Battle of Seattle' (Kahn and Kellner, 2004). In the Philippines, SMS-linked 'smart mobs' quickly converged on protest sites, helping to bring down President Estrada (Rheingold, 2002).

By the 2000s such web uses and strategies were becoming widespread across the campaign sector (Atton, 2004; Pickerill, 2004; de Jong et al., 2005; Dean et al., 2006). Established NGOs, such as Greenpeace and Amnesty began making extensive use of the technology. So too, new social movements appeared, developed especially to use the opportunities offered by the new technology. These included such groups as MoveOn and Avaaz (US), GetUp (Australia) and 38 Degrees (the UK). As Fenton (2016a) explained, interest groups generally were benefiting from three net-enhanced advances in: 'speed and space', 'connectivity and participation', and 'diversity and horizontality'.

This decade, new social movements and new technologies came together in dramatic fashion (Castells, 2012; Gerbaudo, 2012; Mason, 2012; Bennett and Segerberg, 2013; Chapter 8, this volume). 2011 was the year of the anti-capitalist Indignados and Occupy Wall Street movements, which sprung up in Spain and New York respectively before gaining support from around the world (DeLuca et al., 2012; Gerbaudo, 2012; Juris, 2012a and b). So too came the 'Arab Spring' as Tunisia, Syria, Libya and Yemen became embroiled in civil war, with violent anti-government protests taking place across the Middle East (Howard et al., 2011; Eltantawy and Wiest, 2011; Tufekci and Wilson, 2014). For authors documenting things on the ground, new ICTs did not just prove crucial for informing and organizing large protest movements, they created an alternative kind of social movement altogether. For Bennett and Segerberg (2013), these movements operated with 'the logic of connective action'. Digital networks enabled more fluid, deliberative, non-hierarchical organizational structures to flourish. These engaged and mobilized large numbers of people quickly, taking governments and corporations by surprise.

A fourth area is online news and political information websites. The internet immediately opened up fresh possibilities, both for traditional news producers and new entrants. A series of early studies documented the potential of the net for reporters (Miller, 1998; Deuze, 2001; Garrison, 2001; Pavlik, 2001; Gunter, 2003). As the web expanded, established journalists found they could tap into a wealth of information sources. The pace of data transfer and the ability to publish instantly online, cut printing and distribution costs and sped up coverage. With no constraints on space, and the ability to publish without deadlines, correspondents could also file additional reports, comments and blogs. Potential audiences and associated advertising expanded too.

Perhaps more significantly, the news publishing field was opened up. So, came the arrival of online only news sites such as *Indymedia*, South Korea's *OhmyNews*, and the US's *Huffington Post*. Such enterprises were unconstrained by traditional source relations and practices. They operated with far smaller budgets but could also call on a wide range of amateur or 'citizen' journalists to produce user-generated content. Armed with smart phones anyone could now take photos and video footage of those in authority, documenting duplicitous politicians and instances of police brutality (Curran, 2016). Thousands of new political websites appeared, offering stories, gossip and unconventional commentary and instant opinions. Many of these, such as the *Drudge Report*, the *Daily Kos*, *Guido Fawkes* and *Left Foot Forward*, gained millions of visitors and began generating substantial advertising (Gillmor, 2004; Lowrey, 2006; Carlson, 2007). Wikileaks and other organizations used the new platforms to disseminate secret and classified information from whistle-blowers, such as the Edward Snowden files, the Panama and Paradise Papers. In parallel came Wikipedia, file and video sharing sites like YouTube and Flickr, social media platforms such as Facebook and Snapchat, and microblogging sites like Twitter and Weibo.

The transition had major implications for the old media-supported public sphere with its limited access and restricted set of voices. Now political news and information was more pluralist, more interactive, cheap to produce, spreadable, participatory, uncensored and free-flowing. By the end of the 2000s a series of high-profile advocates were lining up to proclaim the democratic advances of the digital brave new world (Tapscott and Williams, 2007; Beckett, 2008; Jenkins, 2009; Nerone, 2009; Shirky, 2009; Castells, 2012).

Normalization, Digital Disillusion and Techno-Pessimism

In the 2000s, parallel waves of pragmatism and pessimism developed alongside the sense of cyber-optimism. These more critical views hardened in the 2010s as scholars saw democratic gains slowing or even reversing and observed a reassertion of power by traditional media and political institutions. Part of the reappraisal came from critical scholars who had documented earlier eras of over-exuberance and unfulfilled promise (Curran et al., 2012; Fuchs, 2014). Part came from empiricists whose studies and experiments revealed a rather more complex picture of digital media adoption (Tufekci, 2014a; Coleman, 2017).

A key problem with early empirical studies of the internet and politics was that initial expectations had been set too high. They were based on an idealistic set of assumptions and a positivistic scientific stance. They frequently took a technologically determinist approach that believed if new hi-tech capabilities were created they would automatically be taken up. Such optimism has been common during past advances in ICT development (Bell, 1973; Meyrowitz, 1985; Sola Pool, 1990; Castells, 1996). But, they failed to factor in the socio-economic, political and cultural factors that are also decisive influences on ICT creation and use. As Winston (1998) demonstrated, history is littered with rejected gadgets and the delayed adoption of useful technologies. The typewriter was originally patented in 1714, the fax machine in 1847, the television in 1884 and the world wide web conceived in 1945; all well before they became available on a mass scale (see also Curran, 2009).

This base problem was repeated during the digital revolution (see Lievrouw and Livingstone, 2006; Fenton, 2009; Curran et al., 2012; Fuchs, 2014). Those promoting the new world were more likely to be entrepreneurs and journalists rather than social scientists or historians. Claims were driven by speculation, and continually focused on new 'killer applications' that were confidently predicted to supersede older media systems. But, as Fuchs (2014: 37) explained, new communication technologies do not just appear in a vacuum and then conquer all before them:

> Media are techno-social systems, in which information and communication technologies enable and constrain human activities ... in a dynamic and reflexive process that connects technological structure and human agency.

A similar problem existed with optimists' assumptions about democracy and the 'public sphere'. The ideal model of democracy aspired to in these techno visions, was a more direct, inclusive and deliberative one, as imagined in the Athenian polis or early European bourgeois public spheres (Habermas, 1989). New ICTs would somehow recreate this communicative architecture so restoring what had been lost. However, this approach side-stepped the many non-technical obstacles to such forms of democracy (see Polat, 2005; Brandenburg, 2006; Dahlberg, 2007; Davis, 2007b). Such a democratic model does not exist in today's 'actually existing democracies' (Fraser, 1992), except to a limited extent in small island or city states. The huge majority of citizens in democracies reside in large, complex representative ones with limited participation for most. As Habermas himself conceded in his later work (1996) not much of his mass mediated public sphere conception is really applicable now.

Instead, so much civil society communication takes place in multiple linked networks or public 'sphericules' (Gitlin, 1998; Curran, 2000) rather than *a public sphere.*

Connected to misconceptions about democracy are misunderstandings about public participation. The problematic assumption is that most people want to participate in national-level politics and to use the web to do so. But, as a series of early studies in the UK revealed, the introduction of new media political fora did little to increase public engagement with Westminster politics (Hansard, 2004; Ward et al., 2005; Lusoli et al., 2006; Ofcom, 2007). In the lead up to the 2005 UK election, Ward et al. (2005) found that only 2% of people had visited their local MP's website and 5% the Parliamentary website in the last twelve months. In a more recent Swedish study (Dimitrova et al., 2014) pre-election surveys found that 39.6% of citizens had visited the site of the tabloid paper *Attanbladat* but no political party website had been viewed by more than 3.6% in the same period. As Chapter 7 showed many citizens are no less interested in politics per se; they are just turning their back on traditional politics and media and participating in other ways. For Brandenburg (2006: 218):

> public discontent with political elites and representative systems, in general does not amount to a widespread demand for inclusion in a deliberative system that affords active participation.

Lastly, techno-optimists who looked to the new digital era for democratic improvement, assumed the market-led expansion of new ICTs could only be good. Although governments everywhere have been instrumental in encouraging the roll-out, the digital world has been above all a commercial endeavour. Corporate profit motives rather than social and political ideals have driven its expansion. Weakly regulated market conditions have resulted in non-democratic outcomes.

Thus, new ICTs have become just as subject to concentration and conglomeration as old media. First, Microsoft and Apple very quickly came to dominate the home computer market in the last decades of the twentieth century. In the late 1990s, 90% of PCs sold world-wide had Microsoft software. For Srnicek (2016) mature economies have become highly dependent on 'platform capitalism' with an increasing amount of commerce operating through a small number of niche platforms. Apple, Amazon, Facebook, Google, Spotify, YouTube, Uber, Microsoft and others have exploited their monopoly positions accordingly. Thus, by 2012, Google was being used in 90% of searches in the UK. In the US, Apple was involved in 70% of all legal music downloads, YouTube provided the platform for 73% of online videos and Amazon was used to purchase a fifth of all goods bought online (Freedman, 2012). If one wants to participate in politics and communication, whether a President or NGO campaigner, they all have to work with these platforms.

The other consequence of market-led digitization is inequality and a set of 'digital divides'. These exist on many levels: between international regions and nations, and within nations. Several early studies noted that internet access and political participation was correlated with income, education and other demographic factors (Golding and Murdock, 2000; Norris, 2001; Bonfadelli, 2002). Two decades on and large divides persist. In 2016, internet penetration rates were 100% in Iceland, 93% in the UK and Sweden, but only 52% in South Africa, 35% in India and less than 10% in some of the poorest nations of Africa and Asia (Internet Live Stats, 2017). Large differences have also been found within countries, including wealthy democracies with high penetration rates (Dutton and Blank, 2013; Curran, 2016: 8). In 2013, 92% of US homes with an annual income over $100,000 had web access compared with only 48% of those earning less than $25,000 a year.

Each of these factors meant that optimists' visions were rarely borne out in reality. As various studies came up with their data, early enthusiasm was replaced by more sober assessments of new media adoption. In terms of governance and party communication, research showed that politicians and administrators were slow to adopt the deliberative and interactive elements of digital media (Gulati, 2004; Jackson and Lilleker, 2004; Chadwick, 2006; Davis, 2009b). Quite simply, those at the top did not have the time or resources to interact on a personal level, in person or electronically. Instead websites and email were more likely to be used as tools for political organization or service delivery, to be used as an additional one-to-many promotional medium. For example, Jackson and Lilleker's analysis of UK MP websites (2004) recorded that only 4.3% attempted online surveys, and 1.6% used online discussion forums. A few years later, Davis (2009b) found that less than one in five MPs used email to communicate directly and extensively with their constituents. Instead they used the new channels more to communicate with other politicians, journalists and those within their existing political networks. After two decades of observing digital democracy applications in Westminster and other parliaments, Coleman's (2017) assessment was that 'huge opportunities' had been missed. Despite multiple reviews and digital initiatives, governance was still very much a top-down and insular affair. Real discussion and deliberation from outside rarely fed into policy-making machines.

Similar outcomes were recorded in established political parties. Much was made of Barack Obama's use of digital media to engage ordinary supporters. However, the large majority of online activity was not about increased dialogue or deliberation with supporters but instead involved fund-raising, organization and mass promotion (Hendricks and Denton, 2010; Magleby, 2011). Although 83% of Obama's donors were small, they only supplied 26% of the funds raised in his 2008 election, leaving his campaign still dependent on a few big benefactors (Farrar-Myers, 2011: 52). Studies show that social media has become as dominated by a limited number of politicians as mainstream media is. Bode and Dalrymple (2016) found that a wealthy political elite in US politics remained highly prominent on Twitter. Van Aelst et al. (2017) recorded the same in their study of Twitter in Belgian politics. At one end, 44% of political candidates had fewer than two hundred followers. At the other, the top 8%, almost all with existing high legacy-media profiles, had more than 5,000 followers. And, for those democratic leaders most able to use social media, such as Barack Obama, Donald Trump and Narendra Modi, follower numbers have now reached the tens of millions.

Meanwhile, governments everywhere, both democratic and authoritarian, have become more proficient at controlling, censoring and tracking online activities (Diamond and Plattner, 2012; Tufekci, 2014a; Hintz, 2015; Woolley and Howard, 2017). The Edward Snowden files revealed just how far Western governments had gone in using the net for surveillance of citizens and governments. Woolley and Howard (2017) found high levels of social media abuse, automated social media bots, and junk news creation and dissemination in all nine countries they looked at, including in the US, Canada and Germany, as well as Russia and China. In 2015, there were an estimated 50,000 Chinese internet police routinely monitoring individuals, disabling critical sites and launching cyber-attacks on interest groups (Fenton, 2016a: 177). Approximately 50,000 automated accounts, active in the US 2016 election, were operated from Russia and reached some 126 million citizens' Facebook accounts (Narayana et al., 2018). As Tufekci (2014a) explained, the current combination of big data, computational methods, modelling, behavioural science, real-time social network experiments, platform power and 'algorithmic governance', has provided a frightening combination of tools for monitoring and influencing citizens without their knowing. The outcome is rather more far-reaching than George Orwell ever envisaged.

The limits of e-participation and e-deliberation have also been documented in the world of NGOs and social movements. Once again, encouraging more exchange and deliberation using internet tools has proved difficult and impractical. Such difficulties were observed in local online forums such as Minnesota E-Democracy, (Dahlberg, 2001; Dahlgren, 2005; Polat, 2005; Wikland, 2005), as well as across established NGOs such as Amnesty, Oxfam and Friends of the Earth (Pickerill, 2004; Kavada, 2005, 2015).

Returning to the new social movements of the last decade, later reviews sound rather more restrained when discussing the part played by ICTs (Fuchs, 2014; Tufekci, 2014a; Fenton, 2016b; Coleman, 2017). One survey of participants of the Tahrir Square demonstrations (Fuchs, 2014: 85), recorded that 93% of people thought face-to-face interactions were a primary means of communication, with 92% saying the same about television. In contrast, 42% mentioned Facebook and 13% Twitter. Most of the movements which had harnessed the new digital 'logic of connective action', from Occupy Wall Street to Tarir Square, either rapidly declined or were suppressed by state authorities (see Chapter 8). Web-based activism works well for rapid engagement and organization but has been poor for building lasting networks, developing long-term policies or impacting on mainstream politics.

The digital era has also had a mixed impact when it comes to democratizing the supply of news and political information. On the one hand, it has undoubtedly increased pluralism and broken down the gate-keeping power of national media, political parties and institutions. However, while large numbers of alternatives have appeared, few have managed to gain a strong foothold or long-term financial stability. By 2009 (Pew, 2009b), 7% of online news sites, almost all digital versions of legacy operations, drew 80% of news traffic. In 2015, legacy online sites still dominated in the US and UK, taking eight of the top ten spots in both countries. Many high-profile new entrants, such as *OhmyNews*, *openDemocracy*, *Vice* and *Vox*, have struggled to be profitable and had to scale back (Curran, 2016; Benson, 2017). Research has also made clear that most alternative sites remain heavily dependent on legacy producers for core content and traffic (Allan, 2006; Quandt et al., 2006; Reese et al.,

2007; Benson, 2017). According to Reese et al.'s study (2007) 99% of the content of blogging sites covered already published material, just with added analysis or comment.

Meanwhile, although legacy news operations retain a dominant web presence, paradoxically, their operations have been devasted by the digital economy itself. The long-term business model of journalism, which has relied on a limited number of news operations with stable advertising and audiences, has now broken down (see Chapter 5). Earlier studies in the US and UK (Cohen, 2002; Singer, 2003; Kovach et al., 2004) began recording these negative internet-related impacts. More than a decade later and web-based changes have left much of the sector in crisis (see Anderson et al., 2015; Pew, 2016c; Reuters, 2017). Competition has intensified in every direction, globally as well as locally. News content, including investigative journalism and scoops, has become devalued as it can be instantly adapted or copied by rivals. Advertising, including once lucrative classified advertising, has mostly gravitated towards specialist advertising platforms, news aggregators and click-bait sites, none of which fund traditional journalism.

The digital environment has had problematic consequences for legacy news content too. Mainstream operations have increasingly turned to watching and following rivals online, ready to steal and reproduce any big story or eyeball-catching content (see Davis, 2007b; Phillips, 2009). They have inadvertently participated in the spread of 'junk' or 'fake' news pumped out and disseminated using social media on an increasing scale (Woolley and Howard, 2017; Narayana et al., 2018). Such fake news was particularly prominent in the 2016 US election. In 2018 Facebook, by far the most dominant global social media platform, was heavily criticized by law-makers in the UK, US and the EU. Hearings revealed its blasé attitude to safeguarding its users' privacy, selling their data to companies such as Cambridge Analytica, and poor attempts to deal with widespread fake news and computational propaganda operations.

In effect, increased plurality turned out to be something of a myth. All alternative news and comment sites rely on old, off-line news operations, but such operations are becoming a shadow of what they once were. News media fragmentation has set in. There are clear problems of veracity and reliability leading to declining trust in legacy news. Seeing the differences between unreliable and poorly resourced news from legacy operations, and hyperbolic coverage and propaganda, became less clear.

Digital Democracy Now: Fragmented, Anarchic and Polarized Public Spheres?

This last part briefly evaluates the positions taken by the two opposing camps before then attempting to assess the wider implications for democracy of recent digital developments.

In constructing future research agendas, it is important to move on from past mistakes, clarify conceptual starting points and use robust research methods. What is clear is that, all too often, new media scholarship has relied on simplistic ideas, positivist assumptions and models, and its funding is frequently determined by political and business agendas. There is also a widespread tendency to use online tools to generate data, ignoring the significant biases that then occur (see summary in Tufekci, 2014b). Such methods generate large-scale survey data which is non-representative, self-selecting and self-reported, and thus not a realistic public sample. It underplays the human biases and fallibilities of the algorithms created for such research too; something ignored all too often as findings are then used in institutional practices (O'Neill, 2017).

On one side, it is now apparent that less critical empiricists and techno-optimists must adjust their frameworks and norms. For one, that means avoiding a technologically determinist starting point. As some scholars in media, and science and technology studies (STS), have stressed (MacKenzie and Wajcman, 1999; Lievrouw and Livingstone, 2006: 4) 'recombinant' and 'social shaping' approaches are key. In these, ICTs are part of 'a mutual shaping process in which technological development and social practices are co-determining'.

Second, they must forget about past, ideal models of direct democracy. Instead, they need to enquire and experiment with 'actual existing democracies' (Fraser, 1992), with their large, representative and multi-layered elements. They are made up of smaller sphericules and fluid networks rather than large, stable public spheres, with multiple areas of expertise and limited scope for wider participation and deliberation. Thus, it should be asked: how might such representative democracies in large, complex societies, be changing with the internet and associated ICTs? How might political and media actors and institutions be significantly altered by these, become unsustainable, or replaced by other types of actor and institution?

Third, the emphasis on the 'new' and different should not blind researchers to the maintenance and continuing influences of the 'old' or the mundane. One should not dismiss new media being used in similar but not identical 'old' ways, nor old media and practices adjusting to the new media environment. Neither should one ignore 'soft' and informal, emotional and non-rational forms of political engagement (Pickerill, 2006; Butsch, 2007). Digital political communication, like non-digital, does not have to be formal, direct and deliberative. Indeed, much of it is not.

On the other side, critical scholars need to acknowledge the extent of change facilitated by the latest wave of new ICTs. These have not simply resulted in established institutions and power structures reasserting themselves after a period of disruption. Yes, corporation conglomeration, political centralization and top-down hierarchies, inequality and abuses of power, still continue. However, it is also important to note that real tipping points have been reached in many foundational institutions and media that have traditionally sat at the heart of national democratic systems. Legacy news media, political parties and the economic systems of nations, as well as the bases and forms of communicative power, are changing substantially; and the digital era is a powerful part of that change.

Is there a bigger picture now developing that all can see? Such stock-taking is difficult as it is impossible to keep up with the multiple changes, new players and types of application emerging. It is likely that as soon as this manuscript has gone into production, important new technologies, platforms, organizations and apps will appear. However, a few key trends are currently fairly clear. Cumulatively, they suggest that what still existed of the mediated public sphere, has metamorphosed into something quite different.

The most dramatic shift has been in the reconfiguration of many organizations that traditionally linked citizens, public discourse and institutional politics. Political and business networks are rather less coherent and stable than they once were (Mizruchi, 2013; Naim, 2013; Davis, 2018). They may be richer than ever, but their positions of power and influence are increasingly temporary. Established political parties are being wiped out, destabilized and fragmented (see Chapter 4). They are riven by internal splits and camps or challenged by brand new mass parties that can appear in months (Chiaramonte and Emanuele, 2017; Hershey, 2017; Conti et al., 2018). New social movements are equally precarious. They can organize rapidly but decline and fizzle out just as quickly (Tufekci, 2014a; Fenton, 2016b; Coleman, 2017). As some have recently suggested (Bode and Dalrymple, 2016; Chadwick and Stromer-Galley, 2016: 282), 'parties are renewing themselves from the outside in', operating like new social movement networks and offering 'dual identifications' with parties and single issues. But, such a shift, if the new 'connective action' movements are anything to go by, simply suggests further declines in stability and longevity.

The news media and political information ecology is now unrecognizable from what existed at the start of the twenty-first century. Legacy news operations now struggle to retain the small fraction of paying customers they once had (see Chapter 5). They operate with ever diminishing budgets, produce diluted and suspect content, and are increasingly viewed with suspicion and mistrust (Reuters, 2017; Pew, 2017).

Instead of relatively extensive, shared and stable public spheres, we now have volatility, fragmentation and polarization. The potential for new ICTs to produce such fragmentation and polarization was initially suggested in the work of Sunstein (2001) and Rheingold (2002). Individuals, given the choice would gravitate towards certain news and information sources and opinions and cut themselves off from others. A decade later and such predictions have become manifested in multiple ways (Turow, 2012; Dunlap et al., 2016; Ofcom, 2017; Pew, 2017; Reuters, 2017; Narayana et al., 2018; Sunstein, 2018). Democrats choose certain affiliated legacy media and share news items with specific allied networks. Republicans do the same with quite different media and networks. Certain news stories, fake or legitimate, only circulate across social media networks, never to be seen by others. The young increasingly get news from social media on mobile phones while the old get far more of it from television. The gaps, between left and right, old and young, highly and poorly educated, wealthy and poor, politically engaged and apathetic, are opening up further than ever. Thus, comes the incredulity of different sides about how and why others think what they do around key policy areas and vote as they do in recent elections.

What is emerging in many democracies of all kinds is a sort of anarchic, wild west of a public sphere where the standard norms, values and rules of engagement have been jettisoned. In this environment, information gushes out from and to every direction. Trusted sources and neutral commentators are harder to find, and are continually undermined by other sources, legitimate or otherwise. It becomes ever harder to separate 'fake' or 'junk' news from real, authentic news. In the invisible networks of digital media, float all manner of automated twitter bots, troll and fake review factories, big data harvesters, state-sponsored propagandists, click-bait news creators, shadowy political consultancies and populist rhetoricians, each seeking to covertly target consumer-citizens. Understandably, trust, even in long-established legacy media and legitimate public institutions, has declined markedly (Mair, 2013; Pew, 2017; Reuters, 2017). In effect, the public sphere is disintegrating and that is proving very difficult for democracies everywhere.

Conclusion

In many respects, the impacts and influences of new ICTs on political and media systems can still be analysed and interpreted using existing methods and frameworks. In other respects, that will no longer do. The pace of these shifts, and the disruption they are bringing to democracies, suggest something more profound is happening. Some of this disruption is undoubtedly beneficial and progressive but some is also extremely destabilizing and regressive.

Such digitally facilitated trends as described here include: the seismic shocks to political organizational structures and mass news media; the migration of users to social media, bringing fragmentation and polarization; the exponential rise in information and opinion with its problems of veracity, accountability and overload; the power of electronic surveillance and big data; and the complexity of regulating such virtual and international communication systems and platforms.

Whether these developments are considered equalizing and positive or normalizing and negative, together they are breaking up what still existed of national, mediated public spheres, and completely reconfiguring citizen-media-political relations. Supporters of healthy democracies have long supported moves towards achieving greater pluralism, space for more voices to be heard, greater information abundance and the end of biased gate-keeping arbiters in politics and media. New ICTs have helped bring about these things but, perhaps, they have gone too far, moving beyond what is optimal for large, representative democracies to function?

11

Globalization, the State and International Political Communication

This chapter draws together some of the diverse literatures on globalization and international political communication. Both are interdisciplinary topics with strongly contested accounts and interpretations of their development. Each complicates national politics and communication and poses complex challenges to states of all kinds.

Neither topic offers a clearly defined territory in the field of political communication. Globalization criss-crosses several other disciplines, including international relations, global trade and finance, human migration, popular culture and the environment. International political communication is an ambiguous concept, as theories of democracy and public communication have traditionally developed out of state-based notions of governance, citizenship, and mediated public spheres. However, there is no doubt that both increasingly impinge on nation-state politics, media and communication. Thus, each can be considered to be disruptive forces with the potential to thoroughly destabilize contemporary democracies.

The chapter is in three parts. The first sketches out the wide-ranging debates on globalization that emerged in the 1990s and 2000s. For sceptics responding to the early enthusiasm of hyperglobalists, globalization was neither clear cut nor as positive as made out. It was damaging to nation-state democracy as governments were increasingly constrained in a number of policy areas. In contrast, for its many advocates, globalization has been largely positive for states and the global citizenry as a whole. Peace, stability, economic growth and multi-cultural understanding have improved as global governance and a wider sense of cosmopolitan identity have spread.

The second part reviews a parallel set of debates on international political communication. For critics, the transnational mediascape, as it developed at the end of the twentieth century, was one dominated by mainly Western-based states and multinationals. Its expansion was driven by national competition, conflict, propaganda and the promotion of Western-style capitalist democracy. For its supporters, however, something more pluralist, multi-directional and 'glocalized' has managed to emerge this century. This has interwoven the disparate parts of an international civil society, generating a nascent global public sphere in the process.

The third part takes stock of these trends over the last decade, reviewing recent developments with rather less enthusiasm. Many of the foundational elements of the globalist vision – the end of the Cold War, agreements on trade and nuclear proliferation, the international trend towards liberal democracy and capitalism – have seemed to stutter or reverse. International finance has extended its influence while national economies have floundered. A new set of transnational digital companies have grown rapidly, often undermining local economies and polities as they go. As nationalism has thrived again, the existing international political and economic order has been significantly weakened. We have returned to a new cold war era with additional forms of cyber warfare and propaganda. Under such circumstances, the turn to 'tough-guy' nationalist political leaders from Trump and Putin to Erdogan and Duterte is no surprise.

Globalization and the Disruption of Nation-state Democracy?

There are many competing definitions of 'globalization'. As one simple summary puts it (Steger, 2009: 15):

> Globalization refers to the expansion and intensification of social relations and consciousness across world-time and world-space.

Taken like that, globalization is not new. Modern (Westphalian) nation states, since conception, have always had to deal with other states and engage with affairs beyond their borders. Over the last century, issues of empire, national security, trade, migration and cultural identity have regularly occupied the minds of national leaders (Held and McGrew, 2003). The concept remains contested in multiple ways, in terms of: periodization (when, definable eras), normative values (good or bad), core elements (political, economic, cultural, environmental), whether unidirectional or multidirectional, an inevitable, continuous process or something cyclical and reversable (see overviews in Steger, 2009; Cohn, 2016; Martell, 2017).

Despite its long history, the term became far more common from the 1990s onwards as politicians, commentators and publics became more focused on its varied international flows and influences. The topic led to scholars across a range of fields, from media and culture to high finance, re-engaging with their subjects through the lens of globalization. What seemed evident in all such accounts was that national politics, media and communication appeared to be increasingly interconnected with the global.

Advances in transport and communication have facilitated more international, mobile networks of industry, finance, culture, communication and people. Since the mid-nineteenth century, there has been a proliferation of international laws, treaties, institutions, banks and regional organizations (Held, 2002). An increasing amount of state politics has become bound up with inter-governmental and transgovernmental exchanges, covering: industrial policy, labour markets and immigration, finance and investment, international crime and terrorism, energy and food production, media and communication, environmental concerns, transport policy, welfare systems and culture. All this has stark implications for nation-based political and media systems.

This first section now briefly sketches out opposing interpretations of how globalization is affecting national politics. On the one side, sceptics and critics see it as being driven by the non-democratic agendas of financialization, Western imperialism, neoliberal economics and multinational corporations. This erodes nation-state autonomy and imperils democracy. On the other side, advocates argue that globalization has become more multi-dimensional and multi-directional. Ultimately, it has strengthened nations by boosting global prosperity and stability.

Globalization became a buzz word in the 1990s, embraced across business, politics and academia. Early 'hyperglobalizers', as they became labelled (Ohmae, 1990, 1995; Reich, 1991; Albrow, 1996), described the phenomenon as an inevitable historical process. Sceptics soon responded (Hirst and Thompson, 1996; Rhodes, 1997; Cerny et al., 2005). They were quick to point out that previous eras appeared more 'globalized' and that many current trends were more about regionalization than globalization. More importantly, their concern was with a concept being heavily promoted by self-interested technocrats, political and business leaders. It was a self-fulfilling vision that failed to engage with the implied threats to national sovereignty and democracy.

For Rhodes (1997) these trends contributed to state control being 'hollowed out'. Power was being ceded upwards to supranational bodies and powerful market actors. Politicians and bureaucrats increasingly saw their nations as participants in a global competition, for investment, trade, people, ideas, resources and innovation. This was leading to a 'race to the bottom' as welfare states, with labour and consumer rights, were transformed into 'competition states' with disempowered citizens (Hutton, 1996; Crouch, 2004; Cerny et al., 2005). Inevitably, such developments undermined and fragmented national sovereignty (Mann, 1997; Habermas, 2001). As Habermas (1999) concluded, states were being left with a stark choice: embrace the new competition orthodoxy on globalization, retreat into 'ethnocentric protectionism', or as Tony Blair's New Labour and Bill Clinton's Democrats attempted, chart an awkward 'third way' path. Arguably, Habermas's three options remain the same today.

The main concerns of these authors and other sceptics was that globalization was really about the roll-out of a 'turbo-charged' form of international capitalism (see also Strange, 1996; Scholte, 1997; Keane, 2001; Stiglitz, 2002). This began when the Bretton Woods system of international exchange rate regulation was abandoned in the 1970s. It proceeded with the deregulation of global trade and finance in the 1980s and 1990s. It was promoted through international economic institutions, such as the IMF (International Monetary Fund), World Bank and WTO (World Trade Organization, previously GATT). Their 'Washington consensus' economic blueprint for dealing with struggling nations always demanded the same: less state intervention, more privatization, reduced trade barriers and free-flowing international financial investment.

In addition to dealing with international institutions, states also had to contend with the rapid growth of transnational corporations (TNCs) and international financiers. By 2001, 65,000 such TNCs were responsible for $18.5 trillion worth of goods and services and 70% of all trade (Held and McGrew, 2003: 26). By 2004 the fifty largest TNCs each had revenues greater than the GNPs (Gross National Product) of 133 UN Member States (Willetts, 2008: 333). By 2007, on the eve of the financial crash, corporate foreign direct investment (FDI) had grown to $1.8 trillion annually (Martell, 2017: 126–7) and over £3 trillion worth of currency was being traded on international exchanges on a daily basis (Steger, 2009: 49). The international banking system operated funds of $516 trillion or 35 times the GDP value of the US economy, or ten times that of the entire world economy (Cable, 2009: 146).

The consequences were that nations were less able to manage their own economies with respect to trade, investment, currency values, inflation, state borrowing and industrial production. They also felt obliged to offer favourable tax and regulatory regimes to attract international companies and investors. National governments could be thrown into crisis by decisions made elsewhere in the international system. Thus, came Britain's failed attempt to join the ERM in 1992, the Asian financial crisis of 1997, or the dot.com bubble in the United States in 2000. But it took the 2007–8 financial crisis to show that all nations, the biggest included, had limited means to deal with the fallout when huge international banks and corporations started to collapse.

Moving beyond economics and finance, it has also became clear that a wider series of global problems are producing difficult challenges to national polities. These have come to include global warming, energy and food supply security, population expansion and migration, international crime and tax evasion, waste and environmental degradation. In each case, these problems are becoming more acute (see Ferguson and Mansbach, 2012; Cohn, 2016; Martell, 2017). Most nations, even those the size of China or the US, cannot fix them unilaterally.

Despite the strong case made by sceptics, as the 2000s advanced globalization advocates grew in numbers and strength. There were two reasons for this. For one, scholars stepped back from their stronger visions of hyperglobalization. Instead, 'transformationalists' (Held and McGrew, 2007) or 'moderate globalizers' (Cohn, 2016), presented more nuanced and complex accounts of change. As many argued, states might be more intertwined with the global but, that did not mean they were being over-run. They preferred the terms 'reconstituted' or 'transformed', suggesting new configurations strengthened as well as weakened national sovereignty (Mann, 1997; Slaughter, 2000; Keane, 2001; Held, 2002; Swank, 2002; Richards and Smith, 2002). Slaughter (2000) described a process whereby each government was 'disaggregating into its component institutions', each of which linked horizontally with external state equivalents. This 'transgovernmentalism' suggested that states were more active in such international developments. Thus, as Richards and Smith (2002) maintained, on balance, the 'reconstituted' state remained 'the dominant actor', something affirmed by many international political economists (see Cohn, 2016).

Second, globalization had become the new orthodoxy of politicians of both centre-left and centre-right parties across the globe. Business leaders, technocrats and commentators all fully embraced the trends. An international consensus developed in a number of areas of politics, each of which spurred positive associations with globalization. These included notions of liberal democracy, free trade and free-market economics (see Cohn, 2016; King, 2017). After 1989, Russia and much of Eastern Europe began adopting the template of Western capitalist democracy. As the Cold War finished Francis Fukuyama declared that the world had arrived at 'the end of history' (1992). China ended its international isolation, embracing international markets and institutions. Think tanks (IDEA, EIU) recorded the steady advance of democracy across the world. There were also signs of global consensus in several policy areas, such as reducing nuclear arsenals, agreements on land mines and chemical weapons, banning CFCs, commitments to minimize global warming, and international cooperation in tackling organized crime and terrorist movements. If there remained disagreements on how to tackle these issues, there was still a wide acknowledgement of the problems and the need to cooperate on fixing them.

Such developments encouraged scholars to envisage and embrace a new future of international governance. Beck (2006) implored political leaders to move beyond state-centric 'methodological nationalism', to adopt an alternative 'cosmopolitan vision' of global governance for world citizens. Held (2003) and Fraser (2007) sketched out the international values and guiding principles that would apply, such as 'inclusiveness', 'equality', 'autonomy' and 'impartialist reasoning'. Others offered competing philosophies for achieving 'liberal internationalism' or 'cosmopolitan democracy', 'radical democratic pluralism' or 'deliberative/discursive democracy' (see McGrew's overview, 2002). Certainly, there seemed to be concrete steps being taken across international institutions to spread power and influence beyond large, Western powers. When the GATT was replaced by the WTO in 1995, it was on a more democratic basis. In 2009, the voting strengths of the US, UK, Germany and others at the World Bank and IMF were significantly reduced, as those from China and other growing economies were upped.

In parallel to discussions of global governance came accompanying accounts of an emerging global civil society (Anheier et al., 2001; Kaldor, 2003; Della Porta and Tarrow, 2004; Albrow and Glasius, 2008). As international institutions and corporations grew so too did the number and size of INGOs (international non-governmental organizations). INGO numbers had grown from 176 in 1909 to 47,098 in 2000 (Held and McGrew, 2003: 12). By 2005 some 2,800 of them had gained 'consultative status' at the United Nations (Willetts, 2008: 339). In 2006, 389 achieved 'participatory status' in the Council of Europe (Albrow et al., 2008: 324–5). Thus, the same transnational architecture that had developed to support international governance was also supporting a global civil society of INGOs and citizenship.

Quite separately, others enthused about the positive effects of the global economic system on nations both rich and poor. Swank (2002) and Mosley (2003) found that international investment occurred regardless of levels of taxation and regulation, being influenced more by other basic economic indicators and factors like security and political stability. States that had actively embraced international corporations and investment had been rewarded with increased growth, productivity and employment (Keane, 2001; Gilpin, 2001; Swank, 2002). Indeed, the growth rates of several developing economies in Asia and Latin America rose steadily and at rather higher rates than those of developed economies. Greater cooperation on trade and integration across regional markets such as NAFTA, ASEAN and the EU, was sustaining growth, employment and improved living conditions. This all fed through to declines in poverty and improvements in health, education and life expectancy. In 1990, 36% of the global population were classified as 'living in poverty' (living on less than $1.25 per day), but by 2011 the number had dropped to 15%. Likewise, global life expectancy increased from 64 in 1990 to 71 in 2013 (Martell, 2017: 144–6).

In effect, through the 2000s, a broader political and economic global vision had achieved a degree of international consensus and appeared to be producing multiple positive outcomes. This vision was based on international cooperation, global institutions, liberated markets, free trade and free flows of capital. When the great financial crisis hit in 2007–8, leading nations from China to the US and Europe came together in a new spirit of cooperation. Central bankers everywhere pulled together and managed to keep the global financial system from collapsing. Their joint efforts did much to bring the world economy back from the brink.

International Political Communication

In many ways, the very notion of international political communication is problematic. This is because theories of politics, media and democracy have been conceived in relation to boundaried nation states (see Habermas, 1989, 2001; Keane, 1991; Dahl, 1999). Government, party and mass media communication is primarily directed to national citizens about national concerns. Ruling administrations are held to account via national elections. So, what exactly is international political communication?

Those tackling the topic tend to take one of two conflicting paths. The first interprets international political communication as being an arena in which nation states compete for definitional advantage over global public discourse. Nations, particularly rich Western ones, disseminate their news and culture beyond their borders to further their interests, be they commercial, cultural, political or military. The second pathway focuses less on nation-state media and communication and looks more towards other organizations and communication formats. It offers a positive vision of an increasingly connected and multi-directional, global communicative architecture. Like globalization advocates, this envisages the spread of global civil society and a sense of cosmopolitan citizenship. In effect, it foresees a global public sphere emerging, one that can counteract nation-state rivalries and nationalism.

For the first group, although global news operations have spread, publics and most coverage remain far more nationally than internationally focused. The actual viewing figures for transnational news operations have been fairly tiny next to national or local outputs (Curran, 2002; Sparks, 2005). What is reported on a daily basis tends to be more 'soft news'. As Cottle and Rai (2008: 175) discovered, only 6.3% of international news reporting of *CNNI*, *BBC World*, *Fox News* and *Sky*, could be considered depth, contextualized or investigative reporting (see also Aalberg and Curran, 2012). What constitutes the main 'hard' reporting topic in international coverage is conflict and war (Herman and Chomsky, 1988; Bennett and Paletz, 1994; Thussu and Freedman, 2004; Knightley, 2004; Thussu and Freedman, 2012). Such content is repackaged for national audience consumption, generating a sense of national rather than international identity and comprehension (Downey and Koenig, 2006; Eide et al., 2008; Hanitzsch and Mellado, 2011; Dencik, 2012). Thus, coverage of 9/11, the 2003 Iraq invasion, and responses to publishing cartoons of the Prophet Mohammed in 2005, was reframed in each case according to nation and region.

For McNair (2017), international political communication is in the main about conflict; the reporting of war and the communication operations of nations embroiled in war, from the Vietnam War to George W. Bush's 'war on terror'. To this end, governments attempt to manage national and international media coverage of rival nations, most especially in times of war. In effect, they are engaged in the production of rival national propaganda campaigns. Authors such as Miller (Miller, 1994, 2004; Miller and Sabir, 2012), and Herman and Chomsky (1988; Herman and Peterson, 2011) have extensively documented the global propaganda operations of the US and UK, as they attempt to demonize the enemy and justify military aggression (see also Stauber and Rampton, 2003).

Whether reporting conflict or offering other types of international coverage, world news is not so much global as Western (Schiller, 1992; Boyd-Barrett and Rantanen, 1998; Thussu, 1998). For most of the twentieth century, four global news agencies, from the US, UK and France, dominated the collection and dissemination of international news to national broadcasters. By the twenty-first century, Anglo-American control was further enhanced as *Reuters* (UK) and *Associated Press* (US) built up a virtual duopoly over the wholesale international news supplier market. Of the six truly transnational news companies that came into operation, five were English language, US and UK enterprises (*CNNI, BBC World, CNBC, News Corporation, Bloomberg*) and one was not (*Al Jazeera*). In effect, Anglo-American media had been instrumental in globally promoting a particular 'Occidental' discourse (Said, 1978).

This Western dominance of international communication operates through other channels too. Since its inception there have been huge disparities between nations and regions when it comes to creating the infrastructure for the internet (Albrow et al., 2008). Internet penetration rates are over 80% in many European countries but remain less than 10% in the poorest Asian and African nations (Internet Live Stats, 2017). Curran and Witschge's (2009: 110–11) study of the international online magazine *openDemocracy*, found that 71% of contributors, and 83% of visitors, came from North America and Europe. Likewise, international popular culture over the last century has been dominated by the outputs of wealthy Western nations, in particular the US (Herman and McChesney, 1997; Zhao and Hackett, 2005; Sparks, 2007; McPhail, 2014). Everything, from Hollywood film and television to music and fast food chains, have been produced and exported on an ever-larger scale. Smaller and poorer nations, with limited budgets and/or audiences, are all the more dependent on such imports. At the start of this century, seven of the top ten transnational media corporations were American, two were Japanese, and one was French (Albrow et al., 2008: 277). In 2011, eighteen of the twenty top grossing films worldwide were made by Hollywood studios (UNESCO, 2013).

This international communication infrastructure has also served as a base for exerting various forms of 'soft power' (Nye, 2004), persuading foreign nations and publics in more subtle ways. Seib (2012), for example, documents how governments and others use social media and popular culture in their 'public diplomacy' as they attempt to gain ideological advantage. One such example is 'Sesame Workshop' which has developed multiple, locally shaped versions of *Sesame Street* to advance particular US values and attitudes. Shaheen (2008) and Kellner (2009) offer a similar account of Hollywood film depictions of Muslims post 9/11 and of international politics in the Bush era (all the more important given Hollywood's global impact). In the 1990s, Anholt (1998) first talked about nations developing their brands to compete in the global arena. Two decades later, a 'transnational promotional class' has emerged to advise governments on cultivating their international images, to attract investment, trade and skilled labour, as well as achieve a degree of diplomatic legitimacy (Aronczyk, 2013; Kaneva, 2014).

Together, these works give an impression that international political communication remains very much dictated by national rather than global interests. There may be much greater levels of international governance, economic exchange, migration, tourism, media and culture, as well as a heightened sense of global citizenship. However, democracy, its media and political communication, operated largely at a nation-state level. This makes any notion of an international-level public sphere fairly far-fetched (Baisnee, 2007; Dencik, 2012). What does exist on this level serves transnational political, corporate and bureaucratic elite purposes and visions rather than international public ones.

The second approach to international political communication is more global rather than national in its interpretive framework. It views the world as edging ever closer to becoming an international community. Marshall McLuhan's 'global village' perspective (1962) is an early touch point here. More recently, notions of a 'transnational public sphere' and 'global civil society' have come to the fore.

At the start of the twenty-first century there was much to suggest that this more optimistic vision was more achievable. First, as mentioned above, there seemed to be increasing areas of international consensus and cooperation in a number of diverse policy areas. As the Cold War ended, the great Western and Soviet propaganda machines were cut back. The 'war on terror' and the 'threat of radical Islam' was a trope that many rival nations, including Russia and China as well as the US and UK (Thussu and Freedman, 2012), could now share.

Second, the combination of new, cheaper communication technologies and wealthier, non-Western economies, meant that international flows of news and culture were becoming more multi-directional. In news terms, McNair (2006) and Chalaby (2009) noted the emergence of a number of more powerful national and regional news players, including *Al Jazeera, Xinhua, Russia Today* and *France 24*. Chalaby's (2009: 63) detailed study showed how a mix of new technologies, an evolving advertising industry and European harmonization policy, had together enabled a pan-European television system to develop. By 2006, some 279 million people in 32 European countries had access to such channels. Volkmer (2005) documented the liberal, internationally minded basis on which *CNNI* expanded its World operations. Likewise, Dencik (2012: 69) recorded how *BBC World* came to operate forty-one international bureaux and gained a truly global audience: 20% North American, 20% European, 17% Asian and Asia-Pacific, 15% UK and 14% Latin American.

Similar trends were also recorded in relation to popular culture outputs (Kraidy, 2005; Rantanen, 2005; Thussu, 2007). Along with the BRIC nations (Brazil, Russia, India, China), Mexico, Egypt, Hong Kong and Japan have all expanded their production and exports of popular culture, in areas of film, television, music, animation and computer games. Tunstall (2007), who had earlier documented the global spread of US media, now declared that 'the media were American'. By 2012, Japan had developed a dominant position in video games production, India's Bollywood was making twelve hundred films a year, 50% more than the USA, and China 600 a year (UNESCO, 2013). In place of Western 'cultural imperialism', a number of accounts talked instead of 'counter-flows', 'hybridization', and 'glocalization' (Tomlinson, 1999; Rantanen, 2005; Flew, 2007).

New ICTs, although unevenly adopted throughout the world, have still done much to link citizens everywhere to an emerging global communication ecology. Thus, although fixed line internet penetration is low in many poorer nations, mobile phone use and wireless web access is far higher. In 2015, only 1.2% of Africans had fixed lines but 71.2% had mobiles. In the Asia Pacific territory 11.9% had fixed lines but 90.6% had cell phones (Martell, 2017: 62). The adoption of social media is also more wide-spread than imagined. In 2012, only one of the top ten cities using Facebook was Western (London). The list was led by Bangkok, Jakarta and Istanbul. They, along with Bogota, Sao Paulo and Mexico City each had more users than the likes of New York or Los Angeles (Volkmer, 2014: 96).

The international NGO sector has also made ample use of new ICTs to develop transnational communications across an emerging global civil society network (Cottle and Lester, 2011). As this evolved there were several early examples of the 'CNN effect' (Robinson, 1999; Volkmer, 1999) or 'boomerang effect' (Keck and Sikkink, 1998), whereby global coverage forced national and international government responses. Successful such campaigns were documented by: environmentalists against polluting energy firms (de Jong, 2005; Kavada, 2005; Hutchins and Lester, 2011), anti-poverty campaigners pushing for national debt amnesties and increased aid spending (Chouliaraki, 2006; Sireau, 2009), and global justice and human rights campaigns (Bowers, 2011; Gerbaudo, 2012; Juris, 2012a).

Such trends and examples gave a growing boost to those who foresaw civil society and democratic public spheres being reproduced on a more international scale. These global communicative networks may not be recreating deliberative public spheres, but they were inspiring a sense of international citizenship and connecting national publics in more limited ways. As Volkmer (2014: 6–7) explained: 'I can live in Australia, vote in Germany, read news sources from the USA, watch live-streaming from Kenya … it is the new calibration of "polis" and "demos".' Some suggested that 'a European layer' was being added 'to the identities of Europeans' and traced the emergence of a nascent European public sphere (Trenz, 2004; Beck, 2006; Gripsrud, 2007). Others went further, predicting the creation of a global public sphere (Rantanen, 2005; Volkmer, 2005, 2014; Albrow and Glasius, 2008; Spichal, 2012). As Albrow and Glasius (2008: 10) proudly proclaimed, there was a growing sense that: 'global civil society and the global public sphere' were either 'an existing reality' or at the minimum, an 'achievable ideal'.

Back to the Future: Globalization and International Political Communication Now

Approaching the end of the second decade of the twenty-first century, there is a feeling that globalization and international communication are going 'back to the future'. On the one hand, our sense of global connectedness is as strong as ever. Satellite broadcasting and the internet propel news and information ever quicker across the planet. Signs of other cultures, ideas and values are everywhere. Flows of goods, services, people and capital continue to grow.

On the other hand, history seems to be repeating itself, albeit with a modern twist. A decade after the financial crash, the global economy remains precarious, and faith in Western-style free-market capitalism has been shaken. Like the 1930s, nationalism is on the rise with populist leaders aggressively challenging other nations, putting up trade barriers and demonizing immigrants and minorities. A new cold war has begun as Russia reasserts its imperial ambitions and Eastern European countries lurch back towards authoritarianism.

In many ways, problems can be traced back to the global financial crisis of 2007–8. For a couple of decades, the developed economies of Europe and North America seemed to have tamed the economic cycles of 'boom and bust'. Various earlier economic collapses, such as the Asian financial crisis in 1997 and the 2000 dot.com bust had been dealt with. The first international responses to the 2007–8 crash were promising. However, the global recession that followed also revealed the larger, long-term build-up of economic problems (see Krugman, 2008; Cable, 2009; UNCTAD, 2009). It became clear that financialization and waves of deregulation had hugely increased the dysfunction of the global financial system and now made economic recovery much more difficult. Nations everywhere had to bail out their banks and began flushing money around their economies. All of this then created huge debts for sovereign states, bankrupting many developed economies such as Iceland, Greece and Italy in the process. Personal debt levels also rose and welfare safety nets were severely cut back. By 2017, almost a decade after the crisis began, UK national debt was approaching 90% of GDP, France 97%, the US 108%, Greece 180% and Japan 239%. Even China, whose economic growth had been relatively unaffected, saw its debt grow to 50% (IMF, 2017).

What also became clear was the extent of growing imbalances across the international system, in terms of trade and rates of income inequality. Countries like the US and UK had been building up trade deficits for decades while others, like China, Japan and Germany had increasing surpluses. In 2013, the US had an annual trade deficit in goods and services of $701 billion. China has a trade surplus of $183 billion and Germany one of $251 billion (Cohn, 2016: 133). Although many poorer economies had grown so had inequalities within those nations, as well as between nations and regions. In 2014 the poorest two thirds of the population were gaining only 13% of world income and half the world's wealth was owned by the top 1% (Martell, 2017: 149). Indeed, the power and income of the global top 1% had become increasingly clear everywhere. In 2014, Knight Frank calculated that there were some 172,000 UHNWIs (Ultra High Net Worth Individuals) with more than $30 million of assets world-wide.

It is these ranks of the super-rich that have come to make up the ranks of the 'cosmocracy'. This highly mobile class of CEOs, political leaders, technocrats and others, moves between global cities and connected international 'hubs' with great frequency (Freeland, 2012; Birtchnell and Caletrio, 2014; Davis and Williams, 2017). They operate with minimal transparency or accountability to national publics. They are many steps removed from ordinary, nation-bound publics, often feeling more socially and culturally connected to each other than to their national citizenry.

Each of these now apparent shifts undermined the idea that Western forms of capitalism, globalization, deregulation and free trade still functioned for the greater global good. Likewise, reform of international institutions, such as the World Bank and IMF have stalled since 2010 (see accounts in Cohn, 2016). It was also clear, even before 2007, that international negotiations around free trade and environmental protections were no longer making much progress. The successes of the Uruguay round of GATT negotiations, completed in 1993, and the Kyoto Protocol on climate change signed in 1997, have not been repeated. Subsequent conventions have failed to make similar progress. Worse still, in recent years nations have started to withdraw from their earlier commitments. Added to this, international migration, after a period of relative decline during the 2000s, began increasing significantly after 2011 as a consequence of conflicts and regional poverty. By 2015 the number of migrants had grown to 320 million. This included fifteen million refugees, the highest figure for thirty years (Martell, 2017: 99). This issue added to the tensions building between nations.

Cumulatively, these developments have encouraged the return of nationalism and populist national parties. A large proportion of the rhetoric of such parties and their supporting media has involved overt attacks on globalization, liberal democratic values, cosmopolitanism and immigration (Diamond and Plattner, 2016; Inglehart and Norris, 2016; Barnett, 2017; EIU, 2017; Goodhart, 2017; Luce, 2017). Leaders such as Donald Trump, once in power, have rapidly gone about tearing up international peace and trade treaties and demonizing immigrants. Others, such as Vladimir Putin or Xi Jinping have resuscitated older claims to foreign territories, engaged in proxy wars and other expansionist tendencies abroad. European nations like Italy, Austria and Poland now have far-right populists in power. Even relatively secure and stable nations, such as Germany and Holland, have had to fend off far-right party growth by sounding tough on immigration and pandering to nationalists.

All of which suggests disturbing parallels with the 1930s depression-era trudge towards dysfunction and eventual war. For several observers (Cohn, 2016; King, 2017; Luce, 2017) the existing world order, built on Western liberalism and capitalist democracy, is breaking down. Globalization, as envisaged by its advocates, is going into reverse. In King's terms, the era of 'post-Columbus globalization' is being replaced by its 'pre-Columbus' version of isolated and uncooperative nations competing globally. A new cold war is clear to see between Russia and the West. The failure of the Arab Spring, along with erratic foreign military interventions, has increased instability across the Middle East. Several Eastern European nations are drifting back towards nationalism and authoritarianism (EIU, 2017). China, Russia and India, among other rising powers, have their alternative approaches to governance and conflicting international interests. As US hegemony continues to weaken, so a competing, weakly allied group of authoritarian capitalist states is offering their own contrary vision of globalization.

On the communication side, the new global media environment, in addition to aiding INGOs, has also created an elite-dominated form of international news. Coverage of national elections and global meetings at the UN or Davos, are framed by their norms and values (Durham, 2007; Kantola, 2009; Ojala, 2017; Knowles et al., 2017). Thus, they continue to promote the virtues of globalization and free-market economies and political parties, while ignoring the problems of declining state sovereignty, inequality and exploitation.

It is also clear that transnational digital communication can be just as undermining as enabling of nation states and the global public sphere. The digital giants of platform capitalism have even greater dominance over the new global communication architecture than their legacy predecessors (Freedman, 2012; Bagdikian, 2014; Srnicek, 2016; Birkinbine et al., 2017). In 2014, Google and Apple operating systems were contained in some 90% of smart phones and tablets worldwide, Google and Baidu accounted for 87% of all internet search activity, and Microsoft and Google web browsers were used in almost 80% of all computers (Birkinbine, 2017: 400). Amazon, YouTube, Spotify, Twitter, Weibo and others are similarly establishing dominant regional or global positions. Most of these international digital entities are undermining national economies in various ways. They avoid local taxes, basing their headquarters and operations in low-tax jurisdictions. They undercut local, tax-paying businesses and have caused the break-down of the business model of content producers in music, book publishing and journalism. Global digital networks, harnessed to international finance, have been instrumental in enabling tax evasion and avoidance schemes by TNCs and the super-rich (Shaxson, 2011; Urry, 2014; TJN, 2015).

Lastly, we have returned to a new, intensified era of international mediated conflict. Propaganda is no longer simply disseminated by nation-based news media. It is also generated and transferred through international news channels and increasingly spread through social media. Russia, North Korea and others now actively engage in 'cyber terrorism' and fake news campaigns designed to undermine national elections and destabilize rival nations (Woolley and Howard, 2017; Narayana et al., 2018). The media cold war has returned once again but now operates on multiple new levels.

Conclusion

By the 2000s, scholars and political and business leaders were all embracing a new vision of globalization that would benefit all. This would bring increased prosperity and international stability. Nation states might lose certain elements of their autonomy, but they would also gain, and humanity would benefit overall. Ideals of Western liberalism, capitalist democracy and cosmopolitan spirit appeared to unite disparate nations. Global media and new digital ecology would be part of that transformation, facilitating a new global public sphere and global civil society.

However, nearing the end of the second decade of the twenty-first century, this grand vision has proved naïve and fanciful. Current circumstances offer something rather bleaker; something that looks backward rather than forward. International points of ideological consensus have become contested again. Cooperation on trade, the environment, free markets and human rights, has faltered. Nationalism and conflict have returned even stronger. Media, both old and new, are very much part of international competition rather than exchange and cooperation.

12

Conclusions: Post-Truth, Post-Public Sphere and Post-Democracy

The Crisis of Twenty-First-Century Democracy

As Chapter 3 argued, the indicators of crisis are far clearer now than at the start of this century. Then, arguments about cycles of change and renewal over the longue durée had a clear, historical rationale. They could draw on century-long trends, such as rises in global life expectancy and wealth, new waves of nation-state democracy, or international surveys showing a continuing faith in democracy per se.

However, they can no longer simply dismiss the problem of declining levels of trust in news media, politicians and governments everywhere. Nations like the US have seen measures of income, education, health and life expectancy stalling or dropping for some time. After recording decades of new global waves of democracy, the trends have gone into reverse for most of this decade. Some established democracies have been reclassified as 'flawed democracies' (EIU, 2018). Newer or semi-democracies, such as Poland, Hungary, Turkey and Brazil, have changed course, moving back towards the authoritarian end of the spectrum. The strong adherence to democratic ideals, recorded in past world values surveys, are edging down. A greater number of citizens in democracies are more attracted to non-democratic alternatives and leaders.

The appeal of the non-democratic in many ways comes down to the fact that capitalist democracy now repeatedly fails to deliver on its promises. On the one side, this is because political sovereignty is increasingly challenged by global forces that emanate beyond borders and are entirely detached from democratic accountability structures (Chapter 11). International flows of capital, migrants and industries make national economic and welfare state management very difficult. The availability and pricing of resources, from food to energy, fluctuate wildly. Environmental problems are global and progressive with no agreement on a unified response from international leaders.

On the other side, the economic thinking that has driven Western-style capitalism since the late 1970s is no longer operating well (Chapter 9). Long established corporations, industrial regions and occupations are dying at an ever-quicker pace. Middle-class and professional incomes have stagnated for over a decade with less-skilled workers experiencing this for a lot longer. Globalization and financialization moved corporate operations and employment across the world, or siphoned investment into financial markets rather than the real economy. The new digital economy with its trading platform logic then made other companies and local high streets strain for survival or broke their business models entirely (Chapter 10). Globalization, financialization and new ICTs have also combined to move trillions in taxes out of the hands of nation states. If most democracies are built on capitalism, and capitalism is malfunctioning, then democracies are imperilled too (Streeck, 2017).

One clear response has been a rise in support for parties and politicians who either eschew core democratic principles and practices or overtly challenge them (Chapter 4). The leaders who have emerged, like Donald Trump, Boris Johnson, Marine Le Pen, Matteo Salvini and Benjamin Netanyahu, do not simply hold strong nationalist views and an attachment to 'traditional social values'. They repeatedly challenge democratic institutions, journalist autonomy, legal process, the rights of immigrants and minorities, and are happy to make up 'the truth' as they go. In many ways they sound and operate like populist, authoritarian leaders such as Recep Erdogan, Vladimir Putin, Rodrigo Duterte and Xi Jinping. Elsewhere, while such far-right populist leaders have not gained a foothold in government, they have still propelled mainstream parties in their direction in countries like the UK, Germany and Holland.

On an international scale (Chapter 11), the global vision of liberal cosmopolitanism and Western-style capitalist democracy, is also being challenged by a new world order. US economic and military influence is waning. The European Union limps on, riven with divisions and disparities. Both are confronted by Chinese, Indian and Russian alliances and alternative visions of globalization. The West can no longer rely on its superior funds and technologies to dominate world trade, geopolitical conflict and international regulatory institutions.

In effect, democracies are experiencing a level of peace-time crisis akin to that witnessed in the 1930s and 1970s. The 1930s, of which there are many parallels, led to the Second World War. The 1970s ended in the advance of a radical new conservative political and economic agenda that pulled nations in new directions. After 2007–8, no such radical agenda gained sufficient political purchase. Established institutions, media and corporations resisted fundamental change. Thus, core causal elements of the crisis have not been resolved.

The Fourth Age of Political Communication

Throughout the book, a number of longer-term trends and changes have been discussed. Over the last decade several of these have reached crucial tipping points for politics and communication. Transformational claims that once appeared hyperbolic at the start of this century, are now here or very visibly on the horizon. Cumulatively, it is not too big a leap to suggest that such changes have propelled us into a fourth age of political communication. Some of these changes have enhanced democracies while others have done more to destabilize them.

Perhaps the most obvious of these changes, and very much part of the fourth age, has been the impact of the internet and associated technologies (computer processing power, digitalization and convergence, wireless technologies, social media, platform capitalism). For Blumler (and Gurevitch, 1995, and Kavanagh, 1999), each new 'age' is associated with a big shift in the communication ecology of politics. The press dominated politics until the 1950s, limited channel national television the next few decades (Blumler's second age), and multi-channel broadcasting the last part of the twentieth century (his third age). Since 2010, increasingly, it has been online mobile communication, as it has come to reshape all aspects of commerce, culture and politics. For better or worse, the new wave of ICTs has fundamentally reconfigured social movements, political parties, capitalism, news media and social relations (Chapter 10). We still have a 'hybrid media system' (Chadwick, 2013) but the digital is becoming the dominant part of that. In very different ways, Donald Trump's 2016 victory and Jeremy Corbyn's unlikely success in the UK, are testament to the changing balance of electoral influence, away from legacy and towards digital-social media.

A second fourth-age feature is the growing instability and precariousness of the core representative organizations of democracy itself. Established parties everywhere have been fractured and split, marginalized by voters or wiped out altogether (Chapter 4). The major parties of the UK and US are utterly divided. They have been shunted to the edges of politics in nations like France, Italy and Greece, or forced into unstable coalitions in Germany, Sweden and Holland. This also poses questions to those electoral professionals who have dominated party organizations; not just questions around representation but also ones related to competence and pragmatic politics. Such experts proved redundant in the 2016 US election, the 2017 UK election and the 2018 Italian election. The margin of error in polls seems to be getting ever greater. Seasoned political commentators appear as out of touch as the political elites they observe in Washington, Berlin, London, Rome and Wellington.

Public-oriented interest groups (Chapter 8) as yet are not an adequate replacement for political parties. They increasingly struggle to compete with the wealth, power and purchased expertise of large corporations and super-rich individuals. This latter group of well-resourced, organized interests operate far better inside the technocratic maze that modern government has become. In frustration, many have turned to the practices and communication methods of new social movements, like Occupy or the Indignados. However, while these have formed and grown with great rapidity, most have also faded into obscurity with equal speed.

In effect, the organizations through which modern, representative democracies have come to operate, are themselves too insecure and fragile too effect real change. In struggling to maintain themselves, too many established parties and related groups have downgraded their roles as citizen representatives. Where alternatives offering greater representation have emerged, they have had too little stability and limited influence over core institutions of political power. In some ways, the repeated failures of such movements and parties to effect real change in 2011 and since, has left a space into which far-right populist groups and parties have moved into. On the whole, these are even less interested in representing ordinary citizens.

A third key feature of the fourth age is the break-down of what was left of nation-based public spheres (Chapters 5 and 10). With the arrival of each new communication medium, from cable TV to the internet, optimists have enthused about the rejuvenation of the public sphere. More outlets mean greater media pluralism, less top-down control and gatekeeper-led news, a greater variety of voices and exchanges made. All this is true. Unfortunately, it has also meant the complete fragmentation of the public sphere; something that is becoming clearer now that the full dynamics of web-based societies are becoming visible.

Part of the break-down is due to the fact that much of the mass, legacy news media, has been fatally weakened as its business model collapses (Chapter 5). A tiny minority of all age groups now picks up and pays for a hard print copy of a newspaper. Even fewer are willing to pay for online news. Many still view broadcast news, but advertising income for all news producers is leaching away. It is either being redistributed across a larger number of outlets or, more often, being snapped up by digital giants and entertainment media alternatives. Reporting standards have suffered accordingly with increasing amounts of content coming from PR, rivals, social media spats, op ed pieces and gossip.

Part of the break-down relates to the fragmentation and polarization that is facilitated by the online news and political information environment. At this point, more people in the thirty-six countries surveyed by Reuters (2017) get their news via algorithms and sharing on social media than by actively seeking it from recognized news operations. The different ways they seek it results in polarized publics. For example, the modes of consumption are completely different for young and old. The young are more than twice as likely to get their news from the internet (including social media) than from television, whereas the old are twice as likely to get it from television than the internet. Democrats and Republicans, Labour and Conservatives now inhabit media networks of their own making which rarely venture beyond their information ghettos. These link social media networks with professional and partisan news and political websites. Such separations also cut across rich and poor, gender and race, highly and poorly educated, activists and passive members of groups, and so on (see Chapter 7). The polarization of views and camps, on such things as the environment, state regulation, immigration and equality, is getting stronger each year.

A related fourth feature is the problem of locating truth and real 'expertise' in public discourse. For over three decades, leaders and commentators everywhere have pushed three similar narratives with great authority: globalization, free-market economics and new ICTs. Each of these was wrapped up in a discourse of inevitability that forward-thinking political and business leaders had little choice but to adopt. These developments were also promoted on the basis that they would advance the health, wealth and peace of citizens in all nations. Accordingly, leaders everywhere have embraced such shifts, jumping on every associated new innovation. Many initiatives indeed delivered much. But, at the same time, large numbers of citizens barely benefited at all economically while also feeling a lot less happy, healthy and secure. For them, the grand stories of progress have proved to be just that – stories, with only partial truths.

Meanwhile, as the amount of news and opinion available grows exponentially, so the real problem for publics and political actors alike is locating reliable and well-researched information. Unfortunately, expertise and objectivity have been compromised as all manner of politicians, institutes, think tanks and others create partial, agenda-driven and spun material (Chapters 6 and 8). In some cases, it is simply 'fake', or presented by 'fake experts' or ignorant authority figures. In an age of complexity and specialization, where risks are multi-dimensional and global, this poses ever larger conundrums for policy-makers and voters (Chapter 11).

Faith in public media has also declined substantially (Chapter 5). Even serious, long-established news operations are viewed with cynicism by a majority of people in many democracies. They are regarded as no more than propaganda or 'fake news' by sizeable minorities. Ironically, while the trends are towards increased consumption through social media, surveys reveal that people are even more distrusting of news and information from such sources (Chapter 10). This severely inhibits public understanding and rational debate (Chapter 7).

A fifth feature is the growing gap between public and private politics (Chapter 8). Public politics, even more than ever, is about projected personalities, party brands and popular culture (in part, a legacy of professionalization, Chapter 4). Both news media and parties, struggling for citizen attention, drive this shift (Chapter 6). Celebrities do politics and politicians operate as celebrities. Entertainment and policy, hyperbole and ideology, all merge seamlessly at times. Popular culture, amusing memes and gifs, flimsy propaganda and fake news are spread across online networks. Political ideas and individuals rise and fall like high-street fashions.

All this gives a distorted impression of actual politics and policy-making behind the Wizard of Oz-style curtains (Chapter 8). There, beyond the cameras and camera phones, are the invisible bureaucrats, lawyers, lobbyists and technical experts, each engaged with politicians. Reams of documentation, full of technical terms and specialist information, personal and organizational agendas, is fed to politicians with modest understandings, who then turn to horse-trading with other politicians and their intermediaries. All operate on a plane (or bubble) far distanced from the voting public and the public culture of social movements, populist media and social media networks.

Seeking Options for Democratic Renewal?

If the fourth age of political communication offers such challenges to democracy how might we think about solutions? Three approaches are briefly sketched out here. One looks to comparative work in the field, seeking to find what political and media systems work best. A second focuses on the problems of existing institutions and media and sets out good principles for reorienting them back to publics. The third comes down to rethinking the norms, values and expectations associated with modern democracy itself. Each of these approaches is not exclusive.

Starting with the first, many turn to comparative work on democracies, on their political, media and other systems. One could ask which nations are 'more democratic', 'happier', more sustainable, less divided and conflicted? This has its drawbacks. Firstly, there are disagreements on which ideals, such as equality or freedom, are more desirable for a healthy democracy to function. Secondly, no one can entirely escape the norms and values of their own system, and that includes those who set the parameters of evaluative schema in the first place (see Chapter 2).

Despite that, in 2010 (Davis, 2010a), I attempted just this, as have several other scholars and democracy-rating institutes (Freedom House, IDEA, EIU). I compared twelve very different nations on a range of measures, from their electoral systems, political checks and balances, and voter turnout, to freedom of the press scores, educational levels and news consumption, to inequality levels, per capita CO_2 emissions and confidence in institutions. The three that came out best most often were Sweden, Finland and Switzerland. In many recent such comparison tables, be it democratic indicators, human development measures or happiness surveys, these three continue to feature in the top ten. Frequently, so do the other Scandinavian countries (Norway, Denmark, Iceland), along with New Zealand, Canada, the Netherlands and Australia.

These ten have a few common denominators. They are long-established democracies and they are wealthy nations. With the exception of Canada and Australia, they are small states with between 330,000 (Iceland) and ten million people (Sweden). Canada and Australia have medium sized populations spread over large territories. Most countries cannot get around issues of wealth or size. But, there is an argument for a much greater devolution of power and finance, away from national capitals and towards the local regions, states and councils of any large nation. There is always a tendency for top-down politics and large, centralized corporations to become too distant from local economies and democracies and to disconnect themselves from publics. People may not want or feel able to engage with national-level politics, but they are much more inclined to do so with local issues and institutions. So, concerted institutional and system efforts need to be made to counter centralization and facilitate local participation.

All but one of the ten have some kind of proportional representation and only one (Canada) has a simple first-past-the-post electoral system. They are more 'consensual' rather than 'majoritarian' (Lijphart, 1984). Most of them have higher than average welfare state expenditures with higher tax rates and more coordinated market systems (Hall and Soskice, 2001). Most also support public service media and intervene more to regulate media in terms of ownership, advertising and electoral coverage. This suggests healthy democracies are more likely to be found within more consensual, coordinated systems with support for welfare, state economic intervention and public media.

That said, even Scandinavian countries have their share of disconnected billionaires, cynical voters and growing far-right populist parties. New Zealand and Australia are clear liberal market economies with weak public service media. Healthy democracy does not have a one size fits all model. However, it might be tentatively argued that the odds of a strong democracy enduring might be improved if following the Scandinavian template.

The second approach is to look at the failings of existing institutions, practices and dominant ideas in many democracies, and then to ask what principles might be applied to improve them. Again, this is problematic as there are considerable disagreements about what are the key causal factors of break-down or what goals might be more important (see Chapter 3). But, going on the arguments and conclusions of earlier chapters, I might make a few suggestions.

News media and other public information sources (e.g., libraries, legal advice, the internet) need to be treated like any other fundamental national resource, like water, education, transport etc. That means finding ways to fund and manage them properly, whether through private, regulated or public means. It also means guaranteeing their autonomy from states, corporate owners, advertisers and others. They need to be adequately resourced to enable this and to fund depth and expert inquiry, especially if stronger levels of public trust are to be restored.

Political parties, think tanks and organized interests, all need to be made more transparent when it comes to their funding, policy development and campaigns. Donations, particularly large single ones, need to be more tightly regulated or restricted. Ideally, parties and other organized interests would gain the bulk of their funds from ordinary members, possibly topped up by state funding calculated on the basis of paid member numbers. Think tanks and pressure groups need stronger, enforced codes of conduct and transparency about their activities. The same needs to apply to many, now over-powerful intermediary professions, such as accountancy and lobbying, each of which have multiple conflicts of interest and lack transparency.

State and public institutions need to be made more transparent too, with more details made public about governance procedures, board members, staff exchanges with the private sector, managerial incentives and so on. Such institutions should not be allowed to police and regulate themselves as far too many currently do. Bodies holding them to account must be arms-length, have no conflicts of interest or be linked to those they evaluate.

Many aging capitalist democracies have to make a concerted effort to tackle the huge economic inequalities that have built up and continue to grow. This begins with a reappraisal of the conventional free-market economics that has guided policy-making in recent decades. Extreme inequalities are not just morally unjust, they are increasingly detrimental to economies and the wider health and functioning of democracies and societies generally. Far too much money now sits with the super-rich and large financial institutions, untaxed and circulating outside the real economy.

Greater steps and cooperation are needed to tackle some of the negative consequences of globalization too. In many ways, this seems extremely difficult. What can single nations do, even larger ones, to deal with problems of a global nature: climate change, international investment, conflicts and mass refugee crises, growing resource scarcity in an age of ever-expanding populations?

One positive step would be to aim at truly democratizing international institutions, such as the UN or World Bank; to make them independent and representative of the global population rather than a legacy of past Western stitch-ups. Greater cooperation is badly needed when it comes to tackling large TNCs, international financial institutions and global digital giants, such as Facebook, Google and Amazon. It is becoming essential to clamp down on international tax evasion, fraud and the easy flows of trillions of dollars in and out of economies. A level playing field needs to be established, between TNCs and nations, international businesses and local economies and markets. It is equally essential to recognize the work and opinions of the 97% of the scientific community who declare human-made climate change a reality, rather than the engineered rhetoric of the fossil fuel lobby and free market zealots of the political classes.

Of course, much of this, particularly on the global scale seems fanciful. But, looking around, several countries or individual states within nations are taking unilateral steps. Many have, for example, retained higher tax rates, regulated party funding, tackled corporate tax evasion, enforced living wage levels and so on, all without seeing their economies dive. Many have also taken great steps to reduce carbon emissions and waste beyond any international treaties. Tackling global problems on a national scale is more possible than many politicians and bureaucrats admit.

A third, alternative approach is to look critically at the theoretical foundations and norms of democracy itself (Chapter 2). That does not mean ditching norms and values such as equality, individuality, pluralism and representation. But it does mean scholars asking difficult questions about the conditions of their validity and their practical enforcement within modern, 'actually existing', large, representative democracies.

For one, perhaps we should admit that the Greek Agora or Habermassian-style public spheres of a past Europe are not real models to compare with. As Bennett and Pfetsch (2018: 46–7) argued, such is the level of 'dysfunction' and 'disruption' to contemporary public spheres, the discipline itself needs to re-evaluate everything from first principles, including idealist 'textbook democracy' models: 'It is time to rethink assumptions – long grounded in idealized normative conceptions of democratic politics – about media systems and press/ politics interactions'. Thus, new lines of enquiry and research need to make a commitment to avoiding approaches that merely evaluate or confirm old canons and ideas.

For example, perhaps aiming to increase participation in all aspects of politics may not be desirable. In a world of increasing technical expertise, where most voters and even politicians are not equipped to intervene in complex policy consultations, maybe they should not. This might mean thinking how we might develop better means of holding politicians and bureaucrats to account by setting up neutral and pluralist panels and organizations of more informed experts from diverse sectors. Most citizens do not want to engage in national politics, but most do in local matters like school provision or safe neighbourhoods. Again, how might systems and institutions better facilitate these forms of participation?

We might similarly interrogate other democratic ideals, like pluralism and deliberation, in relation to developing better systems and institutions for large, representative democracies. Any radical rethink should ask whether the types of institution and organization, traditionally associated with basic democracy, are still appropriate. Political parties, as they have emerged and been funded, may no longer be the best means of representing publics and nations. Independent news media organizations may no longer be tenable or sustainable without a concerted effort to rethink the assumed ethics, management and autonomy of the profession.

Each of these three non-exclusive approaches have their draw-backs. However, even if, as the optimists believe, we are just experiencing a temporary down cycle in democracy's advance, it wouldn't harm to imagine the alternatives; to go back to first principles with a clean slate and think how twenty-first-century political communication might operate for the good of the many, achieving social, economic and environmental stability for decades to come.

References

Aalberg, T. (2017) 'Does Public Media Enhance Citizen Knowledge? Sifting Through the Evidence' in Davis, A. ed., *The Death of Public Knowledge?* London: Goldsmiths-MIT Press.

Aalberg, T. and Curran, J. (2012) *How Media Inform Democracy: A Comparative Approach*, London: Routledge.

Aalberg, T., Esser, F., Reinemann, C., Stromback, J. and de Vreese, C. eds. (2018) *Populist Political Communication in Europe*, London: Routledge.

Abbott, A. (1988) *The System of Professions: An Essay on the Division of Expert Labor*, Chicago: Chicago University Press.

ABC (2017) Audit Bureau of Circulation, at: https://www.abc.org.uk/

Adonis, A. and Pollard, S. (1997) *A Class Act: the Myth of Britain's Classless Society*, Penguin: London.

Akerlof, G. and Shiller, R. (2009) *Animal Spirits: How Human Psychology Drives the Economy, and Why it Matters for Global Capitalism*, Princeton, NJ: Princeton University Press.

Albrow, M. (1996) *The Global Age: State and Society Beyond Modernity*, Cambridge: Polity.

Albrow, M., Anheier, H., Glasius, M., Price, M. and Kaldor, M. eds. (2008) *Global Civil Society 2007/08: Communicative Power and Democracy*, London: Sage.

Albrow, M. and Glasius, M. (2008) 'Introduction: Democracy and the Possibility of a Global Public Sphere' in Albrow, M., Anheier, H., Glasius, M., Price, M. and Kaldor, M. eds. *Global Civil Society 2007/08: Communicative Power and Democracy*, London: Sage.

Allan, S. (2006) *Online News: Journalism and the Internet*, Maidenhead: Open University Press.

Allan, S. (2010) *News Culture*, 3rd edn, Maidenhead: Open University Press.

Allan, S., Adam, B. and Carter, C. eds. (2000) *Environmental Risks and the Media*, London: Routledge.

Almond, G., Bingham Powell, G., Dalton, R. and Strom, K. (2010) *Comparative Politics Today: A World View*, 9th edn, New York: Pearson.

Altheide, D. (2004) 'Media Logic and Political Communication', *Political Communication*, 21 (3): 293–6.

Altheide, D. and Snow, R. (1979) *Media Logic*, Beverly Hills, CA: Sage.

Amoore, L. ed. (2005) *The Global Resistance Reader*, London: Routledge.

Anderson, A. (1997) *Media, Culture and the Environment*, London: UCL Press.

Anderson, C., Bell, E. and Shirky, C. (2015) *Post Industrial Journalism: Adapting to the Present*, New York: Tow Centre for Digital Journalism.

Ang, I. (1985) *Watching Dallas*, London: Methuen.

Anheier, H., Glasius, M. and Kaldor, M. (2001) 'Introduction' in Anheier, Glasius and Kaldor, M. eds. *Global Civil Society Yearbook 2001*, Oxford: Oxford University Press.

Anholt, S. (1998) 'Nation Brands of the 21st Century', *Journal of Brand Management*, 5 (6): 395–406.

Ansolabehere, S. and Iyengar, S. (1995) *Going Negative: How Political Advertisements Shrink and Polarize the Electorate*, New York: The Free Press.

Aresse, A. (2018) 'Austerity Politics in the European Press: A Divided Europe?' in Basu, L., Schifferes, S. and Knowles, S. eds. *The Media and Austerity: Comparative Perspectives*, London: Routledge.

Armingeon, K. and Schadel, L. (2015) 'Social Inequality in Political Participation: The Dark sides of Individualisation', *West European Politics*, 38 (1): 1–27.

Aronczyk, M. (2013) *Branding the Nation: The Global Business of National Identity*, Oxford: Oxford University Press.

Åström, J. Hinsberg, H., Jonsson, M. and Karlsson, M. (2013) *Citizen Centric E-Participation*, Tallinn: Praxis Centre for Policy Studies.

Atton, C. (2004) *An Alternative Internet*, Edinburgh: Edinburgh University Press.

Bachrach, P. and Baratz, M. (1962) 'Two Faces of Power', *American Political Science Review*, 56 (4): 947–52.

Bagdikian, B. (2004/14) *The Media Monopoly*, 7th/20th edns, Boston: Beacon Press.

Baisnee, O. (2007) 'The European Public Sphere Does Not Exist (At Least it's Worth Wondering …)', *European Journal of Communication*, 22 (4): 493–503.

Ball, T. and Dagger, R. (2013) *Ideals and Ideologies: A Reader*, 9th edn, London: Routledge.

Bandura, A. and Walters, R. (1963) *Social Learning and Personality Development*, New York: Rinehart and Winston.

Bandura, A., Ross, D. and Ross, S. (1961) 'Transmission of Aggression Through Imitation of Aggressive Models', *Journal of Abnormal and Social Psychology*, 63 (3): 575–82.

Barnett, A. (2017) *The Lure of Greatness: England's Brexit and America's Trump*, London: Unbound.

Barnett, S. and Gaber, I. (2001) *Westminster Tales: The Twenty First Century Crisis in Political Journalism*, London: Continuum.

Basu, L. (2018) 'Media Amnesia and the Crisis' in Basu, L., Schifferes, S. and Knowles, S. eds. *The Media and Austerity: Comparative Perspectives*, London: Routledge.

Basu, L., Schifferes, S. and Knowles, S. eds. (2018) *The Media and Austerity: Comparative Perspectives*, London: Routledge.

Baumgartner, F. R., Berry, J., Hojnacki, M., Kimball, D. and Leech, B. (2009) *Lobbying and Policy Change: Who Wins, Who Loses, and Why?* Chicago: University of Chicago Press.

Baumgartner, F. R. and Jones, B. (1993) *Agendas and Instability in American Politics*, Chicago: University of Chicago Press.

Baumgartner, F. and Jones, B. (2014) *The Politics of Information: Problem Definition and the Course of Public Policy in America*, Chicago: Chicago University Press.

BBC (2016) *EU Referendum: The Result in Maps and Charts*, London: BBC.

Beck, U. (2006) *Cosmopolitan Vision*, Cambridge: Polity.

Beckett, C. (2008) *Supermedia: Saving Journalism so it Can Save Itself*, Oxford: Wiley-Blackwell.

Bell, D. (1973) *The Coming of the Post-Industrial Age: A Venture in Social Forecasting*, London: Penguin.

Benavides, J. (2000) 'Gacetilla: A Key Word for a Revisionist Approach to the Political Economy of Mexico's Print News Media', *Media, Culture and Society*, 22 (1): 85–104.

Bennett, W. L. (1990) 'Towards a Theory of Press–State Relations in the United States', *Journal of Communication*, 40 (2): 103–25.

Bennett, W. L. (2016) *News: The Politics of Illusion*, 10th edn, Chicago: University of Chicago Press.

Bennett, L. and Paletz, D. (1994) *Taken by Storm: The Media, Public Opinion, and US Foreign Policy in the Gulf War*, Chicago: University of Chicago Press.

Bennett, W. L. and Entman, R. M. eds. (2001) *Mediated Politics: Communication in the Future of Democracy*, Cambridge: Cambridge University Press.

Bennett, W. L. and Iyengar, S. (2010) 'The New Era of Minimal Effects? The Changing Foundations of Political Communication', *Journal of Communication*, 58: 707–31.

Bennett, W. L. and Pfetsch, B. (2018) 'Rethinking Political Communication in a Time of Disrupted Public Spheres', *Journal of Communication*, 68: 243–55.

Bennett, W. L. and Segerberg, A. (2013) *The Logic of Connective Action: Digital Media and the Personalization of Contentious Politics*, Cambridge: Cambridge University Press.

Benson, R. (2004) 'Bringing the Sociology of Media Back In', *Political Communication*, 21: 275–92.

Benson, R (2017) 'The New American Media Landscape' in Davis, A. ed. (2017b) *The Death of Public Knowledge?* London: Goldsmiths-MIT Press.

Benson, R. and Hallin, D. (2007) 'How States, Markets and Globalization Shape the News: The French and US National Press, 1965–97', *European Journal of Communication*, 22 (1): 27–48.

Berkowitz, L. (1984) 'Some Effects of Thoughts on Anti- and Prosocial Influences of Media Events: A Cognitive-Neoassociation Analysis', *Psychological Bulletin*, 95 (3): 410–27.

Berry, M. (2016) 'The UK Press and the Deficit Debate', *Sociology*, 50 (3): 542–59.

Berry, M. (2018) 'Austerity, the Media and the UK Public' in Basu, L., Schifferes, S. and Knowles, S. eds. *The Media and Austerity: Comparative Perspectives*, London: Routledge.

Beyers, J., Eising, R. and Maloney, W. (2008) 'Researching Interest Group Politics in Europe and Elsewhere: Much We Study, Little We Know', *Western European Politics*, 31 (6): 1103–28.

Bimber, B. (2003) *Information and American Democracy: Technology in the Evolution of Political Power*, Cambridge: Cambridge University Press.

Birkinbine, B. (2017) 'Microsoft' in Birkinbine, B., Gomez, R. and Wasko, J. eds. *Global Media Giants*, New York: Routledge, pp. 383–97.

Birkinbine, B., Gomez, R. and Wasko, J. eds. (2017) *Global Media Giants*, New York: Routledge.

Birtchnell, J. and Caletrio, J. eds. (2014) *Elite Mobilities*, Abingdon: Routledge.

Blumler, J. (2013) *The Fourth Age of Political Communication*, Keynote Address at Frei University, Berlin, 12 September 2013. Available at: http://www.fgpk.de/en/2013/gastbeitrag-von-jay-g-blumler-the-fourth-age-of-political-communication-2/.

Blumler, J. G. and Gurevitch, M. (1995) *The Crisis of Public Communication*, London: Routledge.

Blumler, J. and Katz, E. eds. (1974) *The Uses of Communications*, Beverly Hills, CA: Sage.

Blumler, J. and Kavanagh, D. (1999) 'The Third Age of Political Communication: Influences and Features', *Political Communication*, 16 (3): 209–30.

Bode, L. and Dalrymple, K. (2016) 'Politics in 140 Characters or Less: Campaign Communication, Network Interaction, and Political Participation on Twitter', *Journal of Political Marketing*, 15: 311–32.

Bohman, J. (1996) *Public Deliberation: Pluralism, Complexity, and Democracy*, Cambridge, MA: MIT Press.

Bonfadelli, H. (2002) 'The Internet and Knowledge Gaps: A Theoretical and Empirical Investigation', *European Journal of Communication*, 17 (1): 65–84.

Bowers, A. (2011) 'Protest and Public Relations: A New Era for Non-Institutional Sources?' in Cottle, S. and Lester, L. eds. *Transnational Protests and the Media*, New York: Peter Lang.

Bowman, A. et al. (2014) *The End of the Experiment*, Manchester: Manchester University Press.

Bowman, A. et al. (2015) *What a Waste: Outsourcing and How it all Goes Wrong*, Manchester: Manchester University Press.

Boyd-Barrett, O. and Rantanen, T. (1998) 'The Globalisation of News' in Boyd-Barrett, O. and Rantanen, T. eds. *The Globalisation of News*, London: Sage.

Brandenburg, H. (2006) 'Pathologies of the Virtual Public Sphere' in Oates, S., Owen, D. and Gibson, R. eds. *The Internet and Politics: Citizens, Voters and Activists*, London: Routledge.

Braun, J. (2015) *This Programme is Brought to You By … Distributing Television News Online*, New Haven, CT: Yale University Press.

Buchanan, J. and Wagner, R. (1977) *Democracy in Deficit*, New York: Basic Books.

Burnham, P. (2001) 'New Labour and the Politics of Depoliticization', *British Journal of Politics and International Relations*, 3 (2): 127–49.

Butsch, R. ed. (2007) *Media and Public Spheres*, Basingstoke: Palgrave Macmillan.

Cable, J. (2016) *Protest Campaigns, Media and Political Opportunities*, London: Rowman and Littlefield.

Cable, V. (2009) *The Storm: The World Economic Crisis and What it Means*, London: Atlantic Books.

Cacciatore, M. Scheufele, D. and Iyengar, S. (2016) 'The End of Framing as We Know it… and the Future of Media Effects', *Mass Communication and Society*, 19 (1): 7–23.

Calhoun, C. ed. (1992) 'Introduction' in *Habermas and the Public Sphere*, Cambridge, MA: MIT Press.

Campbell, W. (2003) *Yellow Journalism: Puncturing the Myths, Defining the Legacies*, Westport, CT: Praeger.

Cantril, H., Gaudet, H. and Hertzog, H. (1940) *The Invasion from Mars*, Princeton, NJ: Princeton University Press.

Capella, J. and Hall Jamieson, K. (1997) *Spiral of Cynicism: The Press and the Public Good*, Oxford: Oxford University Press.

Carlson, M. (2007) 'Blogs and Journalistic Authority: The Role of Blogs in US Election Day 2004 Coverage', *Journalism Studies*, 8 (2): 264–79.

Carlson, M. 'The Question of Objectivity in the 2016 Presidential Election' in Lilleker, D., Thorsen, E. and Jackson, D. (2016) *US Election Analysis 2016: Media, Voters and the Campaign*, Bournemouth: CSJCC.

Cassidy, J. (2002) *Dot.Con: The Greatest Story Ever Told*, London: Penguin/ Allen Lane.

Castells, M. (1996) *The Rise of the Network Society*, Oxford: Blackwell.

Castells, M. (1997) *The Power of Identity*, Oxford: Blackwell.

Castells, M. (2001) *The Internet Galaxy: Reflections on the Internet, Business and Society*, Oxford: Oxford University Press.

Castells, M. (2008) 'The New Public Sphere: Global Civil Society, Communication Networks and Global Governance', *The ANNALs of the American Academy of Political and Social Science*, 616 (1): 78–93.

Castells, M. (2009) *Communication Power*, Oxford: Oxford University Press.

Castells, M. (2012/15) *Networks of Outrage and Hope: Movements in the Internet Age*, 1st/2nd edn, Cambridge: Polity.

Cave, T. and Rowell, A. (2014) *A Quiet Word: Crony Capitalism and Broken Politics in Britain*, London: Bodley Head.

Cerny, P., Menz, G. and Soderberg, S. (2005) 'Different Roads to Globalization: Neo-Liberalism, the Competition State, and Politics in a More Open World' in Soderberg, S., Menz, G. and Cerny, G. eds. *Internalizing Globalization: The Rise of Neo-Liberalism and the Decline of National Varieties of Capitalism*, Houndsmill, Basingstoke: Palgrave Macmillan, pp. 1–30.

Chadwick, A. (2006) *Internet Politics: States, Citizens and New Communication Technologies*, Oxford: Oxford University Press.

Chadwick, A. (2013) *The Hybrid Media System: Politics and Power*, Oxford: Oxford University Press.

Chadwick, A. and Stromer-Galley, J. (2016) 'Digital Media, Power and Democracy in Parties and Election Campaigns: Party Decline or Party Renewal?' *Harvard Journal of Press/Politics*, 21 (3): 283–93.

Chaffee, S. and Metzger, M. (2001) 'The End of Mass Communication?' *Mass Communication and Society*, 17: 803–29.

Chalaby, J. (1996) 'Journalism as an Anglo-American Invention', *European Journal of Communication*, 11: 303–26.

Chalaby, J. (1998) *The Invention of Journalism*, London: Macmillan.

Chalaby, J. (2009) *Transnational Television in Europe: Reconfiguring Global Communications Networks*, London: I. B. Tauris.

Chang, H. (2010) *23 Things They Don't Tell You About Capitalism*, London: Allen Lane.

Chang, H. (2014) *Economics: The User's Guide: A Pelican Introduction*, London: Pelican.

Chiaramonte, A. and Emanuele, V. (2017) 'Party System Volatility, Regeneration and De-institutionalisation in Western Europe (1945–2015)', *Party Politics*, 23 (4): 376–88.

Chinwala, Y. (2016) *Women in UK Financial Services in 2016*, London: New Financial.

Chouliaraki, L (2006) *The Spectatorship of Suffering*, London: Sage.

CIA (2014/16/17) Central Intelligence Agency World Fact Books, at: https://www.cia.gov

Clarke, J. (2001) 'Ethical Globalization: The Dilemmas and Challenges of Internationalizing Civil Society' in Edwards, M. and Gaventa, J. eds. *Global Citizen Action*, Boulder: Lynne Rienner.

Clegg, S. (1989) *Frameworks of Power*, London: Sage.

Coates, D. (2000) *Models of Capitalism: Growth and Stagnation in the Modern Era*, Cambridge: Polity.

Cohen, E. (2002) 'Online Journalism as Market-Driven Journalism', *Journal of Broadcasting and Electronic Media*, 46 (4): 532–48.

Cohn, T. (2016) *Global Political Economy: Theory and Practice*, New York: Routledge.

Coleman, S. (2004) 'Connecting Parliament to the Public via the internet: Two Case Studies of Online Consultations', *Information, Communication and Society*, 7 (1): 1–22.

Coleman, S. (2005) 'New Mediation and Direct Representation: Reconceptualising Representation in the Digital Age', *New Media and Society*, 7 (2): 177–98.

Coleman, S. (2017) *Can the Internet Strengthen Democracy?*, Cambridge: Polity.

Coleman, S. and Blumler, J. (2009), *The Internet and Democratic Citizenship: Theory, Practice and Policy*, New York: Cambridge University Press.

Coleman, S. and Gotze, J. (2001) *Bowling Together: Online Public Engagement in Policy Deliberation*, London: Hansard Society.

Conti, N., Hutter, S. and Nanov, K. (2018) 'Party Competition and Political Representation in Crisis: Introduction', *Party Politics*, 24 (1): 3–9.

Conway, E. (2012) *50 Ideas You Really Need to Know in Economics*, London: Quercus.

Cook, T. (1998) *Governing with the News: The News Media as a Political Institution*, Chicago: University of Chicago Press.

Cook, J. et al. (2016) 'Consensus on Consensus: A Synthesis of Consensus Estimates on Human-Caused Global Warming', *Environmental Research Letters*, 11 (4): 1–7.

Corner, J. (2003) 'Mediated Persona and Political Culture' in Corner, J. and Pels, D. eds. *Media and the Restyling of Politics*, London: Sage.

Corner, J. and Pels, D. (2003) *Media and the Restyling of Politics*, London: Sage.

Cottle, S. and Lester, L. eds. (2011) *Transnational Protests and the Media*, New York: Peter Lang.

Cottle, S. and Rai, M. (2008) 'News Providers: Emissaries of Global Dominance or Global Public Sphere', *Global Media and Communication*, 4 (2): 157–81.

Couldry, N., Livingstone, S. and Markham, T. (2010) *Media Consumption and Public Engagement: Beyond the Presumption of Attention*, Basingstoke: Palgrave Macmillan.

Cracknell, J. (1993) 'Issue Arenas, Pressure Groups and Environmental Issues' in Hansen, A. 'Greenpeace and press coverage of environmental issues' in Hansen, A. ed. *The Mass Media and Environmental Issues*, Leicester: Leicester University Press.

CRE (2005) *Why Ethnic Minority Workers Leave London's Print Journalism Sector*, London: Commission for Racial Equality.

Cronin, A. (2018) *Public Relations Capitalism: Promotional Culture, Publics and Commercial Democracy*, Basingstoke: Palgrave Macmillan.

Crouch, C. (2004) *Post-Democracy*, Cambridge: Polity.

Crouch, C. (2011) *The Strange Non-Death of Neo-Liberalism*, Cambridge: Polity.

Crozier, M., Huntingdon, S. and Watanuki, J. (1975) *The Crisis of Democracy: Report on the Governability of Democracies in the Trilateral Commission*, New York: New York University Press.

CSM (2014) *Elitist Britain*, London: Commission for Social Mobility.

Curran, J. (1978) 'Advertising and the Press' in Curran, J. ed., *The British Press: A Manifesto*, London: Macmillan, pp. 229–67.

Curran, J. (2000) 'Rethinking Media and Democracy' in Curran J. and Gurevitch, M. eds. *Mass Media and Society*, 3rd edn, London: Edward Arnold.

Curran, J. (2002) *Media and Power*, London: Routledge.

Curran, J. (2009) 'Technology Foretold' in Fenton, N. ed. *New Media: Old News*, London: Sage.

Curran, J. (2011) *Media and Democracy*, London: Routledge.

Curran, J. (2016) 'The Internet of Dreams' in Curran, J., Fenton, N. and Freedman, D. *Misunderstanding the Internet*, 2nd edn, London: Routledge.

Curran, J. and Couldry, N. (2003) *Contesting Media Power: Alternative Media in a Networked World*, London: Rowman and Littlefield.

Curran, J. and Park, M. eds. (2000) *De-Westernizing Media Studies*, London: Routledge.

Curran, J. and Seaton, J. (2003/18) *Power Without Responsibility*, 6th/8th edns, London: Routledge.

Curran, J. and Witschge, T. (2009) 'Liberal Dreams and the Internet' in Fenton, N. ed. *New Media, Old News: Journalism and Democracy in a Digital Age*, London: Sage.

Curran, J., Fenton, N. and Freedman, D. (2012/16) *Misunderstanding the Internet*, 1st/2nd edns, London: Routledge.

Curtice, J. (2005) 'Turnout: Electors Stay Home Again' in Norris, P. and Wlezien, C. eds. *Britain Votes 2005*, Oxford: Oxford University Press.

Cutlip, S., Center, A. and Broom, G. (2000) *Effective Public Relations*, 8th edn, Englewood Cliffs, New Jersey: Prentice Hall Inc.

Dahl, R. (1961) *Who Governs? Democracy and Power in an American City*, New Haven, CT: Yale University Press.

Dahl, R. (1989) *Democracy and its Critics*, New Haven, CT: Yale University Press.

Dahl, R. (1999) 'Can International Organisations Be Democratic: A Skeptics View' in Shapiro, I. and Hacker-Cordon, C., eds. *Democracy's Edges*, Cambridge: Cambridge University Press, pp. 19–36.

Dahlberg, L. (2001) 'The Internet and Democratic Discourse: Exploring the Prospects of Online Deliberative Forums Extending the Public Sphere', *Information, Communication and Society*, 4 (4): 615–33.

Dahlberg, L. (2007) 'Rethinking the Fragmentation of the Cyberpublic: From Consensus to Contestation', *New Media and Society*, 9 (5): 827–47.

Dahlgren, P (1995) *Television and the Public Sphere: Citizenship, Democracy and the Media*, London: Sage.

Dahlgren, P. (2005) 'The Internet, Public Spheres and Political Communication: Dispersion and Deliberation', *Political Communications*, 22 (2): 147–62.

Dahlgren, P. (2009) *Media and Political Engagement: Citizens, Communication and Democracy*, Cambridge: Cambridge University Press.

Dahlgren, P. (2013) *The Political Web*, Basingstoke: Palgrave.

Dahlgren, P. and Sparks, C. (1992) *Communication and Citizenship: Journalism and the Public Sphere*, London: Routledge.

Dai, X. and Norton, P. (2013) *The Internet and European Parliamentary Democracy*, London: Routledge.

Dalton, R. (2004) *Democratic Challenges, Democratic Choices: The Erosion of Political Support in Advanced Industrial Democracies*, Oxford: Oxford University Press.

Dalton, R. (2017) 'Party Representation Across Multiple Issue Dimensions', *Party Politics*, 23 (6): 609–22.

Dalton, R. and Wattenberg, M. eds. (2002) *Parties Without Partisans: Political Change in Advanced Industrial Democracies*, Oxford: Oxford University Press.

Darras, E. (2005) 'Media Consecration of the Political Order' in Benson, R. and Neveu, E. eds. *Bourdieu and the Journalistic Field*, Cambridge: Polity.

Davies, N. (2008) *Flat Earth News*, London: Chatto and Windus.

Davies, N. (2015) *Hack Attack: How the Truth Caught up with Rupert Murdoch*, London: Vintage.

Davies, W. (2014) *The Limits of Neoliberalism: Authority, Sovereignty and the Logic of Competition*, London: Sage.

Davis, A. (2002) *Public Relations Democracy: Public Relations, Politics and the Mass Media in Britain*, Manchester: Manchester University Press.

Davis, A. (2007a) 'Investigating Journalist Influences on Political Issue Agendas at Westminster', *Political Communication*, 24 (2): 181–99.

Davis, A. (2007b) *The Mediation of Power: A Critical Introduction*, London: Routledge.

Davis, A. (2009a) 'Journalist–Source Relations, Mediated Reflexivity and the Politics of Politics', *Journalism Studies*, 10 (2): 204–19.

Davis, A. (2009b) 'New Media and Fat Democracy: The Paradox of Online Participation', *New Media and Society*, 11 (8): 1–19.

Davis, A. (2010a) *Political Communication and Social Theory*, London: Routledge.

Davis, A. (2010b) 'Media and Politics' in Curran, J. ed. *Mass Media and Society*, 4th edn, London: Arnold.

Davis, A. (2011) 'The Mediation of Finance: An Inverted Political Economy of Communication Approach' in Winseck, D. and Jin, D. eds. *Media Political Economies: Hierarchies, Markets and Finance in the Global Media Industries*, London: Bloomsbury.

Davis, A. (2013) *Promotional Cultures: The Rise and Spread of Advertising, Public Relations, Marketing and Branding*, Cambridge: Polity.

Davis, A. (2017a) 'Introduction' in *The Death of Public Knowledge?* London: Goldsmiths Press.

Davis, A. ed., (2017b) *The Death of Public Knowledge?* London: Goldsmiths-MIT Press.

Davis, A. (2017c) 'The New Professional Econocracy and the Maintenance of Elite Power', *Political Studies*, 65 (3): 594–610.

Davis, A. (2018) *Reckless Opportunists: Elites at the End of the Establishment*, Manchester: Manchester University Press.

Davis, A. and Walsh, C. (2016) 'The Role of the State in the Financialisation of the UK Economy', *Political Studies*, 64 (3): 666–82.

Davis, A. and Williams, K. (2017) 'Introduction: Elites and Power After Financialization', for *Theory, Culture and Society*, 34 (5–6): 27–51.

Davis, R. (2005) *Politics Online: Blogs, Chatrooms, and Discussion Groups in American Democracy*, Routledge: New York.

de Jong, W. (2005) 'The Power and Limits of Media Based Oposition Politics – a Case Study: the Brent Spar Conflict' in de Jong, W., Shaw, M., and Stammers, N. eds. *Global Activism Global Media*, London: Pluto Press.

de Vreese, C., Esser, F. and Hopmann, D. eds. (2016) *Comparing Political Journalism*, London: Routledge.

Deacon, D. (1996) 'The Voluntary Sector in a Changing Communication Environment', *European Journal of Communication*, 11 (2): 173–99.

Deacon, D. and Stanyer, J. (2014) 'Mediatization: Key Concept or Conceptual Bandwagon', *Media, Culture and Society*, 36 (7): 1032–44.

Dean, J. (2009) *Democracy and Other Neoliberal Fantasies: Communicative Capitalism and Left Politics*, Durham, NC: Duke University Press.

Dean, J., Anderson, J. and Lovinck, G. eds. (2006) *Reformatting Politics: Information Technology and Global Civil Society*, London: Routledge.

Della Porta, D. and Diani, M. (1999) *Social Movements: An Introduction*, Oxford: Blackwell.

Della Porta, D. and Diani, M. (2015) 'Introduction: The Field of Social Movement Studies' in Della Porta, D. and Diani, M. eds. *The Oxford Handbook of Social Movements*, Oxford: Oxford University Press.

Della Porta, D. and Tarrow, S. (2004) *Transnational Protest and Global Activism*, Oxford: Rowman and Littlefield.

Delli Carpini, M. S. and Williams, B. A. (2001) 'Let Us Infotain You: Politics in the New Media Environment' in Bennett, W. L. and Entman, R. M. eds. *Mediated Politics: Communication in the Future of Democracy*, Cambridge: Cambridge University Press.

DeLuca, M., Lawson, S. and Sun, Y. (2012) 'Occupy Wall Street on the

Public Screens of Social Media: The Many Framings of the Birth of a Protest Movement', *Communication, Culture and Critique*, 5: 483–509.

Dencik, L. (2012) *Media and Global Civil Society*, Basingstoke: Palgrave Macmillan.

Denton, R. and Woodward, G. (1998) *Political Communication in America*, 3rd edn, Westport, CT: Praeger.

Deuze, M. (2001) 'Online Journalism: Modelling the First Generation of News Media on the World Wide Web', *First Monday*, 6 (10).

Deuze, M. (2007) *Media Work*, Cambridge: Polity.

Dewey, J. (1927) *The Public and Its Problems*, New York: Henry Holt.

Diamond, L. and Plattner, M. eds. (2012) *Liberation Technology: Social Media and the Struggle for Democracy*, Baltimore: John Hopkins University Press.

Diamond, L. and Plattner, M. (2016) *Authoritarianism Goes Global: The Challenge to Democracy*, Baltimore: John Hopkins University Press.

Dimitrova, D., Shehata, A., Stromback, J. and Nord, L. (2014) 'The Effect of Digital Media on Political Knowledge and Participation in Election Campaigns: Evidence from Panel Data', *Communication Research*, 41 (1): 95–118.

Dinan, W. and Miller, D. (2007) *Thinker, Faker, Spinner, Spy: Corporate PR and the Assault on Democracy*, London: Pluto.

Dindler, C. (2015) 'Negotiating Political News: The Two Phases of Off-the-Record Interaction', *Journalism*, 16 (8): 1124–40.

Dixon, T. and Williams, C. (2015) 'The Changing Misrepresentation of Race and Crime on Network and Cable News', *Journal of Communication*, 65: 24–39.

Domhoff, G. (1967) *Who Rules America?* Englewood Cliffs, NJ: Prentice-Hall.

Dorling, D. (2014) *Inequality and the 1%*, London: Verso.

Dover, D. (2010) *On Message: Television Advertising by the Presidential Candidates in Election 2008*, Lanham: Lexington Books.

Downey, J. and Koenig, J. (2006) 'Is There a European Public Sphere? The Berlusconi-Schulz Case', *European Journal of Communication*, 21 (2): 165–87.

Downing, J. (2001) *Radical Media: Rebellious Communication and Social Movements*, London: Sage.

Dryzak, J. (2002) *Deliberative Democracy and Beyond: Liberals, Critics, Contestations*, Oxford: Oxford University Press.

Dunlap, R., McCright, A. and Yarosh, J. (2016) 'The Political Divide on Climate Change: Partisan Polarization Widens in the US', *Environment*, 58 (5): 4–23.

Dunleavy, P. and O'Leary, B. (1987) *Theories of the State*, London: Macmillan.

Durham, F. (2007) 'Framing the State in Globalisation: The Financial Times' Coverage of the 1997 Thai Currency Crisis', *Critical Studies in Media Communication*, 24 (1): 57–76.

Dutton, W. and Blank, G. (2013) *Cultures of the Internet: The Internet in Britain*, Oxford: Oxford Internet Institute.

Earle, J., Moran, C. and Ward-Perkins, Z. (2016) *The Econocracy: The Perils of Leaving Economics to the Experts*, Manchester: Manchester University Press.

Edwards, B. and Kane, M. (2016) 'Resource Mobilization and Social and Political Movements' in van der Heijden, H. A. ed. *Handbook of Political Citizenship and Social Movements*, Cheltenham: Edward Elgar Publishing.

Eide, E., Kunelius, R. and Phillips, A. eds. (2008) *Transnational Media Events: The Mohammed Cartoons and the Imagined Clash of Civilisations*, Goteborg: Nordicom.

EIU (2016/17/18) *Democracy Index 2016/2017*, 9th/10th edns, London: Economist Intelligence Unit.

Elliott, A. (2014) 'Tracking the Mobile Lives of Globals' in Birtchnell, J. and Caletrio, J. eds. *Elite Mobilities*, Abingdon: Routledge, pp. 21–39.

Elliott, L. and Atkinson, D. (2009) *The Gods that Failed: How the Financial Elite Have Gambled Away Our Futures*, London: Vintage.

Eltantawy, N. and Wiest, J. (2011) 'The Arab Spring. Social Media in the Egyptian Revolution: Reconsidering Resource Mobilization Theory', *International Journal of Communication*, 5: 1207–24.

Elvestad, E. and Phillips, A. (2018) *Misunderstanding News Audiences: Seven Myths of the Social Media Era*, London: Routledge.

Engelen, E. (2017) 'Shadow Banking After the Crisis', *Theory, Culture and Society*, 34 (5/6): 53–75.

Engelen, E. et al. (2011) *After the Great Complacence: Financial Crisis and the Politics of Reform*, Oxford: Oxford University Press.

Entman, R. (1993) 'Framing: Towards Clarification of a Fractured Paradigm', *Journal of Communication*, 43 (1): 51–8.

Entman, R. (2004) *Projections of Power: Framing News, Public Opinion, and US Foreign Policy*, Chicago: University of Chicago Press.

Entman, R. (2005) 'Media and Democracy Without Party Competition' in Curran, J. and Gurevitch, M. eds. *Mass Media and Society*, 4th edn, London: Arnold.

Epstein, G. ed., (2005) *Financialization and the World Economy*, Cheltenham: Edward Elgar.

Ericson, R. V., Baranek, P. M. and Chan J. B. L. (1989) *Negotiating Control: a Study of News Sources*, Milton Keynes: Open University Press.

Esser, F. (2008) 'Dimensions of Political News Cultures: Sound Bite and Image Bite News in France, Germany, Great Britain, and the United States', *Harvard International Journal of Press/Politics*, 13 (4): 401–28.

Esser, F. and Pfetsch, B. eds. (2004) *Comparing Political Communication: Theories, Cases and Challenges*, Cambridge: Cambridge University Press.

Evans, J. and Hesmondhalgh, D. (2005) *Understanding Media: Inside Celebrity*, Milton Keynes: Open University Press.

Fairvote (2008) Presidential Election Inequality: The Electoral College in the 21st Century, The Center for Voting and Democracy, at: http://archive.fairvote.org/media/perp/presidentialinequality.pdf

Fairvote (2013) *Fairvote Maps the 2012 Presidential Campaign*, at: https://www.fairvote.org/fairvote-maps-the-2012-presidential-campaign.

Farrar-Myers, V. (2011) 'Donors, Dollars and Momentum' in Bose, M. ed. *From Votes to Victory: Winning and Governing the White House in the 21st Century*, Texas: Hofstra University.

Fawzi, N. (2017) 'Information Source and Political Arena: How Actors from Inside and Outside Politics Use the Media' in van Aelst, P. and Walgrave, S. eds. *How Political Actors Use the Media*, Cham., Switzerland: Palgrave Macmillan.

Fenton, N. ed. (2009) *New Media, Old News: Journalism and Democracy in a Digital Age*, London: Sage.

Fenton, N. (2016a) 'The Internet of Radical Politics and Social Change' in Curran, J., Fenton, N. and Freedman, D. *Misunderstanding the Internet*, 2nd edn, London: Routledge.

Fenton, N. (2016b) *Digital, Political, Radical*, Cambridge: Polity.

Ferguson, C. (2012) *Inside Job: The Financiers Who Pulled Off the Heist of the Century*, Oxford: Oneworld.

Ferguson, R. ed. (2006) *tellparliament.net Interim Evaluation Report 2003–5*, London: Hansard Society.

Ferguson, Y. and Mansbach, R. (2012) *Globalization: The Return of Borders to a Borderless World*, New York: Routledge.

Fishkin, J. (1992) *Democracy and Deliberation: New Directions for Democratic Reform*, New Haven, CT: Yale University Press.

Fishman (1980) *Manufacturing News*, Austin: University of Texas.

Flew, T. (2007) *Understanding Global Media*, Basingstoke: Palgrave Macmillan.

Flinders, M. 'A Glorious Defeat: Anti-Politics and the Funnelling of Frustration' in Thorsen, E., Jackson, D. and Lilleker, D. eds. (2017) *UK Election Analysis 2017: Media, Voters and the Campaign*, Bournemouth: CSJCC.

Flinders, M. and Buller, J. (2006) 'Depoliticization, Democracy and Arena Shifting' in Christensen, T. and Laegreid, P. eds. *Autonomy and Regulation*, Cheltenham: Edward Elgar.

Frank, T. (2016) *Listen Liberal: Or, Whatever Happened to the Party of the People?* London: Scribe UK.

Franklin, B. (1997) *Newzak and News Media*, London: Arnold.

Franklin, B. (2004) *Packaging Politics: Political Communications in Britain's Media Democracy*, 2nd edn, London: Arnold.

Franklin, B. (2005) 'McJournalism: The Local Press and the McDonaldization Thesis' in Allan, S. ed. *Journalism: Critical Issues*, Maidenhead: Open University Press.

Franklin, B. and Carlson, M. (2010) *Journalists, Sources and Credibility: New Perspectives*, London: Routledge.

Fraser, N. (1992) 'Restructuring the Public Sphere: A Consideration of Actually Existing Democracy' in Calhoun, C. ed. *Habermas and the Public Sphere*, Cambridge, MA: MIT Press.

Fraser, N. (1997) 'Rethinking the Public Sphere: A Contribution to the Critique of Actually Existing Democracies' in *Justice Interruptus: Critical Reflections on the "Postsocialist" Condition*, London: Routledge.

Fraser, N. (2007) 'Transnationalizing the Public Sphere: On the Legitimacy and Efficacy of Public Opinion in a Post-Westphalian World', *Theory, Culture and Society*, 24 (7): 7–30.

Freedman, D. (2008) *The Politics of Media Policy*, Cambridge: Polity.

Freedman, D. (2009) 'The Political Economy of the "New" News Environment' in Fenton, N. ed. (2009) *New Media, Old News: Journalism and Democracy in a Digital Age*, London: Sage.

Freedman, D. (2012) 'Web 2.0 and the Death of the Blockbuster Economy' in Curran, J., Fenton, N. and Freedman, D. *Misunderstanding the Internet*, London: Routledge.

Freedom House (2017) *Freedom in the World 2017*, Washington: Freedom House.

Freeland, C. (2012) *Plutocrats: The Rise of the New Global Super-Rich*, London: Penguin.

Fuchs, C. (2014) *Social Media: A Critical Introduction*, London: Sage.

Fuchs, C. and Mosco, V. (2017) *Marx and the Political Economy of Media*, London: Haymarket Books.

Fukuyama, F. (1992) *The End of History and the Last Man*, New York: The Free Press.

Gallup Polls (2008 archive) all at: http://www.gallup.com/poll/politics.aspx

Galtung, J. and Ruge, M. (1965) 'The Structure of Foreign News', *Journal of International Peace Research*, 1: 64–90.

Gamson, W. (1992) *Talking Politics*, Cambridge: Cambridge University Press.

Gamson, W. and Meyer, D. (1996) 'Framing Political Opportunity' in McAdam D., McCarthy J., Zald, M. N., eds. *Comparative Perspectives on Social Movements: Political Opportunities, Mobilizing Structures, and Cultural Framings*, Cambridge: Cambridge University Press.

Gandy, O. (1982) *Beyond Agenda Setting: Information Subsidies and Public Policy*, New Jersey: Ablex Publishing Corporation.

Gans, H. J. (1979) *Deciding What's News: A Study of CBS Evening News, NBC Nightly News, Newsweek and Time*, New York: Pantheon.

Garrison, B. (2001) 'Diffusion of Online Information Technologies in Newspaper Newsrooms', *Journalism*, 2 (2): 221–39.

Gates, B. (1996) *The Road Ahead*, New York: Penguin.

Gerbaudo, P. (2012) *Tweets and Streets: Social Media and Contemporary Activism*, London: Pluto Press.

Gerbaudo, P. (2017) *The Mask and the Flag: Populism, Citizenship and Global Protest*, London: Hurst and Co.

Gerbner, G., Gross, L., Morgan, M. and Signorielli, N. (1986) 'Living with Television: The Dynamics of the Cultivation Process' in Bryant, J. and Zillmann, D. eds. *Media Effects: Advances in Theory and Research*, Mahwah, NJ: Lawrence Earlbaum.

Gibson, R. and McAllister, I. (2015) 'Normalising or Equalising Party Competition? Assessing the Impact of the Web on Election Campaigning', *Political Studies*, 63 (3): 529–47.

Gillmor, D. (2004) *We the Media: Grassroots Journalism by the People, for the People*, Sebastopol: O'Reilly Media.

Gilpin, R. (2001) *Global Political Economy: Understanding the International Economic Order*, Princeton, NJ: Princeton University Press.

Gitlin, T. (1980) *The Whole World is Watching*, Berkeley: University of California Press.

Gitlin, T. (1998) 'Public Sphere or Public Sphericules?' in Liebes, T. and Curran, J. eds. *Media, Ritual and Identity*, London: Routledge.

Gitlin, T. (2011) 'The Left Declares Its Independence', *New York Times*, New York: News International.

Glasser, T. ed. (1999) *The Idea of Public Journalism*, London: The Guildford Press.

Goldenberg, E. (1975) *Making the Papers: The Access of Resource-Poor Groups to the Metropolitan Press*, Lexington, MA: D. C. Heath and Co.

Goldenberg, S. (2013) 'Secret Funding Helped Build Vast Network of Climate Denial Thinktanks', *Guardian*, London.

Golding, P. and Murdock, G. (2000) 'Culture, Communications and Political Economy' in J. Curran and M. Gurevitch eds. *Mass Media and Society*, 3rd edn, London: Arnold.

Goode, L. (2005) *Jürgen Habermas: Democracy and the Public Sphere*, London: Pluto Press.

Goodhart, D. (2017) *The Road to Somewhere: The Populist Revolt and the Future of Politics*, London: Hurst and Co.

Graber, D. and Dunaway, J. (2017) *Mass Media and American Politics*, 10th edn, Thousand Oaks, California: CQ Press/Sage.

Grant, W. (1978) *Insider Groups, Outsider Groups and Interest Group Strategies in Britain*, Department of Politics Working Paper No. 19, Warwick: University of Warwick.

Graves, L. (2016) *Deciding What's True: The Rise of Political Fact-Checking in American Journalism*, New York: Columbia University Press.

Greenwald, G. (2014) *No Place to Hide: Edward Snowden, the NSA and the Surveillance State*, London: Penguin.

Gripsrud, J. (2007) 'Television and the European Public Sphere', *European Journal of Communication*, 22 (4): 479–92.

Grunig, J. ed. (1992) *Excellence in Public Relations and Communication Management*, Hillsdale, NJ: Lawrence Erlbaum Associates.

Grunig, J. and Hunt, T. (1984) *Managing Public Relations*, New York: Holt, Rinehart and Winston.

Gulati, G. (2004) 'Members of Congress and Presentation of Self on the World Wide Web', *Harvard Journal of Press/Politics*, 9 (1): 22–40.

GUMG (1976) *Bad News*, Glasgow University Media Group London: Routledge.

GUMG (1980) *More Bad News*, Glasgow University Media Group, London: Routledge.

Gunter, B. (2003) *News and the Net*, London: Lawrence Erlbaum.

Gunther, R. and Mughan, A. (2001) *Democracy and the Media: A Comparative Perspective*, Cambridge: Cambridge University Press.

Habermas, J. (1977) *Legitimation Crisis*, Cambridge: Polity.

Habermas, J. (1987) *The Theory of Communicative Action*, Cambridge: Polity.

Habermas, J. (1989 [1962]) *The Structural Transformation of the Public Sphere: An Inquiry into a Category of Bourgeois Society* (trans. Burger, T.), Cambridge: Polity.

Habermas, J. (1992) 'Further Reflections on the Public Sphere', trans. by Burger, T. in Calhoun, C. ed. *Habermas and the Public Sphere*, Cambridge, MA: MIT Press.

Habermas, J. (1996) *Between Facts and Norms*, Cambridge: Polity.

Habermas, J. (1999) 'The European Nation State and the Pressures of Globalization', *New Left Review*, Issue 235: 425–36.

Habermas, J. (2001) *The Postnational Constellation: Political Essays*, Cambridge, MA: MIT Press.

Hague, R. and Harrop, M. (2013) *Comparative Government and Politics*, 9th edn, Basingstoke: Palgrave Macmillan.

Hall, P. and Soskice, D. eds. (2001) *Varities of Capitalism: The Institutional Foundations of Comparative Advantage*, Oxford: Oxford University Press.

Hall, S., Critcher, C., Jefferson, T., Clarke, J. and Roberts, B. (1978) *Policing the Crisis – Mugging, the State, and Law and Order*, London: Macmillan.

Hall Jamieson, K. (1996) *Packaging the Presidency: A History and Criticism of Presidential Campaign Advertising*, 3rd edn, Oxford: Oxford University Press.

Hall Jamieson, K. (2005) *Electing the President, 2004: The Insiders' View*, Philadelphia, PA: University of Pennsylvania Press.

Hallin, D. (1994) *We Keep America on Top of the World – Television Journalism and the Public Sphere*, London: Routledge.

Hallin, D. and Mancini, P. (2004) *Comparing Media Systems: Three Models of Media and Politics*, Cambridge: Cambridge University Press.

Hallin, D. and Mancini, P. eds. (2011) *Comparing Media Systems Beyond the Western World*, Cambridge: Cambridge University Press.

Hanitzsch, T. and Mellado, C. (2011) 'What Shapes News Around the World: How Journalists in 18 Countries Perceive Influences on their Work', *Harvard Journal of Press/Politics*, 16 (3), 404–26.

Hansard (2004/2009/2015/2018) *An Audit of Political Engagement*, 1st/6th/12th/15th Reports, London: Hansard Society and Electoral Commission.

Hansen, A. ed. (1993) *The Mass Media and Environmental Issues*, Leicester: Leicester University Press.

Hansen, A. (2010) *Environment, Media and Communication*, London: Routledge.

Hardy, J. (2008) *Western Media Systems*, London: Routledge.

Harvey, D. (2007) *A Brief History of Neoliberalism*, Oxford: Oxford University Press.

Hay, C. (2007) *Why We Hate Politics*, Cambridge: Polity.

Heath, A., Jowell, R. and Curtice, J. (2001) *The Rise of New Labour: Party Policies and Voter Choices*, Oxford: Oxford University Press.

Heffernan, R. (2003) 'Political Parties and the Party System' in Dunleavy, P., Gamble, A., Heffernan, R. and Peele, G. eds. *Developments in British Politics 7*, Basingstoke: Palgrave Macmillan.

Held, D. (2002) 'Laws of States, Laws of Peoples', *Legal Theory*, 8: 1–44.

Held, D. (2003) 'Cosmopolitanism: Globalisation Tamed?' *Review of International Studies*, 29: 465–80.

Held, D. (2006) *Models of Democracy*, 3rd edn, Cambridge: Polity.

Held, D. and McGrew, A. (2003) 'The Great Globalization Debate: An Introduction' in Held, D. and McGrew, A. eds. *The Global Transformations Reader: An Introduction to the Globalization Debate*, Cambridge: Polity.

Held, D. and McGrew, A. (2007) *Globalization/Anti-Globalization: Beyond the Great Divide*, Cambridge: Polity.

Hendricks, J. and Denton, R. eds. (2010) *Communicator in Chief: How Barack Obama Used New Media Technology to Win the White House*, Lanham: Rowman and Littlefield.

Hennigan, K., et al., (1982) 'Impact of the Introduction of Television Crime in the United States: Empirical Findings and Theoretical Implications', *Journal of Personality and Social Psychology*, 42: 461–77.

Hepp, A., Hjarvard, S. and Lundby, K. (2015) 'Mediatization: Theorizing the Interplay Between Media, Culture and Society', *Media, Culture and Society*, 37 (2): 314–22.

Herbst, S. (1998) *Reading Public Opinion: Political Actors View the Democratic Process*, Chicago: University of Chicago Press.

Herman, E. and Chomsky, N. ([1988] 2002) *Manufacturing Consent*, 2nd edn, New York: Pantheon.

Herman, E. and McChesney, R. (1997) *The Global Media: The New Missionaries of Global Capitalism*, London: Cassell.

Herman, E. and Peterson, D. (2011) 'Legitimizing Versus Deligitimizing Elections: Honduras and Iran' in Sussman, G. ed. *The Propaganda Society: Promotional Culture and Politics in Global Context*, New York: Peter Lang.

Hershey, M. (2017) *Party Politics in America*, 17th edn, New York: Routledge.

Hess, S. (1984) *The Government/Press Connection: Press Officers and Their Offices*, Washington DC: Brookings Institute.

Heywood, A. (2017) *Political Ideologies: An Introduction*, 6th edn, Basingstoke: Palgrave.

Hibbings, J. and Theiss-Morse, E. (2002) *Stealth Democracy: Americans' Beliefs About How Government Should Work*, Cambridge: Cambridge University Press.

Himmelweit, H., Oppenheim, A. and Vince, P. (1958) *Television and the Child: An Empirical Study of the Effect of Television on the Young*, Oxford: Oxford University Press.

Hintz, A. (2015) 'Social Media Censorship, Privatised Regulation and New Restrictions to Protest and Dissent' in Dencik, L. and Leistert, O. eds. *Critical Perspectives on Social Media Protest*, London: Rowman and Littlefield.

Hirst, P. and Thompson, G. (1996) *Globalization in Question: The International Economy and the Possibilities of Governance*, Cambridge: Polity.

Hoedemann, O. (2007) 'Corporate Power in Europe: The Brussels 'Lobbycracy' in Dinan, W. and Miller, D. eds. *Thinker, Faker, Spinner, Spy: Spin and Corporate Power*, London: Pluto.

Holtz Bacha, C., Langer, A. and Merkle, S. (2014) 'The Personalization of Politics in Comparative Perspective', *European Journal of Communication*, 29 (2): 153–70.

Horton, D. and Wohl, R. ([1956] 2003) 'Mass Communication and Para-Social Interaction' in Corner, J. and Hawthorn, J. eds. *Communication Studies: An Introductory Reader*, 4th edn, London: Arnold.

Howard, P., Duffy, A., Freelon, D., Hussain, M., Mari, W., Maziad, M. (2011) *Opening Closed Regimes: What was the Role of Social Media During the Arab Spring*, Working Paper 2011.1, ITPI, Washington: Center for Communication and Civic Engagement.

Hutchins, B. and Lester, L. (2011) 'Politics, Power and Online Protest in an Age of Environmental Conflict' in Cottle, S. and Lester, L. eds. *Transnational Protests and the Media*, New York: Peter Lang.

Hutton, W. (1996) *The State We're In*, London: Vintage.

IDEA (2016/17) *The Global State of Democracy*, Stockholm: Institute for Democracy and Electoral Assistance.

IMF (2016) International Monetary Fund at: www.imf.org.

IMF (2017) International Monetary Fund data on national debt, at: http://www.imf.org/en/Data.

Inglehart, R. (1977) *The Silent Revolution: Changing Values and Political Styles Amongst Western Publics*, Princeton, NJ: Princeton University Press.

Inglehart, R. (1990) *Culture Shift*, Princeton, NJ: Princeton University Press.

Inglehart, R. (1997) *Modernization and Postmodernization: Cultural, Economic and Political Change in 43 Countries*, Princeton, NJ: Princeton University Press.

Inglehart, R. and Norris, P. (2016) *Trump, Brexit, the and Rise of Populism: Economic Have-Nots and Cultural Backlash*, Harvard Working Paper No. RWP16–026, Cambridge, MA: Harvard University.

Internet Live Stats (2017) at: http://www.internetlivestats.com/.

Ipsos-MORI (October 2014) 'Perils of Perception Survey', London: Ipsos-MORI, at: https://www.ipsos.com/ipsos-mori/en-uk/perceptions-are-not-reality-things-world-gets-wrong.

IPU (2017) *Women in Parliament: The Year in Review,* Geneva: Inter-Parliamentary Union.

Iyengar, S. (1990) 'Framing Responsibility for Political Issues: The Case of Poverty' in *Political Behaviour,* 12 (1): 19–40.

Iyengar, S. (1997) 'Overview' in Iyengar, S. and Reeves, R. eds. *Do the Media Govern?* Thousand Oaks, CA: Sage.

Iyengar, S. and Kinder, D. (1987) *News that Matters,* Chicago: Chicago University Press.

Iyengar, S. and Simon, A. (1993) 'News Coverage of the Gulf Crisis and Public Opinion: A Study of Agenda-Setting, Priming, and Framing', *Communication Research,* 20 (3): 365–83.

Jackson, N. and Lilleker, D. (2004) 'Just Public Relations or an Attempt at Interaction?: British MPs in the Press, On the Web and "In Your Face"', *European Journal of Communication,* 19 (4): 507–33.

Jackson, D., Thorsen, E. and Lilleker, D. (2016) *EU Referendum Analysis 2016: Media, Voters and the Campaign,* Bournemouth: CSJCC.

Jenkins, H. (2009) *Convergence Culture,* New York: New York University Press.

Jenkins, H. and Thorburn, D. (2004) *Democracy and New Media,* Cambridge, MA: MIT Press.

Jenkins, J. (1983) 'Research Mobilization Theory and the Study of Social Movements', *The Annual Review of Sociology,* 9: 527–53.

Jones, N. (1986) *Strikes and the Media: Communication and Conflict,* Oxford: Basil Blackwell.

Jones, O. (2014) *The Establishment and How They Get Away with it,* Allen Lane: London.

Jordan, G. and Moloney, W. (2007) *Democracy and Interest Groups,* Houndmills, Basingstoke: Palgrave Macmillan.

Judis, J. (2016) *The Populist Explosion: How the Great Recession Transformed American and European Politics,* New York: Columbia Global Reports.

Juris, J. (2012a) 'Mediating and Embodying Transnational Protest: Internal and External Effects of Mass Global Justice Actions' in Cottle, S. and Lester, L. eds. *Transnational Protests and the Media,* New York: Peter Lang.

Juris, J. (2012b) 'Reflections on #Occupy Everywhere: Social Media, Public Space, and Emerging Logics of Aggregation', *American Ethnologist,* 39 (2): 259–79.

Kahin, B. and Wilson, E. eds. (1997) *National Information Infrastructure Initiatives: Vision and Policy Design,* Cambridge, MA: MIT Press.

Kahn, R. and Kellner, D. (2004) 'New Media and Internet Activism: From the "Battle of Seattle" to Blogging', *New Media and Society,* 6 (1): 87–95.

Kahneman, D., Slavic, P., and Tversky, A. eds. (1982) *Judgement Under*

Uncertainty: Heuristics and Biases, Cambridge: Cambridge University Press.

Kaldor, M. (2003) 'The Idea of Global Civil Society', *International Affairs*, 79 (3): 583–93.

Kaldor, M., Moore, H. and Selchow, S. eds. (2012) *Global Civil Society 2012: Ten Years of Critical Reflection*, Basingstoke: Palgrave Macmillan.

Kaneva, N. (2014) *Branding Post-Communist Nations*, London: Routledge.

Kantola, A. (2006) 'On the Dark Side of Democracy: The Global Imaginary of Financial Journalism' in Cammaerts, B. and Carpentier, N. eds. *Reclaiming the Media: Communication, Rights and Democratic Media Roles*, Bristol: Intellect.

Kantola, A. (2009) 'The Disciplined Imaginary: The Nation Rejuvenated for the Global Condition' in Roosvall, A., Salovaara-Moring, I. eds. *Communicating the Nation*, Stockholm: Nordicom.

Kateb, G. (1992) *The Inner Ocean: Individualism and Democratic Culture*, New York: Cornell University Press.

Katz, E., Blumler, J. and Gurevitch, M. (1973) 'Uses and Gratifications Research', *Public Opinion Quarterly*, 37 (4): 509–23.

Kavada, A. (2005) 'Civil Society Organisations and the Internet: The Case of Amnesty International, Oxfam and the World Development Movement' in de Jong, W., Shaw, M., and Stammers, N. eds. *Global Activism Global Media*, London: Pluto Press, pp. 208–22.

Kavada, A. (2015) 'Creating the Collective: Social Media, the Occupy Movement and its Constitution as a Collective Actor', *Information, Communication and Society*, 18 (8): 872–86.

Keane, J. (1991) *The Media and Democracy*, Cambridge: Polity.

Keane, J. (2001) 'Global Civil Society?' in Anheier, H., Glasius, M. and Kaldor, M. eds. *Global Civil Society Yearbook 2001*, Oxford: Oxford University Press, pp. 23–47.

Keane, J. (2009) *The Life and Death of Democracy*, London: W. W. Norton and Co.

Keck, M. and Sikkink, K. (1998) *Activists Beyond Borders: Advocacy Networks in International Politics*, Ithaca, New York: Cornell University Press.

Keen, S. (2011) *Debunking Economics: The Naked Emperor Dethroned?* 2nd edn, London: Zed Books.

Keen, S. (2017) *Can We Avoid Another Financial Crisis?* Cambridge: Polity.

Kellner, D. (2000) 'Habermas, the Public Sphere, and Democracy: A Critical Intervention' in Hahn, L. ed. *Perspectives on Habermas*, Chicago: Open Court Press.

Kellner, D. (2009) *Cinema Wars: Hollywood Film and Politics in the Bush-Cheney Era*, Oxford: Wiley-Blackwell.

Kellner, D. (2014) 'Habermas, the Public Sphere and Democracy' in Boros, D. and Glass, J. eds. *Reimagining Public Space*, Basingstoke: Palgrave Macmillan.

Kenski, H. and Kenski, K. (2009) 'Explaining the Vote in the Election of 2008: The Democratic Revival' in Denton, R. ed. *The 2008 Presidential Campaign: A Communication Perspective*, Lanham: Rowman and Littlefield.

Kenski, K. and Hall Jamieson, K. (2017) *The Oxford Handbook of Political Communication*, New York: Oxford University Press.

Keynes, J. (1936) *The General Theory of Employment, Interest and Money*, London: Macmillan.

Khan, S. (2011) *Privilege: The Making of an Adolescent Elite at St Paul's School*, Princeton, NJ: Princeton University Press.

Kindleberger, C. and Alibar, R. (2011) *Manias, Panics and Crashes: A History of Financial Crises*, Basingstoke: Palgrave Macmillan.

King, S. (2017) *Grave New World: The End of Globalization, the Return of History*, New Haven, CT: Yale University Press.

Kircheimer, O. (1966) 'The Transformation of the Western European Party Systems' in Weiner, M. and LaPalombara, J. eds. *Political Parties and Political Development*, Princeton, NJ: Princeton University Press.

Klapper, J. (1960) *The Effects of Mass Communication*, New York: The Free Press.

Klein, N. (2015) *This Changes Everything: Capitalism Versus the Climate*, London: Penguin.

Knight Frank (2014) *The Wealth Report*, at: http://www.knightfrank.com/wealthreport.

Knightley, P. (2004) *The First Casualty*, 3rd edn, London: Andre Deutsch.

Knowles, S., Phillips, G. and Lidberg, J. (2017) 'Reporting the Global Financial Crisis: A Longitudinal Tri-Nation Study of Mainstream Financial Journalism', *Journalism Studies*, 18 (3): 322–40.

Knuckey, J. and Lees-Marshment, J. (2005) 'American Political Marketing: George W. Bush and the Republican Party' in Lilleker, D. and Lees-Marshment, J. eds. *Political Marketing: A Comparative Perspective*, Manchester: Manchester University Press.

Kovach, B., Rosentiel, T. and Mitchell, A. (2004) *A Crisis of Confidence: A Commentary on the Findings*, Washington DC: Pew Research Centre.

Kraidy, M. (2005) *Hybridity or the Cultural Logic of Globalization*, Philadelphia: Temple University Press.

Kriesi, H. (1991) 'The Political Opportunity Structure of New Social Movements' *Discussion Paper FS III*, Berlin: Wissenschaftszentrum.

Krippner, G. (2011) *Capitalizing on Crisis: The Political Origins of the Rise of Finance*, Cambridge, MA: Harvard University Press.

Krotz, F. (2007) 'The Meta-Process of "Mediatization" as a Conceptual Frame', *Global Media and Communication*, 3 (3): 256–60.

Krugman, P. (2008) *The Return of Depression Economics and the Crisis of 2008*, London: Penguin Books.

Kunelius, R. and Reunanen, E. (2012) 'Media in Political Power: A Parsonian View on the Differentiated Mediatization of Finnish Decision-Makers', *International Journal of Press/Politics*, 17: 68–76.

Kurtz, H. (1998) *Spin Cycle: Inside the Clinton Propaganda Machine*, London, Pan Books.

Lander, N. (2013) 'Rethinking the Logics: A Conceptual Framework for the Mediatization of Politics', *Communication Theory*, 23 (3): 239–58.

Lapavitsas, C. (2013) *Profiting Without Producing: How Finance Exploits Us All*, London: Verso.

Larner, W. (2000) 'Neoliberalism: Policy, Ideology, Governmentality', *Studies in Political Economy*, 63 (Autumn): 5–26.

Lasorsa, D., Lewis, S. and Holton, A. (2012) 'Normalizing Twitter: Journalism Practice in an Emerging Communication Space', *Journalism Studies*, 13 (1): 19–36.

Lasswell, H. (1927) *Propaganda Techniques in the First World War*, New York: Alfred Knopf.

Laurens, S. (2017) *Lobbyists and Bureaucrats in Brussels: Capitalism's Brokers*, London: Routledge.

Lawrence, R. and Boydstun, A. (2017) 'Celebrities as Political Actors and Entertainment as Political Media' in van Aelst, P. and Walgrave, S. eds. *How Political Actors Use the Media*, Cham., Switzerland: Palgrave Macmillan.

Lazarsfeld, P., Berelson, B. and Gaudet, H. (1944) *The People's Choice*, New York: Duell, Sloan and Pearce.

Lees, C. (2005) 'Political Marketing in Germany: The Campaigns of the Social Democratic Party' in Lilleker, D. and Lees-Marshment, J. eds. *Political Marketing: A Comparative Perspective*, Manchester: Manchester University Press.

Lees-Marshment, J. (2001/08) *Political Marketing and British Political Parties: The Party's Just Begun*, 1st/2nd edns, Manchester: Manchester University Press.

Lees-Marshment, J. (2011) *The Political Marketing Game*, Basingstoke: Palgrave Macmillan.

Lees-Marshment, J. ed. (2015) *The Political Marketing Handbook*, London: Routledge.

Lengauer, G., Donges, P. and Plasser, F. (2014) 'Media Power in Politics' in Pfetsch, B. ed. *Political Communication Cultures in Europe*, Basingstoke: Palgrave.

Lewis, S. and Carlson, M. 'The Dissolution of News: Selective Exposure, Filter Bubbles, and the Boundaries of Journalism' in Lilleker, D., Thorsen, E. and Jackson, D. (2016) *US Election Analysis 2016: Media, Voters and the Campaign*, Bournemouth: CSJCC.

Lewis, J., Williams, A. and Franklin, B. (2008) 'A Compromised Fourth Estate? UK News Journalism, Public Relations and News Sources', *Journalism Studies*, 9 (1): 1–20.

Lichtenberg, J. (2000) 'In Defence of Objectivity' in Curran, J. and Gurevitch, M. eds. *Mass Media and Society*, 3rd edn, London: Arnold.

Lichter, S. and Rothman, S. (1988) 'Media and Business Elites' in Hiebert,

R. and Reuss, C. eds. *Impacts of Mass Media*, New York: Longman, pp. 448–62.

Lievrouw, L. and Livingstone, S. (2006) 'Introduction' in Lievrouw, L. and Livingstone, S. eds. *The Handbook of New Media*, 2nd edn, London: Sage.

Lijphart, A. (1984) *Democracies: Patterns of Majoritarian and Consensus Government in Twenty-One Countries*, New Haven, CT: Yale University Press.

Lijphart, A. (1999) *Patterns of Democracy: Government Forms and Performances in Thirty Six Countries*, New Haven, CT: Yale University Press.

Lilleker, D. and Lees-Marshment, J. (2005) *Political Marketing: A Comparative Perspective*, Manchester: Manchester University Press.

Lilleker, D., Thorsen, E. and Jackson, D. (2016) *US Election Analysis 2016: Media, Voters and the Campaign*, Bournemouth: CSJCC.

Lindblom, C. (1977) *Politics and Markets: The World's Political Economic Systems*, New York: Basic Books.

Lippman, W. (1922) *Public Opinion*, New York: Harcourt Brace.

Lipsey, R. and Chrystal, A. (2015) *Economics*, 13th edn, Oxford: Oxford University Press.

Livingstone, S. (2009) 'On the Mediation of Everything: ICA Presidential Address 2008', *Journal of Communication*, 59 (1): 1–18.

Livingstone, S. and Lunt, P. (2013) 'Media Studies' Fascination with the Concept of the Public Sphere: Critical Reflections and Emerging Debates', *Media, Culture and Society*, 35 (1): 87–96.

Loader, B., Vromen, A. and Xenos, M. (2016) 'Performing for the Young Networked Citizen? Celebrity Politics, Social Networking and the Political Engagement of Young People', *Media, Culture and Society*, 38 (3: 400–19.

Loughborough (2015) *The UK General Election of 2015*, 5 Reports at: http://blog.lboro.ac.uk/crcc.

Loughborough University (2016) 'EU Referendum Research', https://blog.lboro.ac.uk/crcc/eu-referendum/.

Lowrey, W. (2006) 'Mapping the Journalism–Blogging Relationship', *Journalism: Theory, Criticism and Practice*, 7 (4): 477–500.

Luce, E. (2017) *The Retreat of Western Liberalism*, London: Little and Brown.

Lukes, S. (2005) *Power: A Radical View*, 2nd edn, Basingstoke: Palgrave Macmillan.

Lundby, K. ed. (2009) *Mediatization: Concept, Changes, Consequences*, New York: Peter Lang.

Lusoli, W. and Ward, S. (2003) 'Digital Rank-and-File: Party Activists' Perceptions and Use of the Internet', paper for the *American Political Science Association Conference*, Philadelphia, August.

Lusoli, W. and Ward, S. (2004) 'Digital Rank-and-File: Party Activists' Perceptions and Use of the Internet', *British Journal of Politics and International Relations*, 6 (4): 453–70.

Lusoli, W., Ward, S. and Gibson, R. (2006) '(Re)Connecting Politics? Parliament, the Public and the Internet', *Parliamentary Affairs*, 59 (1): 24–42.

Maarek, P. (1995) *Political Marketing and Communication*, Eastleigh: John Libby Press.

Maarek, P. (2011) *Campaign Communication and Political Marketing*, Oxford: Wiley-Blackwell.

MacKenzie, D. and Wajcman, J. eds. (1999) *The Social Shaping of Technology*, 2nd edn, Buckingham: Open University Press.

MacPherson, C. (1965) *The Real World of Democracy*, Toronto: Canadian Broadcasting Company.

Magin, M., Podschuweit, N., Habler, J. and Russman, U. (2016) 'Campaigning in the Fourth Age of Political Communication: A Multi-Method Study on the Use of Facebook by German and Austrian Parties in the 2013 National Election Campaigns', *Information, Communication and Society*, 20 (11): 1680–97.

Magleby, D. (2011) 'Adaption and Innovation in the Financing of the 2008 Election' in Magleby, D. and Corrado, A. eds. *Financing the 2008 Election*, Washington DC: The Brookings Institute.

Mainwaring, S., Gervasani, C. and Espana-Najero, A. (2017) 'Extra and Within System Electoral Volatility', *Party Politics*, 23 (6): 623–35.

Mair, P. (2013) *Ruling the Void: The Hollowing of Western Democracy*, London: Verso.

Mann, M. (1997) 'Has Globalization Ended the Rise and Rise of the Nation State?' *Review of International Political Economy*, 4 (3): 472–96.

Manning, P. (1999) 'Categories of Knowledge and Information Flows: Reasons for the Decline of the British Labour and Industrial Correspondents Group', *Media, Culture and Society*, 21 (3): 313–36.

Manning, P. (2000) *News and News Sources*, London: Sage.

Manning, P. (2013) 'Financial Journalism, News Sources and the Banking Crisis', *Journalism*, 14 (2): 173–89.

Marchand, R. (1998) *Creating the Corporate Soul*, Berkeley, LA: University of California Press.

Marsh, D. ed (1998) *Comparing Policy Networks*, Buckingham: Open University Press.

Marsh, D. and Rhodes, R. (1992) *Policy Networks in British Government*, Oxford: Clarendon.

Marshall, D. (1997) *Celebrity and Power: Fame in Contemporary Culture*, Minneapolis, MN: University of Minnesota Press.

Martell, L. (2017) *The Sociology of Globalization*, 2nd edn, Cambridge: Polity.

Martinez-Torres, M. (2001) 'Civil Society, the Internet, and the Zapatistas', *Peace Review*, 13 (3): 347–55.

Marx, K. and Engels, F. (1938 [1846]) *The German Ideology*, London: Lawrence and Wishart.

Mason, P. (2012) *Why It's Kicking Off Everywhere: The New Global Revolutions*, London: Verso.

Mazzoleni, G. (2014) 'Mediatization and Political Populism' in Stromback, J.

and Esser, F. eds. *Mediatization of Politics: Understanding the Transformation of Western Democracies*, Basingstoke: Palgrave.

Mazzoleni, G. and Schulz, W. (1999) '"Mediatization of Politics": A Challenge for Democracy', *Political Communication*, 16 (3): 247–61.

McCarthy, J. and Zald, M. (1977) 'Resource Mobilization and Social Movements: A Partial Theory', *American Journal of Sociology*, 82: 1212–41.

McChesney, R. (1999) *Rich Media, Poor Democracy: Communication Politics in Dubious Times*, Urbana: University of Illinois Press.

McChesney, R. (2013) *Digital Disconnect: How Capitalism is Turning the Internet Against Democracy*, New York: New Press.

McChesney, R. and Nichols, J. (2010) *The Death and Life of American Journalism*, New York: Nation Books.

McChesney, R. and Pickard, R. eds. (2011) *Will the Last Reporter Please Turn Out the Lights: The Collapse of Journalism and What Can be Done to Fix it*, New York: New Press.

McCombs, M. and Shaw, D. (1972) 'The Agenda-Setting Function of Mass Media', *Public Opinion Quarterly*, 36: 176–85.

McCright, A., Dunlap, R. and Marquart-Pyatt, S. (2015) 'Political Ideology and Views About Climate Change in the European Union', *Environmental Politics*, 25 (2): 338–58.

McGregor, S., Lawrence, R. and Cardona, A. (2016) 'Personalization, Gender and Social Media', *Information, Communication and Society*, 20 (1): 264–83.

McGrew, A. (2002) 'Models of Transnational Democracy' in Carter, A. and Stokes, G. eds. *Democratic Theory Today*, Cambridge: Polity, pp. 269–93.

McLachlin and Golding, P. (2000) in Sparks, C. and Tulloch, J. eds. *Tabloid Tales: Global Debates Over Media Standards*, Oxford: Rowman and Littlefield.

McLuhan, M. (1962) *The Gutenberg Galaxy: The Making of Typographic Man*, Toronto: University of Toronto Press.

McLuhan, M. (1964) *Understanding the Media: The Extensions of Man*, New York: McGraw Hill.

McNair, B. (2006) *Cultural Chaos: Journalism and Power in a Globalised World*, London: Routledge.

McNair, B. (2009/2011/2017) *An Introduction to Political Communication*, 4th/5th/6th edns, London: Routledge.

McNair, B. (2016) *Communication and Political Crisis: Media, Politics and Governance in a Globalized Public Sphere*, Oxford: Peter Lang.

McPhail, T. (2014) *Global Communication: Theories, Stakeholders and Trends*, Chichester: Wiley-Blackwell.

McQuail, D. (2010) *McQuail's Mass Communication Theory*, 6th edn, Los Angeles: Sage.

Mercille, J. (2014) 'The Role of the Media in Sustaining Ireland's Housing Bubble', *New Political Economy*, 19 (2): 282–301.

Merez, S. (2011) 'Using Time Series Analysis to Measure Intermedia

Agenda-Setting Influence in Traditional Media and Political Blog Networks', *Journalism and Mass Communication Quarterly*, 88 (1): 176–94.

Meyer, T. (2002) *Media Democracy: How the Media Colonize Politics*, Cambridge: Polity.

Meyrowitz, J. (1985) *No Sense of Place: The Impact of Electronic Media on Social Behaviour*, New York: Oxford University Press.

Miliband, R. (1969) *The State in Capitalist Society*, London: Weidenfeld and Nicolson.

Miller, D. (1994) *Don't Mention the War: Northern Ireland, Propaganda and the Media*, London: Pluto Press.

Miller, D. ed. (2004) *Tell Me Lies: Propaganda and Media Distortion in the Attack on Iraq*, London: Pluto Press.

Miller, D. and Dinan, W. (2000) 'The Rise of the PR Industry in Britain, 1979–98', *European Journal of Communication*, 15 (1): 5–35.

Miller, D. and Dinan, W. (2008) *A Century of Spin: How Public Relations Became the Cutting Edge of Corporate Power*, London: Pluto Press.

Miller, D. and Sabir, R. (2012) 'Propaganda and Terrorism' in Freedman, D. and Thussu, D. eds. *Media and Terrorism: Global Perspectives*, London: Sage.

Miller, L. (1998) *Power Journalism: Computer Assisted Reporting*, Fort Worth, TX: Harcourt Brace.

Mills, C. Wright (1956) *The Power Elite*, Oxford: Oxford University Press.

Minsky, H. (1982) *Can "It" Happen Again? Essays on Instability and Finance*, London: Routledge.

Mirowski, P. (2009) 'Postface: Defining Neoliberalism' in Mirowski, P. and Plehwe, D. eds. *The Road from Mont Pelerin: The Making of the Neoliberal Thought Collective*, Cambridge MA: Harvard University Press, pp. 417–55.

Mirowski, P. (2014) *Never Let a Serious Crisis Go to Waste: How Neoliberalism Survived the Financial Meltdown*, London: Verso.

Mirowski, P. and Plehwe, D. eds. (2009) *The Road from Mont Pelerin: The Making of the Neoliberal Thought Collective*, Cambridge, MA: Harvard University Press.

Mizruchi, M. (2013) *The Fracturing of the American Corporate Elite*, Cambridge, MA: Harvard University Press.

Monbiot, G. (2017) *How Did We Get Into This Mess? Politics, Equality, Nature*, London: Verso.

Moran, M. (2003) *The British Regulatory State: High Modernism and Hyper-Innovation*, Oxford: Oxford University Press.

Morley, D. (1980) *The Nationwide Audience*, London: BFI.

Morley, D. (1992) *Television, Audiences and Cultural Studies*, London: Routledge.

Morozov, E. (2012) *The Net Delusion: How Not to Liberate the World*, London: Penguin.

Mosley, L. (2003) *Global Capital and National Governments*, Cambridge: Cambridge University Press.

Motta, M. 'Air War?: Campaign Advertising in the 2016 Presidential Election' in Lilleker, D., Thorsen, E. and Jackson, D. (2016) *US Election Analysis 2016: Media, Voters and the Campaign*, Bournemouth: CSJCC.

Mudde, C. and Rovira Kaltwasser, C. (2017) *Populism: A Very Short Introduction*, Oxford: Oxford University Press.

Muller, D. 'Trump, Truth and the Media' in Lilleker, D., Thorsen, E. and Jackson, D. (2016) *US Election Analysis 2016: Media, Voters and the Campaign*, Bournemouth: CSJCC.

Naím, M. (2013) *The End of Power: From Boardrooms to Battlefields and Churches to States, Why Being in Charge Isn't What it Used to Be*, New York: Basic Books.

Narayana, V. et al., (2018) *Polarization, Partisanship and Junk News Consumption Over Social Media in the US*, Oxford: Oxford Internet Institute.

Negroponte, N. (1995) *Being Digital*, London: Hodder and Stoughton.

Nerone, J. (2009) 'The Death and Rebirth of Working-Class Journalism' *Journalism*, 10 (3): 353–5.

Nessman, K. (1995) 'Public Relations in Europe: A Comparison with the United States' in *Public Relations Review*, 21: 151–60.

Newman, B. ed. (1999) *The Handbook of Political Marketing*, Thousand Oaks, CA: Sage.

Newman, K. (1984) *Financial Marketing and Communications*, London: Holt, Rinehart and Winston.

Newman, N. and Fletcher, R. (2017) *Bias, Bullshit and Lies: Audience Perspectives on Low Trust in the Media*, Oxford: Reuters Institute for the Study of Journalism.

Noelle-Neumann, E. (1984) *The Spiral of Silence*, Chicago: University of Chicago Press.

Norris, P. (1999) 'Changes in Party Competition at Westminster' in Evans, G. and Norris, P. eds. *Critical Elections: British Parties and Voters in Long-Term Perspective*, London: Sage.

Norris, P. (2000) *A Virtuous Circle: Political Communications in Postindustrial Societies*, Cambridge: Cambridge University Press.

Norris, P. (2001) *Digital Divide: Civic Engagement, Information Poverty and the internet Worldwide*, Cambridge: Cambridge University Press.

Norris, P. (2002) *Democratic Phoenix: Political Activism World Wide*, New York: Cambridge University Press.

Norris, P. (2004) 'Global Political Communication: Good Governance, Human Development, and Mass Communication' in Esser, F. and Pfetsch, B. eds. *Comparing Political Communication: Theories, Cases and Challenges*, Cambridge: Cambridge University Press.

Norris, P. (2011) *Democratic Deficit: Critical Citizens Revisited*, Cambridge: Cambridge University Press.

NTO/Skillset (2002) *Journalists at Work: Survey by Journalism Training Forum*, London: NTO/Skillset.

Nye, J. (2004) *Soft Power: The Means to Success in World Politics*, New York: Public Affairs.

O'Neill, C. (2017) *Weapons of Math Destruction*, London: Penguin.

OECD (2010) *The Evolution of News and the Internet*, Paris: OECD.

Ofcom (2007) *New News, Future News: The Challenges for Television News After Digital Switchover*, London: OFCOM.

Ofcom (2017) *News Consumption in the UK 2016*, London: Ofcom.

Offe, C. (1984) *Contradictions of the Welfare State* (ed. Keane, J.), Cambridge, MA: MIT Press.

Ohmae, K. (1990) *The Borderless World: Power and Strategy in the Interlinked Economy*, New York: Harper Collins.

Ohmae, K. (1995) *The End of the Nation State*, New York: Free Press.

Ojala, M. (2017) *The Making of a Global Elite: Global Economy and Davos Man in the Financial Times 2001–11*, Published PhD Thesis, Helsinki: University of Helsinki.

OpenSecrets, 2017, at: https://www.opensecrets.org/news/2017/04/election-2016-trump-fewer-donors-provided-more-of-the-cash/.

Oxfam (2017) *An Economy for the 99%*, Oxford: Oxfam.

Painter, J. (2009) *Summoned by Science: Reporting Climate Change at Copenhagen and Beyond*, Oxford: Reuters Institute for the Study of Journalism.

Palley, T. (2013) *Financialization: The Economics of Finance Capital Domination*, London: Palgrave Macmillan.

Pariser, E. (2011) *The Filter Bubble: What the Internet is Hiding from You*, London: Penguin.

Parsons, W. (1989) *The Power of the Financial Press: Journalism and Economic Opinion in Britain and America*, London: Edward Elgar.

Patterson, T. (2016) *News Coverage of the 2016 Election: How the Press Failed Us*, Cambridge, MA: Shorenstein Centre, Harvard-Kennedy School.

Pattie, C., Seyd, P. and Whiteley, P. (2003) 'Citizenship and Civic Engagement: Attitudes and Behaviours in Britain', *Political Studies*, 51: 443–68.

Pattie, C., Seyd, P. and Whiteley, P. (2004) *Citizenship in Britain: Values, Participation and Democracy*, Cambridge: Cambridge University Press.

Pavlik, J. (1996) *New Media and the Information Superhighway*, Boston: Allen and Bacon.

Pavlik, J. (2001) *Journalism and New Media*, New York: Columbia University Press.

Perse, E. and Lambe, J. (2017) *Media Effects and Society*, 2nd edn, New York: Routledge.

Pew News Coverage Indexes (2012) at: http://www.journalism.org/news_index/99.

Pew (2009a) *Dissecting the 2008 Electorate: Most Diverse in US History*, Washington DC: Pew Research Center.

Pew (2009b) *The State of the News Media 2009*, Washington DC: Pew/The Project for Excellence in Journalism.

Pew (2012) *The State of the News Media Report*, Washington DC: Pew/The Project for Excellence in Journalism.

Pew (2016a) *State of the News Media 2016*, Washington DC: Pew/The Project for Excellence in Journalism.

Pew (2016b) *Many Americans Believe Fake News is Sowing Confusion*, Washington DC: Pew/The Project for Excellence in Journalism.

Pew (2016c) *Behind Trump's Victory*, Washington DC: Pew/The Project for Excellence in Journalism.

Pew (2017) *Covering President Trump in a Polarized Media Environment*, Washington DC: Pew/The Project for Excellence in Journalism.

Pew (2018) *Political Engagement, Knowledge and the Midterms*, Washington DC: Pew/The Project for Excellence in Journalism.

Phillips, A. (2009) 'Old Sources, New Bottles' in Fenton, N. ed. (2009) *New Media, Old News: Journalism and Democracy in a Digital Age*, London: Sage.

Philo, G. (1995) *Glasgow Media Group Reader, Vol. 2: Industry, Economy, War and Politics*, London: Routledge.

Picard, R., Selva, M. and Binonzo, D. (2014) *Media Coverage of Banking and Financial News*, Oxford: Reuters Institute for the Study of Journalism.

Pickerill, J. (2004) 'Rethinking Political Participation: Experiments in Internet Activism in Australia and Britain' in Gibson, R., Roemmele, A. and Ward, S. eds. *Electronic Democracy: Mobilisation, Organisation and Participation Via New ICTs*, London: Routledge.

Pickerill, J. (2006) 'Radical Politics on the Net', *Parliamentary Affairs*, 59 (2): 266–82.

Piketty, T. (2014) *Capital in the 21st Century*, Cambridge, MA: Harvard University Press.

Pilger, J. (2005) *Tell Me No Lies: Investigative Journalism that Changed the World*, New York: Basic Books.

PIPA (Programme on International Policy Attitudes), at: http://www.pipa.org

Polat, R. (2005) 'The Internet and Political Participation', *European Journal of Communication*, 20 (4): 435–59.

Postman, N. (1985) *Amusing Ourselves to Death*, New York: Penguin.

Poulantzas, N. (1975) *Classes in Contemporary Capitalism*, London: New Left Books.

Power Inquiry (2006) *Power to the People*, London: The Power Inquiry.

Protess, D., Cook, F. L., Doppelt, J. C., Ettema, J. S., Gordon, M. T., Leff, D.R., and Miller, P. (1991) *The Journalism of Outrage: Investigative Reporting and Agenda Building in America*, New York: The Guilford Press.

Putnam, R. (1993) *Making Democracy Work: Civil Traditions in Modern Italy*, Princeton, NJ: Princeton University Press.

Putnam, R. (1995) 'Bowling Alone: America's Declining Social Capital', *Journal of Democracy*, 6 (1): 65–78.

Putnam, R. (2000) *Bowling Alone: The Collapse and Revival of American Community*, New York: Simon and Schuster.

Putnam, R. ed. (2002) *Democracies in Flux: The Evolution of Social Capital in Contemporary Societies*, Oxford: Oxford University Press.

Quandt, T., Loffelholz, M. Weaver, D. Hanitzsch, T. and Aitmeppen, K. (2006) 'American and German Online Journalists at the Beginning of the 21st Century: A Bi-National Survey', *Journalism Studies*, 7 (2): 171–86.

Quiggin, J. (2010) *Zombie Economics: How Dead Ideas Still Walk Among Us*, Princeton, NJ: Princeton University Press.

Radway, J. (1987) *Reading the Romance*, Chapel Hill, NC: University of North Carolina Press.

Rampton, S. and Stauber, J. (2006) *The Best War Ever: Lies, Damned Lies and the Mess in Iraq*, New York: Tarcher.

Rantanen, T. (2005) *The Media and Globalisation*, London: Sage.

Reese, S., Rutigliano, L. Hyun, K. and Jeong, J. (2007) 'Mapping the Blogosphere: Professional and Citizen-Based Media in the Global News Arena', *Journalism: Theory, Criticism and Practice*, 8 (3): 235–61.

Rehg, W. and Bohman, J. (2002) 'Discourse and Democracy: The Formal and Informal Basis of Legitimacy in Between Facts and Norms' in von Schomberg, R. and Baynes, K. eds. *Essays on Habermas: Between Facts and Norms*, Albany, NY: State University of New York.

Reich, R. (1991) *The Work of Nations*, New York: Simon and Schuster.

Reich, Z. (2006) 'The Process Model of News Initiative: Sources Lead, Reporters Thereafter', *Journalism Studies*, 7 (4): 497–514.

Rennie Short, J. 'The Politics of De-legitimacy' in Lilleker, D., Thorsen, E. and Jackson, D. (2016) *US Election Analysis 2016: Media, Voters and the Campaign*, Bournemouth: CSJCC.

Renwick, A. 'The Performance of the Electoral System' in Thorsen, E., Jackson, D. and Lilleker, D. eds. (2017) *UK Election Analysis 2017: Media, Voters and the Campaign*, Bournemouth: CSJCC.

Reuters (2017) *Reuters Institute Digital News Report*, Oxford: Reuters Institute for the Study of Journalism.

Rheingold, H. (2002) *Smart Mobs: The Next Social Revolution*, London: Perseus.

Rhodes, R. (1997) *Understanding Governance: Policy Networks, Governance, Reflexivity and Accountability*, Buckingham: Open University Press.

Richards, D. and Smith, M. (2002) *Governance and Public Policy in the UK*, Oxford: Oxford University Press.

Richards, S. (2017) *The Rise of the Outsiders: How Mainstream Politics Lost its Way*, London: Atlantic Books.

Rifkin, J. (2014) *The Zero Marginal Cost Society: The Internet of Things, The Collaborative Commons and the Eclipse of Capitalism*, New York: Palgrave Macmillan.

Robinson, M. (1976) 'Public Affairs Television and the Growth of Political

Malaise: "the Case of Selling the Pentagon"', *American Political Science Review*, 70 (2): 409–32.

Robinson, P. (1999) 'The CNN Effect: Can the News Media Drive Foreign Policy?' *Review of International Studies*, 25: 301–9.

Rojek, C. (2001) *Celebrity*, London: Reaktion Books.

Rommele, A. (2003) 'Political Parties, Party Communication and New Information and Communication Technologies', *Party Politics*, 9 (1): 7–20.

Rosengren, K. (1973) 'Uses and Gratification: A Paradigm Outlined' in Blumler, J. and Katz, E. eds. *The Uses of Communications*, Beverly Hills, CA: Sage.

Roudakova, N. (2008) 'Media-Political Clientalism: Lessons from Anthropology', *Media, Culture and Society*, 30 (1): 41–59.

RSF (2016) *2016 World Press Freedom Index*, Reporters Sans Frontières at: https://rsf.org/en.

Said, E. (1978) *Orientalism*, London: Vintage Books.

Savage, M. (2015) *Social Class in the Twenty-First Century*, London: Penguin.

Savigny, H. 'Political Marketing and the 2005 Election: What's Ideology Got To Do With It?' in Lilleker, D., Jackson, N. and Scullion, R. eds. (2006) *The Marketing of Political Parties: Political Marketing at the 2005 British General Election*, Manchester: Manchester University Press.

Scammell, M. (1995) *Designer Politics: How Elections are Won*, London: Macmillan.

Scammell, M. (2003) 'Citizen Consumers: Towards a New Marketing of Politics?' in Corner, J. and Pels, D. eds. *Media and the Restyling of Politics: Consumerism, Celebrity and Cynicism*, London: Sage.

Scammell, M. (2014) *Consumer Democracy: The Marketing of Politics*, Cambridge: Cambridge University Press.

Schattschneider, E. E. (1961) *The Semi-Sovereign People: A Realist's View of Democracy in America*, New York: Holt, Rinehart and Winston.

Schifferes, S. (2011) 'The Financial Crisis and the UK Media' in Schiffrin, A. ed. *Bad News: How America's Business Press Missed the Story of the Century*, New York: The New Press, pp. 148–78.

Schiffrin, A. (2011) 'The US Press and the Financial Crisis' in Schiffrin, A. ed. *Bad News: How America's Business Press Missed the Story of the Century*, New York: The New Press, pp. 1–21.

Schiller, H. (1992) *Mass Communication and American Empire*, Boulder: Westview Press.

Schlesinger, P. and Tumber, H. (1994) *Reporting Crime: The Media Politics of Criminal Justice*, Oxford: Clarendon Press.

Schmidt, E. and Cohen, J. (2013) *The New Digital Age: Reshaping the Future of People, Nations and Businesses*, London: John Murray.

Scholte, J. (1997) 'Global Capitalism and the State', *International Affairs*, 73 (3).

Schramm, W., Lyle, J. and Parker, E. (1961) *Television in the Lives of Our Children*, Stanford, CA: Stanford University Press.

Schudson, M. (2008) *Why Democracies Need an Unlovable Press*, Cambridge: Polity.

Schudson, M. (2011) *The Sociology of News*, New York: W. W. Norton.

Schudson, M. and Anderson, C. (2009) 'Objectivity, Professionalism and Truth-Seeking Journalism' in Wahl-Jorgensen, K. and Hanitzsch, T. eds. *The Handbook of Journalism Studies*, London: Routledge.

Schumpeter, J. (1942) *Capitalism, Socialism and Democracy*, London: Unwin Books.

Seib, P. (2012) *Real Time Diplomacy: Politics and Power in the Social Media Era*, New York: Palgrave Macmillan.

Shaheen, J. (2008) *Guilty: Hollywood's Verdict on Arabs After 9/11*, Northampton, MA: Interlink Books.

Shane, P. (2011) *Connecting Democracy: Online Consultation and the Flow of Political Communication*, Cambridge, MA: MIT Press.

Shaw, D., McCombs, M., Weaver, D. and Hamm, B. (1999) 'Individuals, Groups, and Agenda Melding: A Theory of Social Dissonance', *International Journal of Public Opinion Research*, 11 (1): 2–24.

Shaxson, N. (2011) *Treasure Islands: Tax Havens and the Men Who Stole the World*, London: Vintage.

Shiller, R. (2000) *Irrational Exuberance*, Princeton, NJ: Princeton University Press.

Shirky, C. (2009) *Here Comes Everybody: How Change Happens When Everybody Comes Together*, London: Penguin.

Siebert, F., Peterson, T. and Schramm, W. (1956) *Four Theories of the Press*, Urbana: University of Illinois Press.

Sigal, L. V. (1973) *Reporters and Officials: The Organisation and Politics of Newsmaking*, Lexington, MA: Lexington Books.

Singer, J. (2003) 'Who Are These Guys? The Online Challenge to the Notion of Journalistic Professionalism', *Journalism: Theory, Practice and Criticism*, 4 (2): 139–68.

Sireau, N. (2009) *Make Poverty History: Political Communication in Action*, Basingstoke: Palgrave Macmillan.

Skidelski, R. (2010) *Keynes: The Return of the Master*, London: Penguin.

Slater, M. (2007) 'Reinforcing Spirals: The Mutual Influence of Media Selectivity and Media Effects and their Impact on Individual Behaviour and Social Identity', *Communication Theory*, 17 (3): 281–303.

Slaughter, A. (2000) 'Governing the Global Economy through Government Networks' in Byers, M. ed. *The Role of Law in International Politics*, Oxford: Oxford University Press.

Smith, W. (1988) 'Business and the Media: Sometimes Partners, Sometimes Adversaries' in Hiebert, R. and Reuss, C. eds. *Impacts of Mass Media*, New York: Longman, pp. 444–7.

Sola Pool, I. de (1990) *Technologies Without Boundaries: On*

Telecommunications in a Global Age, Cambridge, MA: Harvard University Press.

Sparks, C. (2005) 'Media and the Global Public Sphere: An Evaluative Approach' in de Jong, W., Shaw, M., and Stammers, N. eds. *Global Activism Global Media*, London: Pluto Press, pp. 34–49.

Sparks, C. (2007) *Globalization, Development and the Mass Media*, London: Sage.

Spichal, S. (2012) *Transnationalization of the Public Sphere and the Fate of the Public*, New York: Hampton Press.

Srnicek, N. (2016) *Platform Capitalism*, Cambridge: Polity.

Stanyer, J. (2007) *Modern Political Communication: Mediated Politics in Uncertain Times*, Cambridge: Polity.

Stanyer, J. (2013) *Intimate Politics*, Cambridge: Polity.

Starkman, D. (2014) *The Watchdog that Didn't Bark: The Financial Crisis and the Disappearance of Investigative Journalism*, New York: Columbia University Press.

Stauber, J. and Rampton, S. (2002) *Trust Us We're Experts: How Industry Manipulates Science and Gambles with Your Future*, New York: Tarcher/Penguin.

Stauber, J. and Rampton, S. (2003) *Weapons of Mass Deception: The Uses of Propaganda in Bush's War on Iraq*, New York: Tarcher/Penguin.

Stefan, R. and Mounk, Y. (2016) 'The Danger of Deconsolidation', *Journal of Democracy*, 27 (3): 5–17.

Steger, M. (2009) *Globalization: A Very Short Introduction*, Oxford: Oxford University Press.

Sevenans, J. (2017) 'What Politicians Learn from the Mass Media and Why They React to it' in van Aelst, P. and Walgrave, S. eds. *How Political Actors Use the Media*, Cham, Switzerland: Palgrave Macmillan.

Stiglitz, J. (2002) *Globalization and its Discontents*, London: Penguin.

Stiglitz, J. (2010) *Freefall: Free Markets and the Sinking of the Global Economy*, London: Penguin.

Stiglitz, J. (2017) *Globalization and its Discontents Revisited: Anti-Globalization in the Era of Trump*, London: Penguin.

Strange, S. (1996) *The Retreat of the State: The Diffusion of Power in the World Economy*, Cambridge: Cambridge University Press.

Streeck, W. (2014) 'How Will Capitalism End?', *New Left Review*, 87, May/June: 35–64.

Streeck, W. (2016) *How Will Capitalism End?: Essays on a Failing System*, London: Verso.

Streeck, W. (2017) *Buying Time: The Delayed Crisis of Democratic Capitalism*, 2nd edn, London: Verso.

Street, J. (2003) 'The Celebrity Politician: Political Style and Popular Culture' in Corner, J. and Pels, D. eds. *Media and the Restyling of Politics*, London: Sage.

Stromback, J. (2008) 'Four Phases of Mediatization: An Analysis of the

Mediatization of Politics', *International Journal of Press/Politics*, 13 (3): 228–446.

Stromback, J. and Esser, F. eds. (2014) *Mediatization of Politics: Understanding the Transformation of Western Democracies*, Basingstoke: Palgrave.

Stromback, J. and Nord, L. (2006) 'Do Politicians Lead the Tango? A Study of the Relationship Between Swedish Journalists and their Political Sources in the Context of Election Campaigns', *European Journal of Communication*, 21 (2): 147–64.

Stromer-Galley, J. (2014) *Presidential Campaigning in the Internet Age*, Oxford: Oxford University Press.

Sunstein, C. (2001) *Republic.Com*, Princeton, NJ: Princeton University Press.

Sunstein, C. (2018) *#Republic: Divided Democracy in the Age of Social Media*, Princeton, NJ: Princeton University Press.

Sussman, G. (2011) *The Propaganda Society: Promotional Culture and Politics in Global Context*, New York: Peter Lang.

Swank, D. (2002) *Global Capital, Political Institutions and Policy Change in Developed Welfare States*, Cambridge: Cambridge University Press.

Swanson, D. and Mancini, P. eds. (1996) *Politics, Media and Modern Democracy: An International Study of Innovations in Electoral Campaigning and Their Consequences*, New York: Praeger Press.

Tapscott, D. and Williams, A. (2007) *Wikinomics: How Mass Collaboration Changes Everything*, New York: Penguin.

Tarrow, S. (1994) *Power in Movement: Social Movements, Collective Action and Politics*, New York: Cambridge University Press.

Tett, G. (2010) *Fools' Gold: How Unrestrained Greed Corrupted a Dream, Shattered Global Markets and Unleashed a Catastrophe*, London: Abacus.

Thompson, J. (1995) *The Media and Modernity: A Social Theory of the Media*, Cambridge: Polity.

Thompson, J. (2000) *Political Scandal*, Cambridge: Polity.

Thompson, P. (2017) 'Putting the Lies into Libor: The Mediation of a Financial Scandal' in Davis, A. ed. *The Death of Public Knowledge?* London: Goldsmiths-MIT Press.

Thorsen, E., Jackson, D. and Lilleker, D. eds. (2017) *UK Election Analysis 2017: Media, Voters and the Campaign*, Bournemouth: CSJCC.

Thussu, D. ed. (1998) *Electronic Empires: Global Media and Local Resistance*, London: Arnold.

Thussu, D. ed. (2007) *Media on the Move: Global Flow and Contra-Flow*, London: Routledge.

Thussu, D. (2008) *News as Entertainment: The Rise of Global Infotainment*, London: Sage.

Thussu, D. and Freedman, D. eds. (2004) *War and the Media Reporting Conflict 24/7*, London: Sage.

Thussu, D. and Freedman, D. eds. (2012) *Media and Terrorism: Global Perspectives*, London: Sage.

Tiffen, R. (1989) *News and Power*, Sydney: Allen and Unwin.

Tiffen, R. et al., (2014) 'Sources in the News: A Comparative Study', *Journalism Studies*, 15 (4): 374–91.

TJN (2015) *The Greatest Invention: Tax and the Campaign for a Just Society*, Tax Justice Network, Padstow, Cornwall: Commonwealth Publishing.

Tomlinson, J. (1999) *Globalization and Culture*, Cambridge: Polity.

Tormey, S. (2012) 'Occupy Wall Street: From Representation to Post-Representation', *Journal of Critical Global Studies*, 5: 132–7.

Tormey, S. (2015) *The End of Representative Politics*, Cambridge: Polity.

Trenz, H. (2004) 'Media Coverage on European Governance: Exploring the European Public Sphere in National Quality Newspapers', *European Journal of Communication*, 19 (3): 291–319.

Trippi, J. (2004) *The Revolution Will Not be Televised: Democracy, the Internet and the Overthrow of Everything*, New York: Harper Collins.

Truman, D. (1951) *The Governmental Process*, New York: Alfred A. Knopf.

Tufekci, Z. (2014a) 'Engineering the Public: Big Data, Surveillance and Computational Politics', *First Monday*, 19 (7), at: http://firstmonday.org/article/view/4901/4097.

Tufekci, Z. (2014b) *Big Questions for Social Media Big Data: Representativeness, Validity and Other Methodological Pitfalls*, Conference Paper, AAAI, pp. 505–14.

Tufekci, Z. and Wilson, T. (2014) 'Social Media and the Decision to Participate in Political Protests: Observations from Tahrir Square', *Journal of Communication*, 62 (2): 363–79.

Tumber, H. and Palmer, J. (2004) *Media at War: The Iraq Crisis*, London: Sage.

Tunstall, J. (1971) *Journalists at Work*, London: Sage.

Tunstall, J. (1996) *Newspaper Power: The National Press in Britain*, Oxford: Oxford University Press.

Tunstall, J. (2007) *The Media Were American*, London: Constable.

Turner, G. (2009) *Ordinary People and the Media: the Demotic Turn*, London: Sage.

Turner, G., Bonner, F. and Marshall, P. (2000) *Fame Games: The Production of Celebrity in Australia*, Cambridge: Cambridge University Press.

Turow, J. (2012) *The Daily You: How the Advertising Industry is Defining Your Identity and Your World*, New Haven, CT: Yale University Press.

UCS (2007) *Smoke, Mirrors and Hot Air*, Report, Cambridge, MA: Union of Concerned Scientists.

UK Electoral Commission (2017), site at: https://www.electoralcommission.org.uk/england.

UNCTAD (2009) *The Global Economic Crisis: Systemic Failures and Multilateral Remedies*, UNCTAD/GDS/2009/1, New York/Geneva: United Nations Conference on Trade and Development.

UNDP (2016) United Nations Development Index at: http://hdr.undp.org/en/data.

UNESCO (2013) *Feature Film Diversity*, Montreal: United Nations Educational, Scientific and Cultural Organisation.

Urry, J. (2014) 'The Super-rich and Offshore Worlds' in Birtchnell, J. and Caletrio, J. eds. *Elite Mobilities*, Abingdon, Oxford: Routledge, pp. 226–40.

US Bureau of Labor Statistics (2010) *National Employment Matrix*, Washington: US Bureau of Labor Statistics, at http://www.bls.gov.

Useem, M. (1984) *The Inner Circle: Large Corporations and the Rise of Political Activity in the US and UK*, Oxford: Oxford University Press.

Useem, M. (2015) 'From Classwide Coherence to Company-Focused Management and Director Engagement', *Research in the Sociology of Organizations*, 43: 399–421.

Vaccari, C., Chadwick, A. and O'Loughlin, B. (2015) 'Dual Screening the Political: Media Events, Social Media and Citizen Engagement', *Journal of Communication*, 65: 1041–61.

Valkenburg, P., Peter, J. and Wather, J. (2016) 'Media Effects: Theory and Research', *Annual Review of Psychology*, 67: 315–38.

Valtysson, B. (2014) 'Democracy in Disguise: The Use of Social Media in Reviewing the Icelandic Constitution', *Media, Culture and Society*, 36 (1): 52–68.

van Aelst, P. and Walgrave, S. eds. (2017) *How Political Actors Use the Media*, Cham., Switzerland: Palgrave Macmillan.

van Aelst, P., van Erkel, E., D'heer, E., and Harder, R. (2017) 'Who is Leading the Campaign Charts? Comparing Individual Popularity on Old and New Media', *Information, Communication and Society*, 20 (5): 715–32.

van Biezen, I. and Poguntke, T. (2014) 'The Decline of Membership-Based Politics', *Party Politics*, 20 (2): 205–16.

van Biezen, I., Mair, P. and Poguntke, T. (2012) 'Going, going ... gone? The Decline of Party Membership in Contemporary Europe', *European Journal of Political Research*, 51 (1): 24–56.

van der Heijden ed. (2016) *Handbook of Political Citizenship and Social Movements*, Cheltenham: Edward Elgar Publishing.

van Zoonen, L. (2005) *Entertaining the Citizen: When Politics and Popular Culture Converge*, Lanham: Rowman and Littlefield.

Vargo, C. and Guo, L. (2017) 'Networks, Big Data, and Intermedia Agenda-Setting: An Analysis of Traditional, Partisan and Emerging Online US News', *Journalism and Mass Communication Quarterly*, 94 (4): 1031–55.

Varoufakis, Y. (2016) *And the Weak Suffer What They Must?: Europe, Austerity and the Threat to Global Stability*, London: Vintage.

Vissers, S. and Stolle, D. (2014) 'The Internet and New Modes of Political Participation: Online Versus Offline Participation', *Information, Communication and Society*, 17 (8): 937–55.

Volkmer, I. (1999) *CNN News in the Global Sphere: A Study of CNN and its Impact on Global Communication*, Luton: University of Luton Press.

Volkmer, I. (2005) 'News in the Global Public Sphere' in Allan, S. ed. *Journalism: Critical Issues*, Maidenhead: Open University Press, pp. 357–69.

Volkmer, I. (2014) *The Global Public Sphere: Political Communication in the Age of Reflective Interdependence*, Cambridge: Polity.

Walgrave, S., Sevenans, J., Ziozner, A. and Ayling, M. (2017) 'The Media Independency of Political Elites' in van Aelst, P. and Walgrave, S. eds. *How Political Actors Use the Media*, Cham., Switzerland: Palgrave Macmillan.

Ward, S., Gibson, R. and Lusoli, W. (2005) *The Promise and Perils of "Virtual Representation": The Public's View*, London: NOP Opinion Survey.

Ward, S., Lusoli, W. and Gibson, R. (2002) 'Virtually Participating: A Survey of Online Party Members', *Information Polity*, 7 (4): 199–215.

Washbourne, N. (2005) *(Comprehensive) Political Marketing, Expertise and the Conditions for Democracy*, Paper Presentation PSA Conference.

Webb, P. (2007) 'Political Parties and the Democratic Disconnect: A Call for Research' in Webb, P. *Democracy and Political Parties*, London: Hansard.

Weber, M. (1948) *From Max Weber: Essays in Sociology* eds. Gerth, H. and Wright Mills, C., London: Routledge.

Wedel, J. (2014) *Unaccountable*, New York: Pegasus Books.

Weeks, B., Ardevol-Abrew, A. and Gil de Zuniga, H. (2017) 'Online Influence? Social Media Use, Opinion Leadership and Political Persuasion', *International Journal of Public Opinion Research*, 29 (2): 214–39.

Wells, C. et al., (2016) 'How Trump Drove Coverage of the Nomination: Hybrid Media Campaigning', *Political Communication*, 33: 669–76.

West, D. and Orman, J. (2003) *Celebrity Politics*, Upper Saddle River, NJ: Prentice Hall.

Wheeler, M. (2014) *Celebrity Politics*, Cambridge: Polity.

Wikland, H. (2005) 'A Habermasian Analysis of the Deliberative Democratic Potential of ICT-Enabled Services in Swedish Municipalities', *New Media and Society*, 7 (5): 701–23.

Wilkinson, R. and Pickett, K. (2010) *The Spirit Level: Why Equality is Better for Everyone*, London: Penguin.

Wilks, S. (2015) report *The Revolving Door and the Corporate Colonisation of UK Politics*, London: High Pay.

Willetts, P. (2008) 'Transnational Actors and International Organizations in Global Politics' in Baylis, J., Smith, S. and Owens, P. eds. *The Globalization of World Politics: An Introduction to International Relations*, 2nd edn, Oxford: Oxford University Press.

Williams, K. (1997) *Get Me a Murder a Day: A History of Mass Communication in Britain*, London: Hodder Education.

Winston, B. (1998) *Media, Technology and Society: A History from Telegraph to the Internet*, London: Routledge.

Wolf, M. (2018) *Fire and Fury: Inside the Trump White House*, London: Little Brown.

Wolfsfeld, G. (2011) *Making Sense of Media and Politics: Five Principles of Political Communication*, New York: Routledge.

Woodward, B. (2006) *State of Denial: Bush at War, Part III*, New York: Simon and Schuster.

Woolley, S. and Howard, P. (2017) *Computational Propaganda Worldwide*, Working Paper No 2017.11, Oxford: Oxford Internet Institute.

World Values Survey (2010–14) World Values Survey 6th Wave, http://www.worldvaluessurvey.org.

Worlds of Journalism (2012–16) at: http://www.worldsofjournalism.org/.

Wren-Lewis, S. (2018) '"Mediamacro": Why the News Media Ignores Economic Experts' in Basu, L., Schifferes, S. and Knowles, S. eds. *The Media and Austerity: Comparative Perspectives*, London: Routledge.

Wright, K. (2018) *Who's Reporting Africa Now? Non-Governmental Organizations, Journalists, and Multimedia*, New York: Peter Lang.

Wring, D. (2005) *The Politics of Marketing the Labour Party*, London: Palgrave.

Zellizer, B. (2004) *Taking Journalism Seriously: News and the Academy*, Thousand Oaks, CA: Sage.

Zetter, L. (2014) *Lobbying: The Art of Political Persuasion*, 3rd edn, Petersfield: Harriman House Publishing.

Zhao, Y. and Hackett, R. (2005) 'Media Globalization, Media Democratization: Challenges, Issues, and Paradoxes' in Hackett, R. and Zhao, Y. eds. *Democratizing Global Media: One World, Many Struggles*, Oxford: Rowman and Littlefield.

Index